POWER AND IMPOTENCE
The Failure of America's Foreign Policy

POWER AND IMPOTENCE

☆

*The Failure of
America's Foreign Policy*

by

Edmund Stillman & William Pfaff

RANDOM HOUSE · NEW YORK

TO

CAROLYN and MARY

The authors owe an acknowledgment of thanks to friends and colleagues at the Hudson Institute, and particularly to Herman Kahn and Max Singer, for their tolerance of these arguments and their sympathetic interest in this book. We must also thank the Rockefeller Foundation for hospitality at the Villa Serbelloni.

Contents

POWER AND IMPOTENCE
The Failure of America's Foreign Policy

I

The American Dilemma

It has been more than twenty years since the Cold War began; in that fifth of a century the American people have moved from the periphery of world events to a central role in contemporary history. We have—after long years of political and moral isolation—undertaken to discharge responsibility and exercise power. We have assumed the burden of defending a vast alliance of free states against aggression and totalitarianism. We have spent vast sums of money. We have, since 1945, given the lives of some of our best men to this cause.

Yet after twenty years the world proves oddly ungrateful, and we ourselves experience deep doubt about our actions. The American people, it seems, are seriously disquieted about the extent and consequences of this world involvement. Yet it is difficult to know what has gone wrong; indeed, for us it is a source not only of anxiety, but of anger, that things have gone so wrong.

That the world is ungrateful is perhaps unimportant. It is not everything to be loved. But more serious is the fact that the United States is not trusted. Our allies, and those whom we would most help, are among those who doubt and challenge us. In our Asian policies we are very nearly alone. Our policy in Europe— our very ambition for a new political organization of Europe in a qualitatively new relationship with the United States—is blocked by Europeans themselves. Our program to bring about a reform in the economic and political condition of Latin America is cynically misinterpreted, and resisted.

Why should all this be? The argument that world leadership

inevitably provokes misunderstanding and hostility is not wholly convincing. And the public debates within the United States in recent months have demonstrated our own loss of confidence: we are no longer at peace with ourselves about the value and necessity of our actions in the world.

There is disquiet, but we are not yet very close to an understanding of the sources of our present crisis. The issue that today divides this country from the other democracies was summarily expressed by an anonymous State Department officer late in 1965 when he said of the West Europeans' failure to help us in Vietnam, "They don't understand that this is a world war." The United States officially insists that Vietnam is but one act in a larger conflict, a universal crisis. Most of the world disagrees.

Our own disagreements within the United States are not so easily defined. Americans are disturbed, but the context of debate remains a set of canonical assumptions about foreign policy which hardly have been challenged. The policy the United States follows today is a consistent and reasonable expression—if only one expression—of attitudes widely held by those who attack and those who defend the present Administration. There *is* an American consensus on foreign affairs, and the Johnson Administration may legitimately argue that its programs carry out in action what the country demands in principle. If there is controversy, it is largely over method; and governments, the Administration might reasonably argue, do not have unlimited freedom in their choice of methods. They are prisoners of the past. Mr. Johnson escalated the war in Vietnam, but so did Mr. Kennedy when he altered the American commitment in that country from one of assistance and counsel to the South Vietnamese government to direct, if still limited, military engagement with the Vietnamese insurgents. So did Mr. Eisenhower "escalate," or more properly, inaugurate, the American involvement when, in 1954, he stepped into the role the exhausted French had abandoned and chose to sponsor and sustain a noncommunist government in Saigon that would prevent the country's unification under the communist Viet Minh movement which had led the war to expel the French.

For many years now there has been an American national commitment, supported by the public, to underwrite a separatist and anti-communist South Vietnamese state. From the beginning the United States has acted in the belief that the independence of

South Vietnam constitutes a crucial test in a confrontation in Asia between the political values we defend and the challenge of communism: the *general* challenge of communism, as a political ideology and mode of national "development," and the challenge of Communist China as a nation hostile to the United States and to our values. Since there has been a general American consensus on this interpretation of the situation in Vietnam, and a consensus on the objectives which American policy ought to seek, the central controversies over Vietnam can only be controversies over method. The marginal controversies often enough either sentimentalize the real possibilities of action or seek drastic and simplistic short cuts to the "victory" of justice everybody wants. The liberal critics of the Administration policy have called for social reforms and foreign aid to pacify a peasant population which they see as having taken up arms against a "corrupt" central government—acting, in short, out of economic despair. The conservative critics have seen the crisis as military, and have sought solutions in direct military action against North Vietnam, or even China.* If there is anxiety today over our prospects in Vietnam—anxieties which the Administration clearly shares—this does not mean that Americans have yet really abandoned their consensus on the significance of the Vietnamese struggle or the objectives to be sought.

* Unfortunately, it seems both sets of critics have had their influence. The desire for a regime of "progress," "uncorruptability," and "social justice" was the motive for the coup against the dictatorship of Ngo Dinh Diem in 1963—a coup in which the United States government was, to say the least, indirectly involved. The belief that carrying the war to North Vietnam would quickly destroy the logistics and will of the Viet Cong motivated the United States to extend the air war to the north of the 17th parallel in early 1965. In both cases the results have been a rapid worsening of the over-all political situation.

Since 1963 there has been a major effort to oversee a program of social progress in Vietnam; but the kaleidoscopic succession of governments in Saigon since Diem's fall have patently failed to win the allegiance of the peasantry, disaffected intellectuals, and Catholic and Buddhist factions. These shadowy governments in fact have forfeited what was Diem's minimum claim to leadership—a truculent independence of United States dictation. As for the bombings, they have no doubt had their effect, but they have proved far from crippling and, in any case, against a primitive economy, less efficient than the bombings of Germany and Japan in World War II (which were themselves not decisive). Similarly defective has been the belief that the Viet Cong would break before the challenge of American soldiers and Marines. Vietnam has been the graveyard of a host of political and military orthodoxies.

If this is true of Vietnam, it is as true of American policy in Latin America and Africa, or of our attempts to deal with the changing nature of the Soviet threat, or with developments in Europe. There is an American consensus—and dilemma—on foreign policy: the nation is substantially in agreement on what it wants, but it is becoming aware that existing policies are unable to accomplish its goals. Our anxiety and sense of impotence in this situation, our furious turning on ourselves in intemperate debate, arise from the fact that while there are many proposals for alternative ways of going about what we want to accomplish, none are clearly convincing. The Administration, the officials of the Departments of State and Defense, of Central Intelligence, and the other federal agencies concerned with international policy may be the prisoners of past actions, but they are equally the prisoners of American goals in foreign policy, and of American assumptions about political action, whose logical results are the acts and policies to which we are today committed. This Administration—the elected officials as well as the professional foreign affairs officers and their auxiliaries in the scholarly community—is largely faithful to the generalized and unanalyzed assumptions which dominate popular discussion of foreign policy.

But this is nevertheless an indictment of leadership. The public today may be ultimately responsible for national policy, yet professionals, elected officials and their staffs and advisors, must give serious leadership. The professional political community has failed to supply the serious analyses and alternatives which would structure public debate. It sometimes seems that the American people today are considerably more troubled, more aware of risk and contingency in international affairs, more alive to the inadequacy of received doctrine and sentimental aspiration in dealing with Asian revolution or Latin American unrest or Chinese ambition, than many of the leaders of our government. When Mr. McNamara said in 1964 that American troops would have completed their work and could begin to come home from Vietnam by Christmas, 1965, the public hardly took him seriously. When Mr. Rusk declares that America's policy goal is worldwide democracy—"victory for all mankind . . . a worldwide victory for freedom"—the assent of the public is qualified and skeptical. By making such statements, these men offend the public judgment, the *common* sense.

But a new foreign policy cannot be initiated by the public. The public can only give or withhold assent to the policies that professional men and the leaders of the Administration, or the opposition, propose to them. The American public, certainly, has demonstrated that it will support costly national policies. It shows today that it will support established policies even when they are questionable—in the absence of responsible alternatives. But there can hardly be doubt that the public would withdraw its support of the present Administration's Vietnam policy, for example, if a serious alternative were put forward. The problem today is that responsible alternatives can hardly be put forward without a challenge to the assumptions which have dominated American foreign policy for the last decade and more.

A NEW DEBATE

The effect of the American consensus has been to stultify debate. The premises of American foreign policy today are generally accepted by Conservatives as well as Liberals, and by much of the New Left as well. The "interventionist" doctrine was held in substance by the Republican Administrations of Mr. Eisenhower; it is evident in most Republican comment on world affairs today. It lies behind the actions both of the Johnson Administration and its predecessor, the Kennedy Administration. These beliefs are widely held in the university and foundation circles concerned with foreign policy. They have little to do with conventional political divisions. It is a matter of belief in principle about foreign policy, about America, about America's proper role in world affairs, and indeed about history.

Yet these American assumptions, so widely held, are by no means self-evidently true. They demand analysis. If they are not challenged there can be no real change in American policy—and no resolution of the American foreign dilemma. The process of analysis may prove painful and bewildering, for it will involve a reappraisal of what the United States has come to stand for in world affairs, and a reappraisal of the significance of the American political experience itself.

The truth, though, is that such a reappraisal of our assumptions is long overdue; we are very close to having the reckoning forced upon us. The outcome of the war in Vietnam might drive us to

this reckoning. Our allies may force us into self-examination—
by abandoning us. The material substructure of our world commitment could collapse—it is strained already. Indeed, it is not
inconceivable that within as short a time as five years, or more
plausibly within ten, this nation may find itself *forced* into a new
isolation: the world indifferent to us, or frankly hostile.

Is this absurd? We think not. This book dissents in principle
from the now canonical American strategy of globalism; and beyond that it is an attempt to explore constructively what foreign
policy can and should be expected to accomplish for a people.

WHAT GLOBALISM IS

Narrowly conceived, what we describe as "globalism" is the specific set of actions that have produced the American commitment
to a large and serious mainland war in Asia, to military intervention in the Dominican Republic in 1965, to the Bay of Pigs invasion of Cuba in 1961, and to other earlier clandestine and semi-
clandestine attempts to overthrow or disrupt the governments of
other states. But this is to define globalism, or interventionism, at
a superficial level.

More broadly conceived, interventionism is the set of assumptions which produced and justified these actions: it is the general
conviction that the affairs of the world today are to be understood
in terms of a universal conflict of values—between freedom and
unfreedom, reason and force, orderly progress and despotism. It
is the belief that the United States, as the leading proponent of a
system of free government, is obligated to use its power (its material power, but also its power of moral suasion and leadership)
to dominate this worldwide conflict. The United States is held to
be compelled to do this for its own security—since as the leader
of the free world it must be the ultimate objective of the hostile
attack—but also in the general interests of mankind.

The specific policies followed by the present Administration—
at the moment largely military in character—are obviously not
the only ones that can be derived from the general interventionist
belief. Many critics to the left of the Administration would insist
on a vastly expanded program of foreign aid, peaceful construction, political tutelage—of "democratic revolution"—out of exactly
the convictions of universal challenge and universal respon-

sibility that justify our military programs. Here again the controversy is one of methods but not of ends. The belief in universal crisis is the crucial interventionist assumption—that and the faith that the crisis can be resolved.*

As for globalism in present government policy, before we turn to extended criticism we owe to the defenders and administrators of this policy a reasonable statement of their case. Obviously we will not be able to define it in language all would accept, but it may be possible to make a fairly dispassionate outline of the interventionist argument.

Secretary Rusk has said that the "distant stars" of today's American policy, the guiding objectives, are "the notion articulated by Thomas Jefferson that governments derive their just powers from the consent of the governed. Some of the erudite have found philosophical weakness in that proposition, but it just happens to be that the American people believe it and are deeply dedicated to the notion. And that explains why we have welcomed the emergence of the new nations of Asia and Africa to national independence; why we have welcomed and encouraged the doubling of the membership of the United Nations; why we have the strongest attachment to the other democracies; and why we are so deeply concerned about the withholding of freedom outside our borders, and why we are acting, even belatedly, to remove the barriers to freedom within our own society.

"Beyond that, I would call your attention to the preamble and articles 1 and 2 of the United Nations Charter.[1] In all sincerity, I would propose those as a succinct summary of the foreign policy attitudes of the American people. It is no accident that this should

---

* Many liberal critics of the present Administration, for example, share its distaste for nuclear proliferation—the spread of nuclear weapons, or their retention by any but the United States and the Soviets. Many such critics, while deploring the Vietnamese intervention, would go so far, in private conversation at least, as to advocate "pre-emptive" action against Chinese nuclear capabilities and, to make this act more palatable to the Soviets, impartially against the French. Economic co-operation, security guarantees, and, in the Chinese case, diplomatic recognition would be offered by way of compensation. Such views might be dismissed as a caricature of the interventionist state of mind, yet they are fairly widespread in the scientific community and in some agencies of the United States government. Critics and officials apparently meet in their notion of bipolarity as a stable international order, and in their habit of thinking of *physical* intervention, if not always military, as a useful technique for dealing with long-range political and social problems.

be so. . . . [They sketch out] a world of independent nations, each with their own institutions, settling their disputes by peaceful means, banding together to resist aggression, striving to establish a rule of law."*

Communism threatens these objectives of our policy because it is an alternative form of world organization which rests on a pernicious system of political values and a pernicious interpretation of the meaning of history, and because it animates the actions of states hostile to us. These include one great power, the Soviet Union; several states of major economic, military, and political resources (China, East Germany, Czechoslovakia, Poland, Hungary, Rumania); and still others of lesser resources but significant influence and even power (North Vietnam, North Korea, Albania and Cuba, and in its own independent but ideologically committed position, Yugoslavia).

Whatever their disagreements with one another, the argument runs, these states reject the essential values and objectives of the

* Secretary Rusk's remarks are drawn from an address entitled "Building a Decent World Order," delivered before the International Congress of Publishers in Washington on June 5, 1965. (*The Department of State Bulletin*, July 5, 1965, pp. 27–31.) Substantially the same remarks appear in Mr. Rusk's "Guidelines of U.S. Foreign Policy," an address at George Washington University on June 6, 1965 (*op. cit.*, June 28, 1965, pp. 1030–1034). The State Department position is defended in detail against "neo-isolationist" criticisms (presumably and notably those made during 1965 by Senator William Fulbright, Walter Lippmann, and Senator Frank Church, among others) by Under Secretary George Ball in "'The New Diplomacy" (*op. cit.*, June 28, 1965, pp. 1042–1048) and "The Dangers of Nostalgia" (*op. cit.*, April 12, 1965, pp. 532–537).

Mr. Walt W. Rostow, former counselor of the State Department and chairman of the Policy Planning Council, made one of many general defenses of American policy in "Peace: The Central Task of Foreign Policy" (*op. cit.*, July 5, 1965, pp. 21–27). All of these statements will be referred to—in a hostile context—in the chapters to come, but they should be commended to readers as authoritative statements of the interventionist case.

The assumptions of globalism can, of course, be found reflected in the great majority of popular press discussions of policy. *Time* magazine's "essay" of August 6, 1965, "Communism Today: A Refresher Course," is a succinct statement of what might be called the conservative interventionist view of the world. The Left or liberal interventionism that would largely substitute measures of worldwide social reform for present programs is almost as widely expressed, but *The Correspondent*, published by a group that includes David Riesman, Erich Fromm, Seymour Martin Lipset, Charles Osgood, and Marcus Raskin, is perhaps the most influential of the journals specifically devoted to these issues (William James Hall 280, Harvard University, Cambridge, Massachusetts).

United States. Their resources, in support of their ideology, are used in general concert, providing a worldwide challenge to the United States, and to the democratic political values which the United States shares with its major allies and commends to the rest of the nations of the world. The hostile power is great; if these nations were to succeed in the policies which they proclaim, there would be no peaceful world community of nations ruled by consent. There would, indeed, eventually be no democratically governed United States.

Since communism attacks freedom—in military aggressions, but also in its diplomatic and economic campaigns—we must respond and seek a victory of our own. Those who discount the communist threat, the interventionist argument goes on, delude themselves as did those who in the 1930's discounted the threat of Nazism.* They ignore the frankly proclaimed objective of communism, which is, as Mr. Khrushchev put it, to "bury" us. And if Mr. Khrushchev and his successors in Moscow mean to do this by means short of international war, their measures nevertheless include subversion and "wars of national liberation" as well as more conventional actions. And the Chinese accept no such limits. They declare themselves committed to radical action to bring about a world revolutionary struggle against the democratic powers—"to destroy the enemy," as China's Marshal Lin Piao has put it, "wherever the enemy can be most easily destroyed." If it should come to nuclear war, the Chinese assert that they will nonetheless stand fast and that the result would be "the turning of hundreds of millions of people to communism and the doom of the United States."[3]

The interventionist argument asserts that where violence and disruption now exist in the awakened but impoverished areas of Africa, Asia, and Latin America, communism has a powerful ap-

---

* An important official interventionist belief is that there is a close analogy between the situation of the democracies today and in the 1930's. A communist victory in Vietnam is held to promise to be for the communists what Hitler's victories were in the *Anschluss* with Austria and the partition and eventual conquest of Czechoslovakia—a stimulation to still further aggression and to eventual world war. Hitler could have been stopped by decisive military action, the argument goes, and the struggle in Vietnam is thus warranted, whatever its costs, to prevent renewed communist aggression in other places. Mr. Rusk says: "Peace, in the world as it is, must be protected—if necessary, by force. . . . Aggression feeds on success. The appeasement of aggressors leads either to surrender or to a larger war."[2]

peal that does not wholly depend on subversion. It seems to
promise a disciplined doctrine of national action to bring about
social change and economic progress. Communist militants can
seize the leadership of revolutionary movements that include people of many political persuasions. A "hard core" of communists
can dominate movements in which they are outnumbered by
people whose ultimate values are actually democratic; and seizing
the key positions of power, communists eventually discard or
suppress those who are unwilling to accept their leadership and,
eventually, their dictatorship.

In a world newly awakened to the possibilities of political and
economic progress, a world newly aware of the chasm between
the life led by the people of the advanced industrial states and
the condition of the masses of the Southern Hemisphere and East
Asia, there is a competition in revolution—a critical struggle between those who would bring orderly and progressive "revolution"
and those who resort to violence and dictation. America's war,
then, is not only with communism but with the conditions which
breed communism and give it its appeal. Our enemy is communism, but communism is really a disorder caused by social evil,
a parisitic growth feeding on injustice. Remove social evil and
injustice, and communism will wane. Ignore them, and communism will mobilize the dispossessed of the world, offering them its
powerful if delusory promises of revolutionary transformation.

The United States bears chief responsibility for dealing with
this crisis. We are the strongest of the free nations; we are an
example of successful revolution; we are uncompromised by an
imperialist past or a history of self-interested policy. But it is not
only that we are uniquely qualified to lead the forces of freedom,
there is no one else to take this burden. The European states are
weak by contemporary standards of power. Moreover, most of
them are morally unqualified since they are compromised by histories of colonial exploitation and selfish policy and nationalism.
They are—most of them—ill-equipped to teach democracy because their own record of democracy is bad. In the struggle with
tyranny they do not have clean hands; they do not, in any event,
have the will to act.

Thus the interventionist case concludes that while there may
seem to be many crises in the world, these are single acts in a
greater drama, a worldwide revolutionary struggle of freedom

with unfreedom. The forces of injustice are multiple, and while today they manifest themselves in communism—and thus our immediate and urgent struggle is with the communist nations and their agents—our real war is with poverty and social backwardness, and with the selfishness of that minority of men who stand in the way of a "world of freedom and opportunity for the whole human race," a world which is, again to quote Secretary Rusk, "the goal of a great majority of mankind."[4]

This, then, is America's hour in history. Our generation has been matched to a great test whose outcome will shape the future of mankind. And if the strain is great, and many misunderstand what we are about and turn against us, this is at worst the result of the lies and subversion of our enemies; but it is also a penalty of leadership, even of greatness. No nation can expect to exercise world power in an enterprise of surpassing importance without meeting resistance and resentment. For us, the true question must not be whether we are "loved" today, but whether future generations will judge us right. We must appeal to the future to vindicate us and to conclude that by fighting tyranny in Vietnam, by organizing resistance to communism in Thailand and Laos, by supporting forces of freedom in Indonesia, Iran, and India, by struggling for the unification of Europe and the Atlantic community, by suppressing the revolutions of Latin America while organizing its economic development and social transformation, we have made a better world.

Many will argue the specific terms of this statement of American foreign policy belief. Many, surely, insist that the problem of social oppression and economic deprivation far outweighs the military threat of communism. Others hold that it is the military and subversive danger that is primary. But the structure of belief we have sketched is substantially that which the officials of the American government today put forward and it seems likely that it would win at least a qualified endorsement by most of those who are and have been involved in the making of recent American policy.

Their qualifications, or disputes of interpretation, are in any case irrelevant to our case. Our argument radically rejects their fundamental belief in universal crisis—a belief, we hold, which derives from the ideological sickness of our time, as well as from the most sentimental and self-indulgent traits of the

American intellectual and political tradition. We believe that there can be no serious reform of American foreign policy until the essential assumptions of interventionism are rejected. Unless that is done the penalty for this country may be worse than mere impotence and isolation. It may be that the United States—talented, powerful, generous—will commit the ultimate folly, in ways still impossible to foresee: like the Europe of 1914, at the pinnacle of power, invulnerable to external assault, we may yet construct that combination of events that will cast us down.

II

The Sources of Intervention

The real source of danger to America in today's world is not so much the Soviets, or Chinese communism, or the nuclear weapon, as that present policy is mired in illusions—and these illusions express the deepest beliefs which Americans, as a nation, hold about the world. The discouraging truth is that the defects of present American policy are not merely defects of technique, of detail, to be cured by one or another refinement of our programs. They are fundamental errors that spring from defects of the national style and political intelligence.

For there has been throughout American history, with only the briefest exceptions, a single style of diplomacy once the United States had turned its attention from the problem of the defense of the Republic and its territorial expansion to distant problems, to the problems of the larger world. That style has been a compound of the American experience of isolation and a moral fervor that is fundamentally theological in its origins. Isolationism is an instinct of withdrawal—a rejection of the world's complexity. Globalism is this impulse turned inside out—a wish to end complexity by reforming the world through the accomplishment of an indefinable process of orderly "revolution." But in their joint vision of a perfect peace both ideologies incorporate a specifically American dream.

The assumptions of globalism—the present American foreign policy—are at bottom identical to the assumptions of isolationism. This may seem a paradox; yet it is a fact which should not really surprise us. Both impulses reject reality, the world as it is, for an ideal and unattainable vision of a national freedom from the repetitive and harrowing crises of history.

For a century and a half America followed a policy of isolationism because isolationism made sense in terms of this country's particular situation in the world. The need of a young republic was for time to build. Our national preoccupations were westward expansion and the assimilation of immigrants, the defining of what this country was to become, the building of a national loyalty that superseded regional loyalties, and the saving of the Union. In this sense classical isolationism expressed a pragmatic wisdom.

But we were also isolationists because we wanted to separate ourselves from the old world, to make clear our differences, for the whole sense of American national identity has been bound up in the idea that we are a *different* society—a new society, a post-European society. From the very beginning there was a profound and necessary conviction in America that ours is a better society than Europe.

Thus isolationism in earlier American history was not simply an expression of political naïveté; nor was it a policy arrived at out of a mere calculation of practical advantage and danger. "Europe," Washington had said, "has a set of primary interests, which to us have none, or a very remote relation. . . . [I]t must be unwise in us to implicate ourselves, by artificial ties, in the ordinary vicissitudes of her politics, or the ordinary combinations and collisions of her friendships or enmities."[1] This was sound advice for an infant nation, but Jefferson was closer to the real temper of Americans and articulated the true source of America's isolationism when he called the United States the "world's best hope." Isolationism was sensible; it was also emotionally necessary, emotionally inevitable. Jefferson added: "We can no longer say there is nothing new under the sun. For this whole chapter in the history of man is new. . . . Before the establishment of the American states, nothing was known to history but the man of the old world, crowded within limits either small or overcharged, and steeped in the vices which that situation generates."[2] Here was the American's sense of his country as a new dispensation. It was as if, by founding the Republic, Americans had made a new covenant with God. No political policy was ever closer than isolationism to the deep sources of a nation's understanding of its role in the world. That role was not really political. Though it was political in form, it was understood to be a moral role. We were participants in a great moral experiment, the creation of a new kind of political community.* We believed—as Reinhold Niebuhr has expressed it—"that we had been called out by God to create a new humanity. We were God's 'American Israel.'"[4] Thus we were, as Lincoln was later to say, "the last best hope of earth." We sang of America: "Humanity with all its fears / With all the hopes of future years / Is hanging breathless on thy fate."

Such a view of America as a peculiar treasure to be preserved from the world's corruption might for a time be reversed, as it was after 1916 and again, and apparently for good, in 1941. But such deep-seated beliefs about America's qualities, and about its meaning as an experiment for the rest of the world, could not easily be given up. As the nation grew in power and responsibility, practical considerations could compel the United States to abandon isolationism. But if the country found new gratifications as well as burdens in responsibility when the tradition of more than a century was abandoned, we did not give up the peculiarly American temper, the American beliefs, which lay behind isolationism. That United States which had casually and querulously condemned the international dealings of others (as, in Wilson's words in 1916, "the . . . jealousies and rivalries of the complicated politics of Europe"[5]) did not, in abandoning its isolationism, substitute an opinion of itself as merely one more petty actor in the workings-out of such complex and squalid rivalries. We had been a special nation when we held aloof; we were a special nation

---

* It is notable that the only serious challenge to the isolationism of the early Republic came when the French Revolution broke out, and there was a passionate American popular sense of identification with what appeared to be a second and kindred experiment in making a new human society. Tocqueville says, "It was then as evident . . . as it is at the present time that the interest of the Americans forbade them to take any part in the contest which was about to deluge Europe with blood, but which could not injure their own country. But the sympathies of the people declared themselves with so much violence in favor of France that nothing but the inflexible character of Washington and the immense popularity which he enjoyed could have prevented the Americans from declaring war against England. And even then the exertions which the austere reason of that great man made to repress the generous but imprudent passions of his fellow citizens nearly deprived him of the sole recompense which he ever claimed, that of his country's love. The majority reprobated his policy, but it was afterwards approved by the whole nation."[3]

with a special and essentially moral role to play in the world when we eventually intervened. As Wilson also said, committed to the world, we would make the world safe for democracy.

Charles Beard, the American historian, once observed that any foreign policy rests "on a view of the world and of the nation as part of that world. However disconcerting the thought may be, it is also an interpretation of all history, out of which all nations, provinces, and empires have emerged, in which they have their being."[6] This is very important to understand, for the basic beliefs about the world that underlie American foreign policy today clearly manifest an interpretation of history that is curiously unsophisticated—in contrast to the self-conscious methodological sophistication of the theories, intellectual analyses, and studies by which the tactics of our foreign policy are developed. Beard's comment is worth additional attention because one thing can be added to it. While policy implies "a view of the world and of a nation in that world," it also is true that policies, which are instruments, are more easily changed than fundamental views of national significance and of history. Thus if necessity requires a change in the scope and form of policy that is contrary to the underlying national temper, the eventual outcome may be a new policy which is only ostensibly new—the old one in disguise. That, we would argue, is what has happened today. There was always an evangelical quality to American isolationism. *Mutatis mutandis,* America's modern global interventionism is only the old moral separateness, the belief in the special goodness of America, projected outward into the world.

AN ISOLATED NATION

There is no single American philosophy, no one and inescapable view of politics and history, which condemns us as a nation to a single style of foreign policy. There is always tension and conflict in what Americans believe, most of all in what we believe about ourselves. But when this is said, it remains true that there has been, on the evidence of the last fifty years, a characteristic American style of foreign policy—a way of looking at the world and a characteristic belief about what political action can and should accomplish abroad. The sources of this style lie in the experience of isolation, in the beliefs which went into our definition of the

Republic and in our development of this country's political society in the nineteenth and early twentieth centuries. But the fact that our style of foreign policy can be explained in terms of the American historical experience does not mean that this style is a good one, or even that it expresses the best tradition of this country. There are ways in which it expresses the worst of us—our most self-indulgent beliefs about ourselves unchecked by the constraints and known limits that operate to give our domestic politics some sense of scale and restraint.

Our domestic politics, after all, function in the thick reality of ambitions, interests, established powers, and local prides. We know intimately what small cities want, what Italians and Jews want, or the urban Negro and rural Southern whites. We know what water means to Southern California, and corn futures to Iowa, highways to small towns, railroads and welfare to the cities. Where local politics is the issue, we know, as well, the limits of our knowledge—the upsets and unpredictable reverses that elections, local and national, can produce, the limits and dangers of oversimplified national mythologies about Negroes or Wall Street or the South. We have Mr. Dooley's knowledge to aid us, and Dr. King's, and Max Lerner and Walter Lippmann and Buchwald and Lubell; we get the gossip from the neighborhood political club and the firehouse, and from the League of Women Voters and the Friendly Sons of Saint Patrick. American politics is a jungle, but all of us have lived in some part of it, and we glimpse what we do not know as well as assert what we do. There is a limit to the folly we are prepared to risk, a cynicism that tells us when to stop, a feeling for the opportunities that change throws up.

In international affairs we are not so well off. Abroad, our knowledge is sketchy and our skepticism deserts us. Tocqueville thought that democracies would do badly in foreign affairs because "foreign politics demand scarcely any of those qualities which are peculiar to a democracy; they require, on the contrary, the perfect use of almost all those in which it is deficient. Democracy is favorable to the increase of the internal resources of a state; it diffuses wealth and comfort, promotes public spirit, and fortifies the respect for law in all classes of society: all these are advantages which have only an indirect influence over the relations which one people bears to another. But a democracy can

only with great difficulty regulate the details of an important undertaking, persevere in a fixed design, and work out its execution
in spite of serious obstacles. It cannot combine its measures with
secrecy or await their consequences with patience. These are
qualities which more especially belong to an individual or an
aristocracy; and they are precisely the qualities by which a nation,
like an individual, attains a dominant position."[7]

This has not proved to be entirely true. The United States has
been capable of pursuing fixed designs with considerable patience
and restraint—when those designs have been concrete. Yet often
the designs themselves have proved defective for the reason that
as policy changed from a defense of concrete American interests,
at which men like Jefferson, Polk, and Lincoln were superb, to
international action in remote quarters, at which Wilson and
Franklin Roosevelt, for all the decency of their vision, were less
successful, America has lacked a deep and dense experience of
what it was about. There has been only a slight American involvement in the world's history—and crimes. And it is experience
that makes accurate perception possible, as well as a sound judgment of what can be accomplished. It is extraordinary that a
nation that understands perfectly well what money and National
Guard action can and cannot accomplish to change the minds
of Mississippians believes what it does about the efficiency of aid
and military intervention abroad.

It is a commonplace of public debate in this country—in the
newspapers, textbooks, and speeches of public officials—to condemn both the isolationism of the 1930's and the legalist internationalism of Woodrow Wilson. Isolationists are dismissed for
failing to understand the dangers of the world of the twentieth-
century dictators, America's vast commercial involvement, our
military vulnerability, and the responsibility which modern communications, weapons, and politics impose. Wilson is treated with
respect for his idealism but criticized for his innocence; his ambition to make the world safe for democracy is regarded today, with
some reason, as a black joke.

But to criticize past errors does not mean that we are liberated
from them. After World War I, Wilson and the isolationists fought
bitterly over what American policy was to be. The battle was
continued in books and articles, town meetings and radio forums,
and in Congress, all through the 1930's, until the Japanese attack

ended the argument on December 7, 1941. It began again, briefly
at least, after World War II in the postwar "Great Debate."*

Yet through all of this the contending factions were really
united in their assumptions about America and the world, and
none of them was very far from Wilson and his ambitions for
ending "power politics" and creating "an organized common
peace," though the naïveté of Wilsonianism was universally denounced. As George Kennan describes Wilson's vision, the League
of Nations "would mobilize the conscience and power of mankind
against aggression. Autocratic government would be done away
with. Peoples would themselves choose the sovereignty under
which they wished to reside. Poland would achieve her independence, as would likewise the restless peoples of the Austro-Hungarian Empire. There would be open diplomacy this time; peoples,
not governments, would run things. Armaments would be reduced
by mutual agreement. The peace would be just and secure."[8] But
the isolationists wanted no less dramatic a reform in the world.
The manifest idealism of Wilson's critics and of the isolationists
of the inter-war years hardly differed. As Kenneth Thompson
writes, they held that "the end of power politics was to be
accomplished in three ways. Ultimately, power politics would
be eliminated through instituting a world government. Practically,
power politics would be abolished when its main exemplars, the
totalitarian states, had been erased. Provisionally, this evil system
would be progressively and decisively undermined through the
example of a moral and upright nation forswearing relations with
corrupted and power-seeking nations, pursuing policies of neutrality, and abstaining from the morally ambiguous exercise of influence or coercion in world politics."[9]

And today? For all the loudly proclaimed coming-of-age of
American foreign policy, our imposing goals hardly differ—as
goals, at least—from the evangelical visions of the past, those
of Wilson *and* the isolationists. Our mission is to create, accord-

---

* It even became a three-way struggle with Henry Wallace and the other
non-communists who allowed themselves to share the Progressive Party with
communist activists, arguing an even more idealistic and trusting internationalism than the internationalism of the Roosevelt Administration which
had produced the Four Freedoms and the Atlantic Charter—conceptions
derived from the Wilsonian tradition. There were unqualified idealists,
cautious idealists, and isolationists debating postwar American policy—but
what is often forgotten is that the isolationists were idealists too.

ing to Mr. Rostow, a leading Johnson Administration planner, "no matter how long it may take, a world community in which men and nations can live at peace. No less is required of us for the safety of the Nation and the continuity of civilized life on this small planet."[10] Mr. Rusk has added that "our goal . . . is a world in which human rights are secure, a world of better life for all. . . ."[11] Not only is this our objective, but it is, as Mr. Rostow says, our responsibility to achieve it. Vice-President Humphrey has added: "Let there be no doubt about it . . . [America's] capacity . . . to help build a cooperative and progressive international community based on common interest is unique in this world and unique in history."[12] It is the sustained quality of the present American world intervention which distinguishes it from the Wilsonian intervention. It is the confidence in the efficiency and naturalness of America's world involvement which provides the chief difference between present policy and the discredited beliefs of the isolationists.

For who in America today is an isolationist? Now that the enemy, as in Vietnam, is communism, and is further identified with Chinese communism, even Republican conservatives are largely silenced. But does this kinship of moral spirit between isolationism and globalism, between Wilsonianism and globalism, demonstrate much more than a continuity of idealism in America's foreign outlook that transcends party? Is it not, in fact, an expression of a valid interest in bringing the conflicts of nations into some kind of organized check? We would argue that however genuine the idealism, this American spirit goes far beyond reasonable ambition, demonstrating a view of political possibility that has dominated, and distorted, American foreign policy for too long. The continuity in American foreign policy—seriously challenged only in the realistic and limited programs briefly followed in the late 1940's—is essentially a continuity of illusion. It is a continuity with a tradition of self-indulgence and sentimentality in foreign affairs which today has brought the United States into dangers more serious than most Americans are prepared to acknowledge. It may be that it is within our power to change this. The practical virtues of our domestic politics are equally valid for foreign policy, and we are an intelligent and resourceful society. But we need to translate our domestic realism and restraint into foreign affairs.

IDEOLOGY AND INTERNATIONAL ACTION

The current fallacies of American foreign policy can be described individually, but in the end they all reflect a single problem, a generalization from the isolated, and immeasurably lucky, American experience and a tendency to believe (and insist) that America's wants and values are universal. Nearly all sectors of American society hold the belief that American history—particularly the success of federalism and material prosperity in damping down social discord—provides a proto-typical solution for the world's disorders. This is a belief of nearly theological intensity, and it is no exaggeration to label it an American ideology. It is an evangelical belief which argumentation and chronic failure can hardly shake.

Before 1914 Americans had, of course, enjoyed a noontime security—a prosperity and power so well established and unthinkingly accepted that, as George Kennan has remarked, they "had forgotten that it had any foundations at all outside our continent. They mistook our sheltered position behind the British fleet and British Continental diplomacy for the results of superior American wisdom and virtue in refraining from interfering in the sordid differences of the Old World."[13] The Spanish-American War of 1898 had been, as much as anything else, an explosion out of boredom. We simply wanted a little gunfire, martial music, and glory, and Spain was the luckless victim (together with Cuba, whose actions to this day bear the marks of the trauma of the relationship with the United States which began in Cuba's liberation of 1898). None of the various contemporary justifications for the Spanish-American War can be dignified as part of serious strategies or political programs for this country. Even the commercial argument, that possession of the Philippines (and Hawaii) would put us in a good position for Far Eastern trade, followed the war rather than led up to it.

World War I put paid to this careless era. The foreign sources of American security—chiefly Britain's power—were destroyed as European civilization, which had hardly seen major conflict since Napoleon's exile a century before, flung itself into a carnage which exceeded the Thirty Years' War in scope and savagery. The United States was at first horrified by the war and condemned it; and then joined it, providing for it a rationale whose effect, if it had any effect on the war itself, was to prolong it and intensify the fighting, and by so doing, contributing ultimately to the conditions that brought on World War II. "The obscure foundations from which [the war's] stupendous flood has burst forth we are not interested to search for or explore."[14] This was Wilson speaking in 1916, as if an American intervention, either as would-be peacemaker or ultimately as a combatant, could be anything but futile or destructive in an international tragedy whose causes we did not wish to understand.

Caught up in the war at last, America rejected compromise, as the other combatants had done. But whereas Germany, France, and England had rejected compromise out of emotion—hatred or stubbornness, or greed—America rejected compromise out of high principle. We introduced a new interpretation of the significance of the war which went far beyond those which the European combatants had put forward. They had argued variously that the war was for national survival, a place in the sun, or that it was provoked by encirclement, or the territorial ambitions of the enemy, or that enemy victory meant the end of their empires or trade dominance or naval superiority. They had also, with what today must seem a terrible innocence, produced atrocity propaganda which was almost wholly groundless but which was to be acted out in reality by Adolf Hitler twenty-five years later —the product of the bleak inter-war years who became in fact what the Kaiser had been called, a "Beast of Berlin." The justifications which the two sides had proclaimed in 1914 and 1915 had borne simple shapes and colors—tyranny challenging the innocent, the homeland threatened by hereditary opponents or by an enemy's imperial greed. What America did when Wilson proposed the Fourteen Points was to provide an entirely new objective for the war; the goal became not simple victory but a fundamental institutional reform of international society. This was, in the now banal, but then exhilarating, phrase, the war to end war; and compromise could not be considered when such an achievement was at stake. If the European combatants had been unwise enough to reject compromise, until America entered the war with its vast power and its high purpose there was nevertheless hope that mutual exhaustion would eventually bring the two sides to reason. The irony of history was that the American intervention compounded a catastrophe.

This was the first of two immensely significant effects of the American intervention in this war. We supplied an ideological rationale for the war which went entirely beyond appeals to nationalism, national interest, even national hatred, or even beyond appeals to justice and against aggression. By relating the war to a fundamental reform in the world political system, America gave the war a moral significance which transcended the particular concerns, causes, or elements of the war. The newly defined purpose of the war was to change the condition of men in history. So doing, we raised the crucial issue of the inter-relationship between morality and political action in history—a fundamental dilemma of American foreign policy to this day.

The second significant effect of our war aims in 1917–1918 lay in the character of the reform we sought, and still seek in today's world (criticisms of the Wilsonian tradition commonly function in the past tense only). The reform we wanted was not to be "political" in the traditional understanding of politics as a kind of brokerage of the contending interests of peoples and civil societies. "We dare not turn from the principle that morality and not expediency is the thing that must guide us," Wilson had proclaimed as early as 1913. ". . . It is a very perilous thing to determine the foreign policy of a nation in the terms of material interest. It not only is unfair to those with whom you are dealing, but it is degrading as regards your own actions."[15] One might observe that this disdain for self-interest in international politics was the ideology of a very wealthy nation which had never suffered at another's hands—an ideology more suitable to a great nation than to a small one. But in any case the effect of this principled diplomacy was to substitute for international bargaining the quite different principle of law—a system which must rest on agreed principles and which requires, if it is to work, an administrative and policing mechanism by which those principles are impartially enforced upon all.

The appealing logic of this plan is that it extends to the international community the achievement which has made the internal life of nations possible. The superficial assumption it makes is that there is in fact a consensus among nations on a sufficient number of principles to make law observance possible—that all, at least, oppose war and aggression and are prepared to accept the same definition of aggression. Implicit too are assumptions about the universality of the democratic impulse, the self-evident character of principles of social justice, and the general validity of the values of individualism, consensus politics, and public altruism which are upheld, on the verbal level at least, in the states of the modern West. Crudely stated, in one contemporary formulation, this is a belief that "where the clash of individual and group interests can find outlets, there need be no resort to violence. Where such avenues are closed—where the economic system will not give people bread, or where the political system will not permit them a hearing, or where the prestige arrangements afford them no chance at dignity—men will appeal to the sword. We must make such adjustments in the international field that no nation need feel that its progress is impossible."[16] So stated, this is perhaps obvious sentimentality; but the essential argument has a tougher form. As summed up by Secretary of State Henry L. Stimson in 1932, it holds that in international conflicts one or the other participant should be named the wrongdoer. "We no longer draw a circle about them and treat them with punctilios of the duelist's code. Instead we denounce them as lawbreakers."[17]*

---

* Curiously enough, Senator Robert Taft, the spokesman for postwar isolationism, made the argument equally clear in 1949 and thus demonstrated that the belief in legal and organizational remedies for conflict is very close to universal in American politics—it exists among Republicans and Democrats, and obviously on both sides of the old isolationism-interventionism controversy. During a Senate debate in which he called for rejection of the North Atlantic Treaty, arguing that it committed the United States to undertakings and conditions which could not be foreseen and thus threatened to involve America in needless war, Taft added that "in the United Nations Charter we accepted the principle that we would go to war in association with other nations against a nation found by the Security Council to be an aggressor. . . . I believe that all nations must ultimately agree, if we are to have peace, to an international law defining the duties and obligations of such nations, particularly with reference to restraint from aggression and war. I believe that there should be international courts to determine whether nations are abiding by that law, and I believe that there should be a joint armed force to enforce that law and the decisions of that court. I believe that in the end, the public opinion of the world will come to support the principle that nations like individuals are bound by law, and will insist that any nation which violates the law be promptly subjected to the joint action of nations guided by a determination to enforce the laws of peace. It is quite true that the United Nations Charter as drafted does not yet reach the ideals of international peace and justice which I have described, but it goes a long way in that direction. . . ."[18]

George Kennan observes that "the mind of American statesmanship, stemming as it does in so large a part from the legal profession in our country, gropes with unfailing persistence for some institutional framework. . . . Behind all this, of course, lies the American assumption that the things for which other peoples in this world are apt to contend are for the most part neither creditable nor important and might justly be expected to take second place behind the desirability of an orderly world, untroubled by international violence. To the American mind, it is implausible that people should have positive aspirations, and ones that they regard as legitimate, more important to them than the peacefulness and orderliness of international life. From this standpoint, it is not apparent why other people should not join us in accepting the rules of the game in international politics. . . ."[19] To this it must be added that Kennan's is a conservative statement which is concerned with the conflicting but reasonable impulses of other nations that lead to war. There are, as well, forces of irrationality and emotion, of egoism, pride, passion, messianism, and ideological ambition, of cultural shock, racism, vengeance, even of nihilism, which have made themselves felt dramatically in the last five decades of world politics.

The American approach to international affairs typically regards the actions which such impulses produce as "outlawry"—crimes which the international community will wish to suppress. But these forces are not always so easily localized and identified. When they manifest themselves in an institution like the Nazi regime, they are, comparatively speaking, the easiest to deal with. What happens when they show themselves less dramatically among our friends, or even among ourselves, is another matter. It is, for instance, a sad commentary on the perversity of human affairs—to say nothing of the relationship between idealism and violence—that no Administration in American history intervened so often, and sometimes brutally, in Latin American affairs as the Wilson Administration. It has been well said of Wilson that rejecting economic imperialism, he practiced a kind of moral imperialism. He began his Administration by devising thirty treaties, of which twenty-two were signed, that abjured the use of force in favor of arbitration. "I am going to teach the South American republics to elect good men," Wilson asserted to a visiting Englishman in 1914.[20] But the practical effect of his noble intentions was to bombard Vera Cruz and to sanction military interventions in Mexico, Haiti, Santo Domingo, and Nicaragua—all notably without teaching the South American republics anything of the kind.

THE FAITH IN LAW

The desire for a system of law which will define "the duties and obligations" of all nations reflects three factors in the parochial American experience. First of all is the success of legal and organizational remedies in our own history. But next and more important is the intellectual appeal of schematic solutions as short-cutting politics—"power politics." Last is the effect upon us of an imprecise but very influential historicism—a deep belief in material progress—which sees men slowly but inevitably improving their lot, and in political affairs moving toward a universal constitutionalism and peace.

The first appeal is easiest to understand, although it is equally apparent that it underestimates the difficulties encountered even in the American experience. There is an impressive foundation of consensus and common purpose in the United States which made, and continues to make, the appeal to law possible and the organizational solution acceptable. But even among ourselves, law and civil administration are resisted by others than criminals. There are those who peacefully oppose what they regard as unjust law by disobeying it—and who create a new kind of problem for the institutions of civil community while providing a new mode of protest whose notable value is that it avoids or sublimates impulses which otherwise could tear the community apart. This is the way chosen by the contemporary civil rights movement, for example. But the United States is also familiar enough with violent dissidence. Often this violence is only verbalized, but too frequently it breaks out in lynchings (for which local juries may refuse to convict), in assassinations, and in beatings and mob action. Except in racial conflict we now have largely confined this kind of thing to the semi-psychotic fringe of society, but other highly civilized countries have not been so fortunate. There, significant internal minorities have traditionally resisted majority government and often have resorted to violence or treason on a mass scale. The record of the terrorist Secret Army Organization in France—a movement led by responsible political figures who had previously given distinguished service to moderate governments, and manned by a segment of both the army and the civilian population too large, too sober in their origins, and too serious in their effort at self-justification to be discounted as equivalent to lunatic-fringe Klansmen or minutemen in America —is only one recent case in point.

In such a country of Latin America as Colombia, where for more than a decade the *Violencia* has flourished, literally killing hundreds of thousands in the backlands, or in such countries of Afro-Asia as the Congo and Indonesia where civil strife seems endemic, it is obvious that no such consensus exists.

In the United States our success in achieving a kind of consensus on law and government reflects as much the lucky fact of geographical isolation and cultural homogeneity in our early national life as it does the fact that this country was founded as a free act of organization and legal compact. The theory of politics in this country, moreover, has always betrayed its origins in the Enlightenment faith, which became a Populist faith—the belief in reasonable action to improve things. The effects of this belief had been felt even before the Revolution and before the Constitution was adopted—in the native habit of democratic decision developed in townships and provincial assemblies. It was possible for this habit to develop, and a federal system to be established on its basis, to quote Tocqueville, not only because "the states have similar interests, a common origin, and a common language, but . . . they have also arrived at the same stage of civilization. . . . I do not know of any European nation, however small, that does not present less uniformity in its different provinces than the American people, which occupy a territory as extensive as one-half of Europe. The distance from Maine to Georgia is about one thousand miles; but the difference between the civilization of Maine and that of Georgia is slighter than the difference between the habits of Normandy and those of Brittany."[21]

All this ought to be self-evident: America is not Europe, still less Afro-Asia. But it is another American article of faith that all men are at bottom the same. The experience of uniformity has created a belief in uniformity, just as the values of national homogeneity resulted in making the United States into a vast assimilative machine that absorbed the great immigrations of Slavs, Italians, Jews, Irishmen, and Scandinavians of the latter nineteenth century. But this nineteenth-century triumph of native American political and ethical standards over the different traditions of the immigrants, while preserving this country's form of political life, does not argue for the inevitability of the process in far less advantageous conditions abroad. To believe this is furthermore to denigrate a brilliant and virtually unique American social feat. The other face of this implacable assimilative power of American civilization is also understood today—and deplored in its more grotesque excesses of Know-Nothingism, McCarthyism, and the Procrustean patriotism of Congressional subcommittees. Yet the excesses of American assimilationism (the anti-Orientalism of our immigration laws, and even the racism which has oppressed American Negoes and Indians), like our political virtues, derive from a national intuition of the importance of homogeneity in American political life. No such homogeneity unites Greek and Turkish Cypriotes, or Israelis and Arabs, or even the six nations of the European Common Market. Nor in any of these cases is there a single standard of politics and morality to which the factions will subordinate themselves as the nineteenth-century Ukrainian and Irish peasant in steerage or the immigrant Jewish peddler stood in awe of the standards of the native American middle class.

That the United States should then turn outward the assimilationist assumptions that have guided our domestic politics is perhaps not surprising. Our founding beliefs and our subsequent historical experience prompt us to assert a belief in an eventual world union—first consciously constitutional and legalist, and later, we assume, proceeding from this phase by an assimilative process which will at last create "world citizens" out of selfish parochialists and nationalists.

But to believe in this peaceful world process, by analogy to our own past, is not even to understand that past well. It is to forget the implications of the Southern challenge of 1861—a revolt of the agrarian, aristocratic, pre-capitalist South against the industrial, middle-class, and commercial ethos of the North. In that titanic conflict, in which nearly half a million died, one "consensus" crushed another by force. This is no optimistic prototype for a nuclear world.

THE FAITH IN UNIFICATION

We have, of course, been taught by recent history, notably the collapse of the wartime alliance with the Soviets and the outbreak of the Cold War, and the impotence of the United Nations, to give up much of that naïve faith in an immediate world law which Stimson expressed and Taft faithfully endorsed. We have substituted another version—another schematic solution which may, we believe, organize the world in a way that will outlaw conflict. Now we see regional federations of nations as the first move in a process whose implied development will be the coming together of United Europe with America into a union of the Atlantic world, and of the Atlantic world eventually with the advanced industrial countries of Asia or with a prospective political system of the Americas.* On the horizon—and nearly all now concede this is a distant horizon, decades away—is the assimilation into this great federation of constitutional and habitually democratic countries of the newer and less experienced states of Asia and Africa. Nevertheless, as Secretary Rusk has said, the "distant stars" of American foreign policy today remain these goals: that all peoples eventually enjoy Jeffersonian government, the powers of governments to be derived from the consent of their peoples; and that all states should eventually be members of a constitutional world federation—"a world community of in-

---

* Daniel Boorstin remarks that the implied thesis of the American plan for a League of Nations after World War I was that "the peoples of France, Germany, Italy, and of many lesser nations would seize the opportunity to deal with each other in the manner of Massachusetts, New York, and California. Wilson's program was not merely an embodied idealism, it was a projection of the American image onto Europe. Many of our historians have shared the Wilsonian illusions. Therefore many of them have written the history of the Peace as if there was something perverse in the unwillingness of the Senate and the American people to go along with Wilson's program for Europe. In the long perspective of our history what is surprising is the opposite: that even a considerable minority of Americans were ready to give up their traditional image of Europe and to begin to think of it as a potential America."[22] The particular forms or plans for European unification which were enthusiastically supported by the United States after World War II again were those which followed the American model (and which clearly provided for an American role in the new Europe). We have resisted—with some bitterness—schemes which reject this model and substitute for American-style federalism and moderation older European traditions which appeal to Europe's pride and sense of grandeur," and include a component of anti-Americanism, excluding America from a major European role.

dependent states, each with its own institutions but co-operating
with one another to promote their common interest and banding
together to resist aggression, a world increasingly subject to the
rule of law . . . We believe that that is also the goal of a great
majority of mankind. This identity of basic purpose gives us
friends and allies in many nations . . ."[23]

Yet the chasm between the American experience of union, constitution, and an assimilative culture, and the prospective world
experience is seldom grasped. Even in the limited conceptions of
a regional federation of Europe—a society, surely, of profound
cultural unity as well as common experience and tradition, of high
intelligence and a recent and terrible experience of nationalist
self-destructiveness—there has perhaps been too little understanding of the chasm between constitutional forms which have grown
organically and federal schemes which are theoretically conceived.

NATO, the first of the modern regional gatherings, was not initiated as a step in international federation. It was a military
alliance established in 1949 to defend Europe from Soviet attack.
It was a means for extending an American military guarantee to
Europe and for providing a legal and organizational basis for
maintaining American troops in Europe outside occupied Germany. The attribution to NATO of a larger ambition and meaning
has come only in the aftermath of what seemed a military emer-
gency in the early years of the Cold War—the expectation of imminent Soviet attack. The argument that NATO could prove to be
the precursor of permanent Atlantic union has actually been developed as the Cold War, and, therefore, the initial military
rationale of NATO, has weakened. In the years since Stalin's
death and the consequent waning of the Soviet threat, a larger
political purpose has been substituted for an original military
function now largely superseded—for institutions become invested with emotion, and more sordid interests as well. If NATO
were merely a defensive military system it might well, on strict
military and political grounds, be reduced or ended today. This,
of course, is the French argument. Only if it is more than a military system is there reason to continue and, as many argue, to
expand and develop NATO into a means for Atlantic co-operation on issues which go far beyond the Cold War. President
Johnson has said: "We must all work to multiply in number and

intimacy the ties between North America and Europe. For we shape an Atlantic civilization with an Atlantic destiny."[24] But this argument assumes that the present alliance of Western Europe with America is really a step in a constitutional drawing together of nations, a process meaningful in terms of political reform rather than of narrow military defense.

The process actually is one by which the conception of "collective security" is given a permanent justification rather than a transitory one; it is a replacement of that traditional British, and American, policy by which "collective" security was sought in the balancing of alliances and the collecting of coalitions to oppose each new enemy. Nicholas Spykman, the Yale geopolitician, once observed that the charm of power politics is that one never need grow weary of one's friends.* Today's American effort to establish a permanent anti-communist coalition foresees it as evolving into an ever larger coalition of associated nations with common values. "Our policy," Mr. Rostow has said, "has been

---

* In this view alliances are normally contracted to counter specific threats, military or diplomatic, and end when the threat fades. Such alliances are, if one likes, temporary liaisons, not marriages of the soul; but therein lies their advantage. A permanent alliance demands a community of values and interests, and where these interests are not in fact identical, one party or another must pretend that they are so, subordinating himself to the other. Thus, in today's world, the United States has come in some sense to play the thrall to German national (and irredentist) sentiment. Because we wish to retain influence in Bonn on such issues as European Common Market politics or NATO integration, we cannot recognize the present division of Germany—which is not necessarily a bad thing for Europe and the world— or the present eastern boundaries of Germany. The United States has become tied to Bonn in an alliance that purports to be more than a simple instrument of pragmatic military defense. It is true that America and West Germany are wholly united on the need to keep the Soviet armies from the territories of the Federal Republic; a Soviet occupation of West Germany would be nearly as great a tragedy to this country as it would be to Bonn, since the ultimate effects on the world balance of power would be exceedingly grave. But this does not mean that German and American interests in other areas —in Eastern Europe, say, or the Caribbean, or Southeast Asia—are at all identical. Bonn, the capital of a highly commercial republic, in fact cares nothing for American policy in Latin Ameria and Afro-Asia. In Washington the exaggerated sense of identification with West German interests impedes American policy in the Soviet satellites; nothing holds the Soviet orbit together so much as a Polish and Czechoslovak fear of Germany. The truth is that by seeking to make the need for military defense in Western Europe into the germ of a larger union, the United States has given new validity to the fading Warsaw Pact. The fear of Germany binds Moscow and its northern satellites long after the common ideology of communism has begun to fail as an amalgam among the Bloc members.

systematically to strengthen the foundations for national independence. As people gather strength and confidence and seek a new status on the world scene, our task is to try to organize these more assertive, stronger, national states in ways which will make the world community more orderly and peaceful. The need for organization arises because simple nationalism has limitations in the kind of world in which we live . . . safety still depends on collective security arrangements and on the continued commitment of the United States. . . ." The objective, he adds, is no "sudden emergence of a peaceful world community overnight. . . . There is a long road ahead; but, despite the continuing crises, despite all sorts of noise and confusion in the world, we are on a path which can lead, not only the free world but the whole world, toward something which we can all recognize as peace."[25] Such an objective clearly transcends the old conceptions of security by means of alliance and attributes to American foreign policy an imposing historical purpose, one which recalls the persistent moral formulations of America's world role which distinguished our World War I debates and professions of purpose.

It is not that the old system of the balance of power and pragmatic alliance has proved itself infallible in history. We know that this is not so, though the hundred years' peace between 1815, the year of the defeat of Napoleon, and the outbreak of war in 1914 was no mean achievement.* We do not know that

---

* "Apart from the Crimean War—a more or less colonial event," writes Karl Polanyi, "England, France, Prussia, Austria, Italy, and Russia were engaged in war among each other for altogether only eighteen months." Yet the hundred years' peace "was certainly not the result of the absence of grave causes for conflict. Almost continuous shifts in the internal and external conditions of powerful nations and great empires accompanied this irenic pageant. During the first part of the century civil wars, revolutionary and anti-revolutionary interventions were the order of the day. . . . During the second half of the century the dynamics of progress were released; the Ottoman, Egyptian, and the Sheriffian empires broke up or were dismembered; China was forced by invading armies to open her door to the foreigner and in one gigantic haul the continent of Africa was partitioned. Simultaneously, two powers rose to world importance: the United States and Russia. National unity was achieved by Germany and Italy. . . . An almost incessant series of open wars accompanied the march of industrial civilization into the domains of outworn cultures. . . . Yet every single one of these conflicts was localized and numberless other occasions for violent change were either met by joint action or smothered by compromise by the Great Powers. . . . Under varying forms and ever-shifting ideologies . . . peace was preserved."[26]

modern theories of collective security can do as well, for one thing is clear: where one system of collective security is counterbalanced by another, as in the opposing alliances of the Cold War, a clash if it comes may be an Armageddon. The chances of localizing the conflict are not great. But neither is it certain that the outbreak of the two world wars testified to the bankruptcy of the old alliance system, any more than today's comparative peace testifies to the efficiency of the new one: World Wars I and II stemmed from darker causes than mere inept diplomacy, and the present state of the world, especially the Cold War, occasional rhetoric in Moscow, Washington, and Peking notwithstanding, suggests that international tempers are remarkably relaxed.

Thus the present American theory of international security, resting as it does on the notion of unities, merits only the noncommittal Scotch verdict—"not proven." Yet to say that the American interest in a legal and organizational remedy to international political problems is one form of projecting onto the world the political habits and assumptions of the United States itself is not to say that this is wholly false, or a foolish or wrong thing to do. Political civilization has been a matter of extending constitutional and legal forms and gaining a voluntary acceptance of arbitration and law to resolve conflict in place of appeals to threat or to force. The criticism to be made is rather that the United States characteristically oversimplifies this process, tends to beg the question of consensus, and makes use of this commitment to intellectually simplified forms of world organization as a substitute for—or evasion of—policy that addresses the complexities of political action. Organization does not resolve conflict, although it may transpose conflict from one level to another. Its purpose is to channel conflict and provide means for its arbitration and containment. But it may intensify it, or even make war.

We have noted that a federation in 1789 did not solve the latent conflict between North and South in this country which was to erupt a half-century later. Yet the two areas, encompassing disparate values and social types, and also competitive economic ethos—the one industrializing, the other agrarian and slave-holding—conceivably could have peacefully coexisted, even in amity, had the Union not been created. Once it was created, the ultimate recourse of North-South competition was the Civil

War. Clearly, then, organization does not obviate force. Force is inherent in it, for as Reinhold Niebuhr has observed: "It cannot be denied that modern nations and empires have been able to extend their dominion and to include within their original community many and various other communities which do not have obvious affinities with the original basis of unity. But this policy is not always successful. . . . It may be recorded as axiomatic that the less a community is held together by cohesive forces in the texture of its life the more it must be held together by power."[27]

So much for internal conflict; but neither are political unities necessarily peaceful in their foreign relations. Usually the reverse is true. Take, for example, the German *Bund* before Bismarck, which loosely associated Austria and Prussia with the lesser German-speaking states. It was called by Gerhard Ritter the "most stable ordering of peace the West has known since the days of the high Middle Ages."[28] Clumsy and unplanned, an awkward historical growth among related peoples, it was, as a contemporary observer called it, "impregnable in defense and incapable of aggression." Bismarck broke the *Bund*, creating in its place an empire, a *Reich*, a centralized Germany with a united government (which excluded Austria). The results for the world—but also for a once peaceful and "impregnable" Germany—are well known.

And to speak of American and German warnings against a simplistic universalism is to invoke the history of the successful unions. The unsuccessful ones include the various pan-Arab schemes of our own day, which express a legitimate desire for union among a culturally homogeneous people but which have actually resulted only in a weary succession of assassinations and *coups d'état;* and the ephemeral unions of the African states, where the collapse of the "East African Common Market" is only the latest failure. We see conflict latent too in the nominal association of American states in the OAS, which is largely a fictional plastering-over of inevitable but unresolvable tensions between the Protestant, aggressive, Anglo-Saxon United States and the Latin American states whose chief source of common political purpose is resistance to the North Americans. (In the words of a Mexican of the revolutionary days of anti-religious proscriptions and self-conscious radicalism, the real attitude to the United States is far from an unambiguous admiration: "Poor Mexico, so far from God and so near to the United States.") And in each of these abortive or halting associations there have been at least some of the ingredients of natural association—a common language or religion, a customary or historical link, a geographical situation or shared strategic interests.

The lesson, surely, is that if political association and agreement on a common international law are defensible general goals in foreign affairs, the process itself is bloody and long. Lewis Namier has remarked of the unions of 1848: "A constitutional regime is secure when its ways have been engrained in the habits and instinctive reactions—*dans les moeurs*—of the political nation: it safeguards civilized life, but it presupposes agreement and stability as much as it secures them; and it can hardly be expected to build up, recast, or dissect the body in which it resides. States are not created or destroyed, and frontiers redrawn or obliterated, by argument and majority votes; nations are freed, united, or broken by blood and iron, and not by a generous application of liberty and tomato sauce. . . ."[29]

One does not always find this very clearly understood in American formulations of the problem. President Johnson has said: "Law is the great civilizing machinery. It liberates the desires to build, and it subdues the desire to destroy. And if war can tear us apart, law can unite us—out of fear or love or reason, or all three."[30] This is a qualified statement of the optimist's case; but the difference between the President's and the historian's version is critical.

THE FAITH IN REASON

The emotional force behind organizational and constitutional solutions to political conflict derives from the fact that they are simple, and they are simple because they beg the question of the ordeal of common experience and of the coming together of communities. They function from the top down, imposing a scheme upon humanity which humanity is expected to recognize as in the common interest. When he was preparing for the Versailles Conference, President Wilson refused to have the experience of the Congress of Vienna studied for any lesson it might provide the treaty negotiators of 1919. He wanted the problems of politics settled "not by diplomats or politicians each eager to serve his own interests but by dispassionate scientists —geographers, ethnologists, economists—who had made studies of the problems involved."[31] But as the Prussian historian Frederick Meinecke said of the influence of theoreticians on German political life: "They could give to their political aspirations a spirit of purity and independence, of philosophical idealism and of elevation above the concrete play of interest . . . but through their defective feeling for the realistic interests of actual state life they quickly descended from the sublime to the extravagant and eccentric."[32]

Wilson himself was expected by Europeans to arrive at Versailles with a comprehensive scheme for implementing his Fourteen Points. Actually he had nothing. At Versailles—according to John Maynard Keynes, who was a British official at the time —he displayed only the most nebulous and ill-informed notions about what might be done to create the new European order. Yet, as a war leader, he had repeatedly demanded a new order as a justification for the prosecution of the war to victory. This failure was obviously not a result of ignorance or simple hypocrisy, but rather a case of naïve faith in the power of reason and a spirit of reform to cut through the dark undergrowths of political passion and historical conflict. Any discussion of American experience in international politics must constantly return to the case of Wilson, not because Wilson was an ignoble figure —he was an imposingly good man—but because Wilson provides the prototype of the dominant modern American encounter with the world. It is an encounter which in Wilson's day was understood in terms of the fresh new world of America, powerful and idealistic, applying its energies to the solution of the crisis of the old world which had all but destroyed itself. In fact, Wilson's intervention made things worse; it proved to be an intervention which brought only naïve good intentions to bear on a crisis whose sources were deeply imbedded in the history and culture of Europe—and, by extension, of America.

Whatever the Calvinist strain in the origins of America may have been, it seems fair to say that as a country we no longer believe in Original Sin. We have instead exaggerated the old Enlightenment faith in reason and believe that full bellies and good will can exorcise demons. Put another way, popular American political theory, at least as applied to the external world, is relentlessly pre-Freudian. There is no place in our public debate for notions of an unconscious destructive impulse or irrational action by nations. Despite the experience of a twentieth century replete with horrors—the hecatombs of the World War I battle-fields on the Marne and the Somme, the mass purges and the concentration camps of the totalitarians, the firestorm raids of World War II, to say nothing of the atomic horrors of Hiroshima and Nagasaki—the American diplomatic credo remains relentlessly optimistic. Though all these things have happened in our time, we believe they are expungeable from future history, and not merely expungeable but, in some sense, easily so. The claims of realism are noted, but in a curiously perfunctory way.

Mr. Johnson has said: "If world conditions were largely satisfactory, it would not be difficult to evolve a rule of law. But we do not live in a satisfactory world. It is stained with evil and injustice, by ruthless ambition and passionate conflict. Only by fighting these forces do we help build a base on which the temple of law may rest."[33] This seems like a post-Wilsonian realism, holding to the ideal of world reform but humbler before the conditions which reform must overcome. Yet the validity of the political realism must still be doubted; in fact, it reflects an American historicism, a faith in the millennial victory of reason, a conception of evil as identifiable and as ultimately subject to defeat—and all of these are beliefs which few, except Americans, can today sustain.

THE FAITH IN PROGRESS

We are all historicists, and an oddly naïve historicism is the third element underlying the characteristic American approach to foreign affairs. Whether we acknowledge them or not, each of us holds opinions about the meaning of history and the destiny of the human race, though the way we order our practical affairs may contradict the beliefs we would seriously profess. But even the practical historicism of the United States is progressive and optimistic. It stems primarily from the eighteenth-century Enlightenment belief in the imminent feasibility of a perfectly reasonable form of human society in which the old crimes and injustices of history are progressively eliminated by intelligent reforms and a just ordering of interests, with an allied influence of perfectionist sectarian Protestant Christianity. The success of the American Republic, combined with that sense of moral separateness and superiority we have already mentioned, supported this faith in America's becoming steadily better and better—not merely richer, but *morally* better. The nineteenth-century American anthropologist Lewis Morgan summed up this powerful faith in man well when he wrote in 1877: "Democracy in government, brotherhood in society, equality in rights and privileges, and universal education foreshadow the next higher plane of society to which experience, intelligence, and knowledge are steadily tending."[34] The emphasis here was on the notion of steady, inevitable advance. And Morgan, though he was American, meant all men. There was nothing in this American faith to warn of the near-catastrophe of 1914, to say nothing of Buchenwald or Hiroshima.

As for the American nation itself, as D. W. Brogan has put it, the American is "convinced that if not all is for the best in the best of all possible countries, it is on the way to becoming so."[35] A good deal might be added to this picture about the alienation and despair which exist amidst the resolute optimism of white middle-class America, about the native streak of violence and nihilism which exists amidst the Rotary stereotypes, breaking out in Ku Klux Klan and Know-Nothing politics, but it is undeniable that the public philosophy of America is largely as Brogan states it. Our public rhetoric—the language of our wisest men in public life as well as the dealers in genial platitudes—is fundamentally optimistic. We have a secure faith in our power to improve our condition, and our destiny to accomplish that improvement, that was only briefly shaken during the economic collapse of the 1930's.

At the conceptual level this naïve faith in progressive improvement is supported by simple analogies between politics and technology. Americans are passionate in their love for technology, and in their mastery of it. Technology is taken as the normative activity of society, so that what man has accomplished in ridding society of grinding labor is thought to presage what can now be done to rid society of cruelty and greed. What is needed, the American faith holds, is a new "science of society" which will match the physical sciences in its certainty and technical mastery. But who will then use this knowledge and for what purpose is not always asked.

In America scientists and engineers are often those with the most unqualified faith in the power of intellect to discern the underlying laws of politics and establish organizations and systems by which these laws will be turned to the good of man. As is clear enough in the voluminous contemporary literature on disarmament and "world order," it is men of scientific temper who are often the new Utopians; or at least who display the most naked faith in the power of organization and logic to obviate conflict. But they are not really alone in these beliefs. An American pessimist today is almost a contradiction in terms.

Yet the outcome of the particular belief in techniques is evident in the repeated attempts—notably in Pentagon appraisals—to find "systems," that is, organizational or technological solutions, capable of achieving political ends. In the political sphere modern America harnesses enormous sophistication of technique to goals which are derived largely from unanalyzed tradition. Thus the government has persistently sought to deal with Vietnam in terms of essentially engineering or organizational solutions. The conviction is that Vietnam's crisis can somehow be remedied by the right combination of military and administrative reforms: new tactics, new systems of rural regroupment and security, new methods for Saigon's leaders to "get through to the people," a new emphasis on civic action by military units, new "quick-response" security forces, new village information and indoctrination programs. American critics of our current policy are just as often convinced of the merit of programmatic solutions, except that they are inclined to see these in terms of new structures of government or administration, a new "commitment to democracy" in Saigon, an aid program to make South Vietnam a "showplace of democracy," schemes for "democratic revolution." All of these are intended to isolate the Viet Cong and win the allegiance of the Vietnamese peasants by outbidding the Viet Cong in what is taken to be the peasantry's quest for justice, prosperity, and free political institutions. Both sides believe that America's values and aims in Vietnam are self-evidently valid and relevant, and that our troubles must stem from failures in translating these into practical action and popular appeal. Obviously there is some truth in the specific critiques both sides make, and in many of the proposed remedies, but both ignore the possibility that Vietnam's upheaval is too deeply rooted, too passionate and particular in its sources, for "reasonable" solution—the possibility that one element in the upheaval might, in fact, be what we would regard as a revolt against "reason," against the meliorist and pragmatic methods of a foreign system, and against its values and goals.

The Pentagon has vainly sought a cure for the difficulties our European policies have encountered in organizational devices or reforms—a Multilateral Nuclear Force, an Atlantic Nuclear Force, "consultation" in American nuclear planning. But the new European challenges to the United States arise from a discontent with the Continent's present power relationship with the United States. France's sense of autonomy and desire for ultimate control over its own nuclear defense, still less its search for a restoration of "grandeur" (as we have ample reason by now to know) can hardly be ended by giving France a minority position on an American strategy committee or in an American command post. Germany's problem lies in its geographical and political division, its desire for reunification, the hostility of its allies, who are also its former victims, to this unification, and its complex desire to have at present the substance of autonomous power and yet to avoid the vulnerabilities, responsibilities, and risks that real autonomy will bring. This is an immense problem and it is not to be solved by mere nuclear consultation or by evading present realities with formulas of an eventual "Atlanticism," which even if it were achieved, could not reunite Germany or bring America to assess its Central European commitments in the same way as a Germany that dwells there. Nor can the American schemes rehabilitate Germany in the eyes of the East European states and the Soviet Union (nor even necessarily of the West Europeans and the Germans themselves). And the Soviets, unless they are defeated in a war we do not intend to fight, must consent to Germany's reunification.

But the American critics of present policy have again tended to look for solutions to deep ideological or national divisions among today's nations in simple organizational schemes—disarmament or arms-limitation plans, or systems of policy consultation, or proposals for co-operative space or foreign aid ventures. But these would properly follow a reconciliation, and in that case, would take on important symbolic meaning; otherwise they function as empty forms, like the Pan-American Union in the days of habitual American military intervention in Latin American affairs.*

The government—this Administration but also its predecessors —has persistently attempted to damp down political crises or buy off revolutionary forces with foreign aid programs. Surely, one such argument goes, a vast development of the Mekong River Valley will so benefit the people of that region that self-destructive civil violence ought to be halted and constructive regional development programs begun. But the revolutionists fight on; the governments involved are indifferent to this great plan. They seem to prefer war to progress and order. The societies we attempt to influence seem to have an unaccountable addiction to violence in place of that pragmatic adjustment of economic and political mechanisms, to say nothing of "prestige arrangements," that American social millenarian critics have recommended as "alternatives to the A-bomb" or as a strategy "beyond deterrence." America must face squarely the implications of the fact that in the face of these sensible norms, men choose destruction and

---

* A case in point is the limited Test Ban Treaty signed by the United States and the Soviet Union in 1963. Coming as it did after the Cuban missile confrontation of the autumn of 1962, and the gradual lessening of Soviet-American tensions which dates back to Stalin's death in 1953, or at least to the First Geneva Conference of 1955 which led to the Soviet evacuation of Austria, the Test Ban Treaty had genuine importance. What it was, in effect, was a weak, or informal, non-aggression pact between the two Cold War blocs, a summation of previous political progress achieved over many months and years. (It was not, and is not, an important means of halting nuclear proliferation, since the two powers, France and China, now acquiring nuclear systems have refused to sign the Treaty and have not thereby been seriously inconvenienced by the functioning of "world opinion." The Soviet Union now seeks out France as a *de facto* ally on a variety of international issues, and even characterizes the general French position as "constructive" or "correct." Peking's admission to the United Nations—which it is doubtful that Peking really seriously seeks—has not been especially hampered in Afro-Asia by China's new nuclear status.)

The point that needs to be remembered is not that the Treaty ended a virulent Cold War (a war which in any event is not quite ended) or even mitigated it, but that it put the official stamp on the previous *de facto* reconciliation of the parties. A mere signing of such a treaty in the midst of extreme cold-war tension would, first of all, have been unlikely, and, second, would no more have mitigated the Cold War than did the fact that the United States and the Soviet Union sat together on the United Nations Security Council when that war broke out.

deprivation. The *bonzes,* and alienated Americans too, drench themselves in gasoline and burn themselves—to our horror and incomprehension.

THE PROJECTION OF AMERICAN VALUES AND PERCEPTIONS

We fail to understand this seeming resistance to reason and progress, first of all because no nation can expect to comprehend another; few individuals can approach even a limited and insecure grasp of the motives of others. That much is common experience; those, even in personal life, whom we know best are also those whose ultimate mystery is most evident to us. Who really knows his parents, his wife, his children?

But in politics—the collective action of men—this dilemma is infinitely multiplied, and the "forces," "trends," policies, ideologies, and movements—those categories which populate our political discussion—are our own inventions to articulate a reality which, we also ought to know, largely eludes us. Thus, for example, to speak of communism, fascism, "reaction," the "left" in the myriad new states of Afro-Asia is a kind of political nominalism—a stubborn insistence that political and economic terms and habits of thought that have meaning, as labels, in modern Europe or America can be transferred to cultures profoundly different from our own, and which even when they are in transit to "modernism," whatever that may be, must underneath remain alien.

There is, however, a particular American problem here. America is an impressively capable society, but we are also a peculiarly parochial society with a poor record of deep or comprehensive interest in other societies. The reason lies perhaps in the intensity of our own national experience, the need we have had to concentrate upon *making* ourselves into a nation. (The states of Western Europe, after all, became modern nations by virtue of being what they already were; the continuity of the British or Italian nation is a continuity of place and society thousands of years old, whereas the continuity of America is less than a few hundred years old; and the American people is a phenomenal in-gathering from the entire world.) One might think that our worldwide origins would have produced an unparalleled knowledge or sympathy for others. Yet this has not been true. Our isolationism manifests itself here too, perhaps as a matter of hardly conscious yet deliberate choice, part of our repudiation of the old world. America, after all, is the creation of men who did not truly like it elsewhere; this, too, is our tradition. So that whatever it is that America is fated to be in world history, we are not well suited to be the world's mentor.

Even at the level of culture we do not manifest a real interest in other societies, even those closely related to our own. Even when American writers like Mark Twain, or Henry James, or Ernest Hemingway, or Henry Miller have written of Europe, it has been to examine the condition of an *American* there, the quality of an American experience abroad. America's imperialist bout after the war with Spain produced no Kipling, who, whatever his jingoism, showed a real understanding and affection for the Indian. No American has written about Mexico or the Caribbean as Wilfred Thesiger wrote about Arabs or André Malraux about East Asia. Or at least there are few American writers who show a real sympathy for, an inner understanding of, foreign peoples as such, apart from their mere function in a political war. What exists, by contrast, is a ponderous academic literature.

Our scholarship in the culture, history, and politics of foreign societies is extensive but not, all things considered, very deep. We have not done, in short, for any other country what Tocqueville did for us, nor even what Rebecca West did for the Balkans. The enormous number of "area studies" and political investigations of foreign countries which the Cold War has produced are rarely distinguished by insight or empathy. And American political science as a discipline has even in recent years interested itself in developing theoretical "models" and "systems," on the example of economic mathematics, whose tendency, whatever their other merit, is to eliminate the need for specific understanding, or intimate data and intuition, in studying foreign affairs.

The significance of this is borne out by the common experience of American soldiers, officials, businessmen, and tourists abroad. Only infrequently do Americans really enter into the texture of a foreign society. Expatriate is an epithet among Americans, and there are few American expatriates who do not succumb to dilettantism. The Irish (and the Poles) made a career of expatriation for centuries, never losing their Irishness but managing to integrate thoroughly into France or Spain or Latin America, as soldiers as well as adventurers, priests, housemaids, artists. The French and English are not good expatriates but they are better than we, and they both have distinguished lists of soldiers, scholars, writers, saints, and cranks who have deeply penetrated foreign societies. The American cases of comparable service are few.

We seem to hoard our Americanism and avoid compromising it. Our way of coping with the foreign world is, characteristically, to define it as another America, since by this means we conjure away a host of complexities. This is a matter first of belief in that fictitious entity, the "common man," who is held to be, everywhere, alike in his essential qualities; and while it is rhetoric to talk of the common man, the rhetoric arises out of serious belief. No American would be likely to deny completely these remarks of President Johnson, speaking of the revolutionary uprising in the Dominican Republic in 1965: the people of that country "do not want government by extremists of either the left or right . . . they want—as we do—food and work and quiet in the night . . . they want—as we do—a constitutional government that will represent them all—and work for all their hopes. . . . Those are the hopes of the Dominican people. But they are our hopes, too. And they are shared by responsible people in every nation of this hemisphere. . . . We want for the peoples of this hemisphere only what they want for themselves—liberty, justice, dignity, a better life for all."[36]

Is this true? At one level it obviously is not true. The Dominican rebels clearly wanted a kind of government which conflicted with the kind of government the United States wanted for their country—and they were by no means a mere conspiratorial band. They have since come to enlist very large sectors of popular support. The Argentinians of the 1940's, the Cubans of the 1960's, the Mexicans of the first thirty years of this century, the Nicaraguans and Panamanians of the nineteenth century—all have struggled against what the United States has stood for in their day. But should it not be said that this has been a misunderstanding, errors on their part as well as ours; that if they *really* knew what the United States wanted for them we would find agreement and unity? That conviction, perhaps vulgarized, is the common apologia; and it is implicit in what Mr. Johnson says.

The truth is that at the simple level of specific interests and ambitions these people have often understood what we wanted better than we ourselves have understood it. The Nicaraguans, Panamanians, and Mexicans have always understood—though they might not phrase it so dispassionately—that our repeated interventions have expressed specific economic or strategic commitments and interests or ambitions to be defended or advanced, and that these commitments and interests were not theirs. That we acted with a gloss of idealistic rhetoric and an admixture of genuine idealism does not spare us from the kind of critique E. H. Carr has made of all the democracies in the years after World War I. "The charge is not that human beings fail to live up to their principles. . . . What matters is that these supposedly absolute and universal principles were not principles at all, but the unconscious reflections of national policy based on a particular interpretation of national interest at a particular time. There is a sense in which peace and cooperation between nations or classes or individuals is a common and universal end irrespective of conflicting interests and politics. There is a sense in which a common interest exists in the maintenance of order, whether it be international order or 'law and order' within the nation. But as soon as the attempt is made to apply these supposedly abstract principles to a concrete political situation, they are revealed as the transparent disguises of selfish vested interests."[37]

Obviously the United States is vulnerable to such a charge, although we are inclined to place our admissions of guilt in the past tense only, as if the Caribbean interventions of recent years—the Bay of Pigs fiasco in 1961 and the Santo Domingo occupation of 1965—can be understood as outside a historical record of almost casual American Caribbean interventions: United States troops in Cuba in 1898–1902, 1906–1909, 1917–1922, plus a permanent naval base at Guantánamo; troops in Haiti in 1914–1934 and a "financial supervision" from 1916 until 1941; troops in the Dominican Republic in 1913 and 1916–1924, plus a "financial supervision" that began in 1905 and only ended in 1941; a military occupation of Nicaragua in 1909–1910, 1912–1925, 1926–1933 and the usual "financial supervision" from 1911 to 1924; and a military occupation of Vera Cruz in 1914.[38]

It is perfectly true that by comparison, say, to the colonial record of the Congo Free State—established by Leopold I in the nineteenth century as a kind of private imperial domain—

the American record is a benign one; it may well be, as in the Philippines and Puerto Rico, that the United States has well and truly tried to discharge its obligation of "the white man's burden" more often than it has not. But imperialism is not only the sordid record of Leopold in the Congo. It is also Britain's civilizing role in India—the gift of a disinterested civil service, a concept of democracy, and a common law. It is the genuine achievements of the French *mission civilisatrice* in Negro Africa and even in Indochina. And as the turbulent political reality of the present-day Philippines and its socio-cultural distraction (a kind of caricatured Americanism superimposed on Spanish and native influences) suggest, our successes of this kind are not so clear. We are not wholly free of the taint of imperialism, past or present. Perhaps we should be inhuman if we were. It may be that the American conviction that "plain ordinary men are the same everywhere" is truer in a harsher sense than we like to admit. At least, and this is the crucial point, Latin Americans would say so.

But whatever the American penchant for self-congratulation, is there not, whatever universal selfishness and error exist in history, an underlying truth to the belief that the people of the world *do* want the peace and freedom and opportunity which we, however clumsily, want for them, and upon which we, with whatever shortcomings and failures, base our national life? There was a time when the American—and America—was a near-mythic figure for much of the world. The American was understood as the citizen of a society which was Everyman's goal. Today this sentimental view of us seems chiefly to survive among those New Guinea tribesmen who practice "cargo-cults," making religious uses of the discarded American equipment of World War II. It was a naïve picture which most Europeans and some Asians had of America in the past, although it had valid sources in our revolution, our practical hospitality to immigrants, and our relatively disinterested acts, as well as words, of liberation during the two world wars. But for the most part—though not entirely —the American image in the world was a projection of the wants and illusions of a depressed mankind. "*Amerika,*" said Goethe, "*du hast's besser.*"

But we were not as good as the illusion. The illusion had to disappear, in part at least, when America showed itself to be a real, and thus flawed, country. It was bound to be undermined by America's Cold War political and military interventions, whatever their substantive necessity and merit. (Yet even the harshest critics of America among the intelligentsia of postwar Europe, seeing greed and imperialism in everything America did, and denouncing us passionately, in that passion sounded often enough like betrayed lovers.) On our part, this identity as the one society which had passed the old limits into a "new world" was cultivated and proclaimed by us, both as humble believers in our calling and as prideful pharisees. In the language of Emma Lazarus, we celebrated liberty's gathering-in of "the poor, the huddled masses" of the world. In Wilson's somber statement of 1919, we asserted that our world role had come about "by no plan of our conceiving, but by the hand of God who led us into this way. . . . It was of this that we dreamed at our birth. America shall in truth show the way."[39]

Here again is the moral passion that dominates our belief about the world. But setting that aside—assuming that we are indeed "better," "purer," more advanced on a "way" which leads toward truth and peace, as well as toward material wealth and industrial power—the problem remains: how accurately do we see the world, and how valid are our judgments when we interpret not the ultimate longings, but the immediate realities and motives of those others, the peoples with whom our foreign policy must deal? Do we really grasp what sends thirteen-year-old boys and grandmothers into battle with U. S. Marines in Vietnam? We speak of the enemy's ideological fanaticism or of men drugged before battle, but what moves the Buddhist priest in South Vietnam to die terribly, or a "reactionary" like Ngo Dinh Diem stubbornly to create the kind of self-defeating mandarin and sectarian government he did establish, and to struggle against our sensible, pragmatic counsels and our material threats until, rather than give in, he met his death?

Our inadequacies in Vietnam might be interpreted as mere tactical errors, but they are not. They spring from deeper causes. Optimistic American society is fundamentally different from most of the world's cultures. Do we urban Americans remotely understand the kind of society where violence is the mark of man's honor and where vendettas are pursued between families for generations? We ought to understand Europe even though we may not understand Vietnam. But can Americans comprehend the Montenegro of fifty years ago and that lingers on in isolated valleys today? A contemporary Montenegrin, Milovan Djilas, writes of his own family, "typical in one respect: the men of several generations have died at the hands of Montenegrins, men of the same faith and name. My father's grandfather, my own two grandfathers, my father, and my uncle were killed as though a dread curse lay upon them. My father and his brother and my brothers were killed. . . . Generation after generation, and the bloody chain was not broken . . . it seems to me that I was born with blood on my eyes. My first sight was of blood, my first words were blood and bathed in blood."[40] Can Americans comprehend this? Sicilians and Andalusians would.

Do we grasp the aristocratic impulse, the elitism of contemporary French society, or the sense of stubborn class identity which still influences the political behavior of French and Italian industrial workers? Do our intelligence and foreign aid agencies understand the stubborn class and family exclusivism of Latin American "oligarchs"? We ought to understand Great Britain, but do we really grasp the dynamics of a society in which class barriers are still savage and real? Do we understand the pessimism amidst wealth of the Swedes, to say nothing of the tortured idealism of those hundreds of French paratroopers—the "centurions" —who performed acts of great cruelty in Algeria, repugnant to themselves, in the desperate belief that they were saviors of France and by extension of Europe?

Andrei Gromyko, *the* Soviet man, once remarked, "My personality does not interest me." Paul Gauguin declared, "Life being what it is, one dreams of revenge." Simone Weil said, "It is better to fail than to succeed in doing harm." These are clearly not Americans speaking. Possibly it is really not important to understand them, since politics must deal in gross shapes and not in private personalities. But it is not unimportant to be able to understand what Baudelaire wrote in his notebooks a century ago: "It is not specifically in political matters that the universal ruin or the universal progress—for the name matters little—will be manifested. That will appear in the degradation of the human heart. Need I describe how the last vestiges of statesmanship will struggle painfully in the last clutches of a universal bestiality, how the Governors will be forced—in maintaining themselves and erecting a phantom of order—to resort to measures which would make our men of today shudder . . . ? So far will progress have atrophied in us all that is spiritual, that no dream of the Utopians, however bloody, sacrilegious, or unnatural, will be comparable to the result."[41] Reading these words, we are now in deeper waters than mere foreign policy, or what ordinarily is taken as politics. But who could deny weight to this prophecy in our generation of death camps, racial extermination, class purges, "rectification campaigns," and depersonalized warfare in which a few men, with the proper equipment, destroy thousands whom they never meet, or see, or touch?

Americans ordinarily prefer to draw back from topics such as this; we like to say that such horrors are either crimes of the past, or that they arise from the forces which we struggle against. When the identifiable enemy is beaten, they will end. "The world," Under Secretary of State George Ball has declared, "has divided like an amoeba into two opposing systems of ideology and power—one based on free choice, the other on the subservience of the individual to rigid dogma."[42] That is one way to attempt to conjure away the horrors which Baudelaire prophetically perceived as latent in the twentieth-century political condition. But such a Manichean view of politics is essentially equivalent to the communist's comfortable perception of the world as a dialectical process in which progress and evil are locked in combat. Ours is the isolationist fiction of a world in which despotism and evil are easily identified and killable; in such a world, victory over evil is finally possible.

Mr. Johnson has said that "the roots of . . . trouble are found wherever the landless and the despised, the poor and the oppressed, stand before the gates of opportunity seeking entry into a brighter land. They can get there only if we narrow the gap between the rich nations and the poor—and between the rich and the poor within each nation. And this is the heart of the purpose of the United States."[43] Though it is a better and more humane statement of the problem than Mr. Ball's, this still evades the issue, since it implies that if the material problems of wealth and its distribution are overcome—a great organizational and technical problem, certainly, but not inconceivably difficult—we would automatically find ourselves in a different kind of world.

Both statements are fundamentally optimistic, since the crises they describe are soluble. If we merely face identifiable enemies, we can beat them if we mobilize enough power. If the world's bloody-mindedness stems primarily from poverty, the unequal distribution of wealth, a belief that is close to being an American faith (but not a Montenegrin, Sicilian, or Vietnamese faith), we can deal with the problem if we only put our minds to it. As Mr. Rostow has put it: "There is a long road ahead; but . . . when a planner scans the whole horizon, he feels an underlying confidence, not only in the general direction in which the United States is going, but also in the prevailing currents of world history."[44] This is language Americans like to hear. "Our goal," Mr. Rusk says, is "a world of independent nations . . . cooperating with one another . . . a world free of aggression; a world which moves towards the rule of law . . . a world of better life for all mankind."[45]

THE MODERN AMERICAN EXPERIENCE

We prefer this interpretation of the world and of history because it coincides with our belief about ourselves and about our own history. The Baudelairean horrors that such a faith denies are, after all, horrors from which Americans have been exempt. We have enthusiastically given up isolationism as a policy but, and this is the point, *emotionally and morally we remain largely an isolated nation.* The terrors of this century—the violence, ideological betrayals, the wars, purges, military occupations, the death camps and population transportations and police torture —have hardly touched the United States.

The last fifty years have seen a series of great world crises which have changed the nature of war and international politics and, with the rise of totalitarian societies, the condition and fate of entire peoples in the quality of their individual lives. While America has played a role in these events, it has been a lucky role: we have largely been spared the intensity of the experience. We have skimmed the surface. We entered World War I three years after it had begun and with no real notion of what war on the Western Front had become, or what that war was likely to accomplish. Our military intervention was an insouciant adventure; the *élan* and dash of the Americans in such battles as Château-Thierry, Belleau Wood, and the Argonne evidenced **not** only courage but innocence and ignorance. Our British and French allies, and the German enemy, veterans of three years of the heaviest casualties in the history of warfare, were impressed; but they also thought the Americans were mad.

In this war our fatal casualties were about fifty-three thousand. The French in World War I lost one in every twenty-eight of their population and their country was the ravaged battleground on which, for five years, trench fighting was waged with artillery and gas barrages on a scale never before, or since, equaled in warfare. The Germans had a casualty total of six million men. The Russians suffered seven million casualties, two million of them battle deaths. Britain, even though it was spared the civil devastation of the countries on the Continent (except for the erratic damage of Zeppelin bombing raids), lost one million men dead on the Western Front and another two million wounded. This, in a nation of less than a fifty-million population, meant that the postwar elegies for a "lost generation" were literally true for Britain, but also for the Continental powers.

Woodrow Wilson had once said that people called him an idealist. "Well," he replied, "that is how I know that I am an American." The Europeans, considering what they had suffered in 1914–1918, might have said that America could afford idealism. In fact they did not; at least they did not until the splendid vision of reform Wilson had proposed to them collapsed ignobly and inter-war Europe had become, on the one side, a society of demoralized or incompetent democracies, and in Germany and Italy, where the war had left radical social disorder, of new, fascist movements.

The first European response to Wilson's idealism—the wartime and armistice response—had been a kind of enthusiasm which went far beyond all realistic expectation. The crowds greeted Wilson when he arrived in Paris for the armistice negotiations with what one observer called "inhuman . . . superhuman" cheers. Disillusionment was to follow, for Wilson as well as for the Europeans. But the experience of Europe's response, its fantastic response, to Wilson's wartime and armistice speeches and policies had a lasting effect on America's own attitude toward world affairs. The interpretation of those events—which later was widely accepted in the United States, taught in American schools in the 1930's and 1940's, and incorporated as a fundamental assumption of our policy-making in World War II—was that Wilson's great plan for a League of Nations would have saved the peace if only the United States had joined the League; but this theory has not been, and can never be, tested against reality.

The United States was thus not forced into a realistic appraisal of the political turbulence and nihilism of the inter-war years—which clearly had far deeper sources than a mere debating society like the League of Nations could have cured. We acted with skill and realism in dealing with our domestic crisis during the Great Depression, but bad as that was, it never produced the political dislocation which the postwar inflations and parliamentary incompetence of Germany and Italy had produced. Despite much alienation among intellectuals and some of the poor, the American political system was never seriously in danger, and the resonant optimism of Franklin Roosevelt expressed an unbroken American national optimism which could burst out in a new explosion of confidence when World War II in Europe provoked both an American economic recovery and a crusade against unmistakable evils abroad.

For Europeans, the 1920's and 1930's were a radically worse experience than the American ordeal of economic depression. The Russians fought a civil war long after the German war was ended. Then came Stalin's succession to Lenin, collectivizations, famine, population transfers, and purges—in which in 1936–1938 alone three to four million Russians, Communist Party members and ordinary citizens alike were killed. The Germans fought on after 1918 for their eastern territories against both the Russians and the Poles, using the so-called *Freikorps* of veterans and adventurers under unofficial commanders. The Poles and the Russians fought one another in 1919–1920 in a war that threatened Warsaw at one point and, at another, penetrated deep into the Soviet Union. There was a brutal war between Greece and Turkey, a kind of guerrilla war between Irish rebels and Britain, and then civil war between factions within Ireland itself. There was a communist *coup d'état* in Hungary, a counter-revolution, and then two decades of right-wing dictatorship. Poland spent the same period under the military dictatorship of Colonel Pilsudski and his incompetent successors. Rumania was a corrupt monarchy, a petty fascist state, in which the so-called Iron Guard threatened the king and was itself butchered in the streets. Czechoslovakia was the only Central European state in which democracy sur-

vived the inter-war years, but it too was torn by struggles among
Czechs, Slovaks, and the German ethnic minority which in the
end were to contribute heavily to the Czechoslovak capitulation
to Hitler. Spain went through mounting disorders and then a
great and exhausting civil war. Italy fell to fascism and suffered
nearly twenty years of political humbug, theatrical war preparations—and concentration camps and the O.V.R.A.'s castor-oil
tortures and beatings of political dissidents. Germany experienced
an inflation which sent money to more than a billion times its
prewar figure, saw troop rebellions, rightist *coups* in Berlin and
Bavaria, street fighting among communists, socialists, conservatives, and Nazis—and then, Nazi government, internal purges,
and political terror, and another war in which seven million
more Germans were to die and the German nation would be
implicated in immense human crimes.

The West European democracies were not spared the inter-war
crisis. Violence had infected them; they too had civil disorders,
political struggles which went into the streets, general strikes.
They had depression, and their governments could do little to al-
leviate conditions. When fascism created a "new order" in Germany there were many in the rest of Europe who were fascinated
and half convinced by its claims, having despaired of democracy.
When the Germans conquered France, for example, only three
or four of the great intellectual figures actively opposed the Nazis
—François Mauriac, André Malraux, Georges Bernanos—and
even such a figure as André Gide could be described as believing
that "politically . . . France is destined to be *protected,* either by
Germany or by the Anglo-Saxons. . . . And will not Hitler . . .
suddenly become transformed into Augustus, a prisoner of his
own greatness and of the grandeur of his mission?"[46]

The meaning of all this was drastically oversimplified in American political discussion of the period and the war years, but more
important is that Americans, as individuals, experienced hardly
anything of the personal horror of this great period of crises. The
political effects of the worldwide collapse of values were muted
by a relative prosperity and social isolation. Leftist radicalism of
a new ideological sort appeared, and there was a resurgent Ku
Klux Klan, now spread to the North as well. But of actual tragedy
on a vast scale we knew nothing, and had known nothing since
our own Civil War a century earlier. Then America had truly

experienced the devastation of cities—the violence of industrial warfare on a scale presaging 1914–1918; and American families had been torn apart by opposing loyalties, and most suffered casualities—when they were not themselves uprooted by the movements of armies. But as a people, America experienced none of these things in the twentieth century. Yet there is hardly a family in Europe today, to say nothing of Asia, which has not been touched by such horrors—or the newer ones of death camps, concentration camps, torture, revolutionary and resistance warfare, and the security measures of the totalitarian state.

Like Wilson, we still could afford idealism as we entered World War II. Again, as in 1918, we could make the creation of a "new world system" our proclaimed war goal, and half convince ourselves, at least, that the defeat of the Axis would make permanent peace a reality. Our battles again were waged overseas. Our fatalities were nearly six times those we experienced in World War I, but this was still less than .25 percent of our population. British battle losses were proportionately three times ours, and Britain, in spite of the Blitz, was the luckiest of the European combatants. The Russian population's deaths from all war causes between 1941 and 1945 are conservatively estimated at twenty million.

It was not until very late in the war, when the Allies began to overrun the death camps, that we got a glimpse of what totalitarianism had really meant in Europe. But even then we did not grasp the character of the Soviet regime. The sentimental glosses on Soviet intentions and policy which marked the late 1940's were no monopoly of deluded or "soft-minded" policymakers. The State Department's actual record of judgment in this period was considerably better than that of either the White House or the vast majority of the press. The Russians, we told ourselves, would co-operate in the new world system which would be created after the war. China would make a splendid democracy. Japan and Germany would be rendered powerless and "re-educated." We believed these things in part, of course, because of the tendency of any nation fighting a war to sustain itself with great hopes about the future; but there was more to the American attitude than that.

The Europeans hoped, as well, for the success of the United Nations and for Soviet co-operation with the West, but they were

far more guarded in their expectations and their policies. Church-
ill obsessively tried to maintain a British presence to check the
Soviets in southeastern Europe. De Gaulle, frankly skeptical of
reliance on world parliaments, made his own unsentimental
agreement with Stalin, and condemned Britain's and America's
Yalta agreements granting Russian demands with respect to
Poland's and Yugoslavia's postwar governments. Americans, at
the time, condemned these actions as a dangerous reversion to
"power politics."

The European public responded to the great aims of the Atlantic
Charter and the United Nations, both of them American initiatives, with a kind of distracted hope, but there were no "superhuman" cheers for America, or for an expected transformation
of the character of world affairs. The postwar European mood,
sobered by the experience of 1938–1945 and the new specter of
the nuclear bomb, was one of considerable pessimism and of
exhaustion. There was some renewal of popular affection for
America as the "young" nation whose optimism and high spirits
might give a new lead to European-American society, but the
attitudes expressed by European writers of the period, the
philosophers and most perceptive political men, was much darker.
Many turned in a kind of self-abasement to the terrible image of
Stalin's Russia, which became in the postwar imagination both
an object of terror and a kingdom of messianic deliverance. Even
those who did not nonetheless believed that mankind had proved
itself incapable of controlling its own violence and cruelty. The
most influential of France's wartime and postwar writers, Albert
Camus, could say, as the war in Europe approached victory:
"Hundreds of thousands of men assassinated at dawn, the terrible walls of prisons, the soil of Europe reeking with millions of
corpses of its sons—it took all that to pay for the acquisition of
two or three slight distinctions which may have no other value
than to help some among us to die more nobly." The "slight distinctions" were that "this world has no ultimate meaning. But
I know that something in it has a meaning and that is man, because he is the only creature to insist on having one. . . . You
will ask me: What do you mean by saving man? And with all
my being I shout at you that I mean not mutilating him and yet
giving a chance to the justice that man alone can conceive."[47]
This kind of philosophy could find little place in it for reliance on

the natural good will of men, or on new political organizations, or on the defeat of Germany and Japan as meaning an enduring defeat of evil in human society.

THE FEAR OF POLITICS

Few Americans could make so narrow and precise an affirmation as Camus in the cauldron of wartime Europe. And Camus, of course, was one of the Europeans capable of an affirmation. Others, ordinary people as well as philosophers, were lost in bitterness and nihilism.

The philosophical questions are the hard questions, and as a nation America has preferred to avoid them. Our beliefs about the fate and prospects of men in history—at least as our public officials and great newspapers voice such beliefs—remain cheerful and hopeful. Yet there is reason to think that, underneath, most Americans have doubts about these formulations, and about the character of politics, which they do not articulate. Fiction is too often easier to live with than reality. Today controversy among Americans over the validity of the grander American plans for the world, or the content of the American mission in history, will often veer suddenly into emotion—which suggests that our opinions in these matters have more than intellectual value to us. It may be that this country preaches a faith in man which it does not, perhaps, always believe; that we place a confidence in man's essential reason and goodness which, we also know, is too often barbarously betrayed. Our foreign policy is, it may be, the projection of what we want to believe, of myths we dare not disbelieve. We shrink from the notion that Nazis were ordinary people. We shrink from the prospect of a world in which communism may not wither, or poverty may not be overcome, a world without organization, without a consensus on what aggression is and how that aggression is to be suppressed. We are not at all sure how we would endure in such a world. We did not give up isolation for this.

Our isolationism was a defense, emotional as well as material; certainly it was never merely a foreign policy briefly pursued and now abandoned. Global interventionism, in fact, is isolationist in everything except action. In action it is a way of making over a world we could no longer ignore—making it over into something tolerable for us.

Interventionism expresses the same rejection of non-America which Jefferson expressed—rejection of that old world, small, overcharged, "steeped in the vices which that situation generates." Today we condemn the old world for its "rivalries of nation states." We regretfully condemn the newer world of Africans and Asians for their immaturity while extending our aid and tutelage to them. We warn the Latin Americans that they are incompetent to deal with popular fronts and domestic subversion. We warn Asians that not only are they too weak to stand alone against China, whom they have had to resist since a thousand years before the United States existed, but warn them, as well, that they do not seem to take their dangers seriously enough. We warn further that all other claimants to world power are compromised either by their present incompetence or their imperial or despotic past. Such warnings as these were all issued by spokesmen of the United States Department of State in a single six-month period of 1965. As for America, "never before in human history has a nation undertaken to play a role of world responsibility except in defense and support of a world empire. . . . [W]e find ourselves in a position unique in world history." The words are those of Under Secretary of State Ball.[48]

How are we to describe what such matters as this really mean in America today? In our domestic affairs and in our intellectual and private lives we are neither ingenuous nor illusionist. The rhetoric of official Washington obviously is a fingering of the smooth coins of rhetoric past, a half-thoughtless indulgence in pieties which Wilson first spoke out of true innocence faced with crisis and anguish; it is a repetition of real warnings and real exhortations first issued against the lurid backdrop of Stalinism, the Greek and Korean wars, and the East European political terror that led to the loss of Poland, Czechoslovakia, Rumania, Hungary, Yugoslavia, Bulgaria, and East Germany. This lurid backdrop is no longer, as we shall see, today's world.

For America, the real question is whether we can free ourselves from the fear of politics, of historical commitment and compromise. Interventionism, as much as isolationism, is a policy of evasion—a policy of fear, fear of the dark. This is a fear of the young, so that the question is, can America accept the world for what it is, for its dismaying and tragic reality—can it accept maturity?

III

The Challenge to America, Myth and Reality — I

What is the reality that the United States faces in contemporary politics? Any serious answer must begin by insisting that this reality—complex, as all the newspaper editorials and official statements tell us—daily grows more complex: the old clear-cut divisions and rivalries between the communist world and the West, between Moscow and Washington, between unfree and free, dissolve into a bewildering welter of contending national forces, bastardized ideologies, and fragmented alliances. The years of the great Cold War between Moscow and Washington may have been years of terror and anxiety, but intellectually they were easy to comprehend.

Apart from the political complexity of today's world (where, to take one recent example, a formal ally of the United States, Pakistan, can ally itself as well to Communist China and battle a neutral India, for whom the United States and the Soviet Union express an anxious and co-operative regard) we encounter the problem of phase. The old doctrinal conflicts are today ending, and new ones are beginning. The class antagonisms which dominated the political formulations of Europe and the United States from 1850 until the end of World War II now begin to be supplanted by something else that is, in part, an antagonism of culture and race. Marxism, a proletarian political philosophy, is increasingly a dead letter in Afro-Asia, with less and less to say to the disturbed elites of what the French have called the *tiers-monde*, or "Third World." Thus the intellectual categories and labels—the conceptual shorthand which all of us resort to when thinking about the world—which were good and useful in 1930 or even 1950 simply do not fit the contemporary causes of political disturbance. We need a new vocabulary of international politics. And behind this new vocabulary there will have to stand new categories of thought.

The task is complicated by the fact that while adjusting to a new reality we cannot simply jettison the old; the speed of the transformation of contemporary politics should not be exaggerated, and the old conflicts cannot simply be dismissed. Class issues are far from dead, even in an America which is surfeited with wealth, still less in backward and depressed regions like Latin America. The Soviets have not joined the West, or the camp of the "haves," so completely that old antagonisms do not linger on, or could not easily be revived and even flare into war. Nevertheless we do stand on the threshold of a new era of politics.* We cannot go on insistently viewing the world in the old ways, tirelessly jamming or trimming every new revolutionary movement to fit the political vocabulary of a dying age.

Apart from this problem of phase, there is another problem in distinguishing between political *reality* and the *perception of that reality*. Assessing international affairs is no simple matter: emotion interferes with reason. Analysis is always clouded, in greater or lesser degree, by pre-existing political commitments and ideologies, by national myth, self-interest, class interest, and, above all, by long-standing habits of thought and intellectual laziness.

---

* The notion that the political passions of the last hundred years are dying is not a new one. Daniel Bell has written of *The End of Ideology*, and he is not alone. There have been other such political watersheds in history, most notably the period that set in with the American and French Revolutions, outmoding dynastic or kingly politics and introducing nationalism and class warfare. There was a similar division between the war and politics of the late Middle Ages and those of the Renaissance. The totalitarian political ambitions of a Cesare Borgia in Italy were light-years removed from the ambitions of a medieval king like Henry V of England. But as the Dutch historian Johan Huizinga has remarked: "The transition from the spirit of the declining Middle Ages to humanism was far less simple than we are inclined to imagine it. Accustomed to oppose humanism to the Middle Ages, we would gladly believe that it was necessary to give up the one in order to embrace the other. We find it difficult to fancy the mind cultivating the ancient forms of medieval thought and expression while aspiring at the same time to antique wisdom and beauty. Yet this is just what we have to picture to ourselves. Classicism did not come as a sudden revelation; it grew up among the luxuriant vegetation of medieval thought. . . . On the other hand, the characteristic modes of thought of the Middle Ages did not die out till long after the Renaissance."[1]

What we see is very often what we *want* to see or are accustomed to see. If there is a single indictment of the multiple and self-contradictory forms that American globalism takes, it is simply that its arguments and rationales are out of date. A fundamental revision of the analysis on which American foreign policy rests is long overdue.

To warn against arguing from emotion is not to prescribe total detachment. Nor it is to call for cynicism. Of all countries, the United States may be the least equipped to pursue a purely pragmatic and self-seeking foreign policy, and it would be futile as well as foolish to prescribe a Machiavellianism for it. Nations, like men, need values; but values in politics reside in what a nation *does*, not in the vision it sets forth as the remote objective of its policies. Most men want a peaceful and lawful world; such an aspiration can hardly be dignified as a moral choice. The moral choices are the immediate choices, the decisions about action now, not generalized ambitions for the world of our children. Values, in any event, are not properly at issue when, as in this chapter, we make a preliminary effort to define the truth about world affairs. Analysis is diagnosis. When a physician examines a patient, the proper issue is whether disease exists. Whatever the physician, as a human being, feels for the patient is irrelevant to this.

The next issue of fact is whether anything can be *done* for the condition. Any physician knows that there are interventions that will speed death, or only compound a disorder. Presumably the physician's commitment against death and suffering was made long ago; the practical question is whether, given the present state of the medical art, the condition of the patient, and a particular physician's skills and available resources, any intervention is wise. The physician who blinds himself to his own and his science's limitations, to the realities of failure and death, and who frivolously deals in good intentions, useless treatments, false optimism, and placebos, is the one against whom the most severe moral case might be made.*

The distinction between realism, or what William James called "tough-mindedness," and expediency is important to bear in mind. Tough-mindedness properly consists in an absence of illusions, a

---

* We will return to this problem of damaging or self-defeating interventions in the following chapters.

dislike for self-deception, not in an absence of ideals. In foreign policy, the self-advertised "tough-mindedness" which justifies all immediate actions by appeals to an American "moment of history" or its call to the "anguish of power" too often confuses the two states of mind; if emotion and moralizing have no place in political diagnosis, they *do* have a place in the framing of policy. The moral consciousness of a nation, perhaps even more than gross national product and the size of an atomic stockpile, is an objective factor in what a nation can accomplish in the world. Men who are prone to dismiss "morality" from the calculations, as if morality and sentimentality were one, too often create policies which lie beyond the actual national commitment. This has already happened to us. There is at best only a mixed enthusiasm for current American actions in Vietnam, and since the United States remains a democracy, it is increasingly necessary to enlist national enthusiasm by appeals to moralism that are couched in terms of cant—empty language. And in the end, there may be disillusionment and bitterness at home, and abroad the loss of public credit and reputation, and even of honor.

SIX OBSTACLES TO REALISTIC ANALYSIS

Nations, like men, have the defects of their virtues, and the United States, a *moral* nation in a very real sense, is excessively prone to self-deception—to that unadmitted hypocrisy about itself and that oversimplification of the beliefs and actions of others which serve to reconcile expedient actions to a moral conscience. This, along with parliamentarianism and the cult of work, the better side of the coin, is a Puritan legacy. Such an inclination is difficult to eradicate, but to identify the problem and raise it to the level of public consciousness is to open up at least the possibility that it can be brought within the bounds of reasonable control. Apart from this predilection to cant, Americans in general need beware of at least six obstacles to honest political diagnosis. These obstacles are worth some comment before going on to a more detailed consideration of the actual state of the contemporary world.

The problem of "lag." We have already referred to this. It may well be that in the 1960's we stand at a watershed between two political eras. The attitudes, commitments, and institutions that stemmed from the Cold War with Stalinism are being carried over into an era in which Soviet capabilities (and, it may be, intentions) are no longer what they were.

Thus, for example, present American habits of thinking about the defense of Europe are far more relevant to the era of virulent Cold War after 1945, when a prostrate Western Europe faced a dynamic, expansionist, overwhelming, and utterly cynical Soviet power, than to an age in which Soviet dynamism is fading and Europe is wealthy and secure enough to begin, at least, to defend itself.* The need for an American direction and physical presence in Europe, indisputable a decade ago, is now taken by many in Washington to be a self-evidently desirable permanent factor in world affairs—even though that continued presence may actually hinder the European settlement which American wartime and early postwar policy in Europe was designed to bring about. American spokesmen speak continually of the need to "maintain and strengthen NATO" as if NATO, a military al-

* The important factors here are the decline of Soviet will and authority within its former sphere, and the reverse growth of a West European ability to match Soviet conventional and nuclear arms—not the "mellowing," *embourgeoisement*, or alleged democratization of Soviet society, or the growing number of "bridges" (contacts) between the Soviets and the West. That there has been a significant mellowing of Soviet society since Stalin's death is hardly arguable; but for military purposes this fact may be irrelevant. There is no historical evidence for the common belief that democratic societies do not make war, or even that they do not make aggressive war. The case of the United States in 1846, in the war against Mexico, is a sufficient refutation of that argument. In 1914 Hohenzollern Germany and Hapsburg Austria each guaranteed its citizens political freedoms far more extensive and advanced than any yet granted by post-Khrushchevian Russia. Both countries were integrally related by common tastes and civilization to Britain and France. Yet in the summer of 1914 Germany and Austria incontinently went to war against the Allies.

The point is that in 1945–1947, when the Cold War began, Stalin disposed of some 150 to 200 full-strength divisions, whereas the Soviet Army in 1965 probably cannot boast more than 65 such divisions—as the result of social and budgetary pressures generated *within* Soviet society, and which are only in the most limited sense the result of United States policy. This slender Soviet conventional force is required to guard not only the Central European frontier of the Soviet empire against the West but the thousands of miles of Inner Asian and Siberian frontier with China. If in 1945–1947 the United States had not taken up a blocking position in Central Europe, the result quite possibly would have been that France, Italy, Germany, the Low Countries, and Scandinavia would have fallen to Stalin. But contemporary Europe is rich and stable enough to generate the conventional and nuclear forces to guard its own frontiers.

liance, were an end in itself and not, as in its inception, merely one means of securing European defense and political tranquillity —an inherently limited policy which was to contribute to a further goal.

That attitudes and institutions appropriate to one era should generate loyalties and intellectual commitments that are difficult to shed as the world evolves is natural enough. But that such loyalties and commitments should strangle debate and prevent America from adapting to new conditions is impermissible.

The problem of the "self-evident." A second obstacle to realistic thinking about the state of the world is the dead weight of notions which are taken to be "common knowledge" when they actually will not stand up to elementary analysis. That they continue to block thought and impede the formation of effective policy is directly attributable to the intrinsic inertia of ideas: such notions, once given currency, are hardly ever given rigorous scrutiny again.

Examples are legion. It was, for example, "common knowledge" in 1957, when the Soviets launched their *sputnik* and proved the existence of an ICBM, that the balance of military power had shifted against the United States. Something close to political panic was engendered by this demonstration, in the United States at least. Even a serious analyst of the political scene could write in December of that year: " . . . Recent Russian achievements have called attention to the fact—of which the intelligence agencies of the government have been aware over a considerable period of time—that the Soviet Union is superior to the United States in the quality and quantity of atomic and conventional weapons . . . that, in other words, the Soviet Union is superior to the United States in almost every department of warfare. . . . The United States will . . . be exposed to the Russian ICBM without being able to retaliate in kind, for its sole weapon of retaliation will then be that fraction of the Strategic Air Force which happens to be in the air at the moment of attack with sufficient fuel to reach its targets."*

* Hans Morgenthau, writing in *The New Republic* of December 9, 1957. The strategic case made by Professor Morgenthau does not deserve detailed refutation. It is sufficient to say that the Russian military missiles of the period, like Russia's space boosters, were few in number, exposed above

There were few qualifications in this, or other, comments at the time; in other words, the case for Soviet military superiority in 1957 was at the same time "self-evident" and false. Hardly a detail of the argument could have stood up to analysis (for example, the alleged superiority of the Soviets not only in quality but *quantity* of atomic weapons, which was close to an absurdity). In point of fact the Soviet Union in 1957 could not have delivered on target in the United States more than a portion of the megatonnage that the British Bomber Command could today deliver against Russia. The Soviet leadership of the time surely harbored no such illusions of crushing superiority, and, verbal bluster aside, behaved with the greatest circumspection in the face of the "obsolete" bombers of the Strategic Air Command—to say nothing of the sea-based nuclear forces which the United States owned.

But unsophisticated notions about the balance of military power are hardly the most pernicious examples of the problem of the "self-evident" but false. In the assessment of political motivations the problem is much greater. It is another commonplace that the revolutionary movements of our time are a struggle by the submerged masses of Afro-Asia and Latin America for elementary human dignity and a just share in the world's wealth. But why has Vietnam, where the living standards were among the highest in Asia, sustained civil violence and a civil war of passionate and undeniably extensive popular commitments? Why did Cuba, whose living standard was one of the highest in Latin America, produce the Fidelistas? Why, if the search is for human dignity, do these revolutionary movements so often take the form of hysterical one-party politics, or xenophobic and militant ideologies in which the claims of the individual are submerged in the needs of the state or the mass?

Why have revolutionary regimes—as in North Korea or North Vietnam—so often been able to create political stability in the midst of great economic hardship, when other societies, on "our"

ground and vulnerable to destruction, might have required as much as twelve to twenty-four hours to arm and prepare for firing, and could not have been held in such readiness for any great length of time—truly no decisive weapons. Subsequent professional studies have suggested that in the event of nuclear war between the Russians and the United States in 1957 the balance of losses might have been greater than ten or fifteen to one, against the Russians.

side of the line, which have notably higher living standards sustained by regular infusions of foreign aid, fail to establish social peace? The steadiness of North Korean troops in 1950 and the impressive ability of the poverty-stricken centralized dictatorship in North Vietnam to dispatch its troops south of the 17th parallel to fight dispersed guerrilla actions against government professionals and American troops, without losing cohesion and discipline, have received little attention. Our intellectual defense against these problems usually takes the form of citing dissidence or rebellions by peasants or intellectuals in these countries. True enough; yet the fact remains that these regimes endure and none of them have faced the kind of internal opposition that Poland did in 1956, or a revolt comparable to the Hungarian Revolution. What stops them? There are no Red Army tank divisions to put down revolution in Cuba. Surely Hanoi—or Peking, for that matter—could be shaken by a mass uprising even half as extensive and intense as the guerrilla movement against the Saigon government in South Vietnam.

We have equally failed to analyze the general notion that underlies our foreign aid programs—that economic development, industrialization, leads to social peace—when the histories of Europe and even America in the nineteenth century, and of Imperial Russia and Japan in the twentieth, suggest precisely the reverse. The ultimate end of economic development and modernization may be social integration and peace when the new gifts of technology are integrated with old values. But Japan performed an economic *tour de force* between 1870 and 1941, transforming itself from an Asian hermit kingdom to a modern industrial power, and nevertheless plunged East Asia into a catastrophic war. Such an experience—to say nothing of the evidence of the "modernizing" China of today—hardly offers very solid grounds for hope that the effort at industrialization in Indonesia or Pakistan (if these two countries can manage to industrialize in this century) will help pacify Afro-Asia, or bring about a new international order of "satisfied" nations.

The problem of sentimentality. The problem of the "self-evident" is the problem of what everyone "knows" to be true but is not. The problem of sentimentality is the reverse: what everyone knows is true but no one will admit. Certain unpleasant truths cannot be said, and since they cannot be said they cannot be used for rational political analysis and policy. Thus, for example, it is an axiom of American foreign aid policy, deriving ultimately from our tradition of egalitarianism—the notion that all men are equal in endowments as well as rights—that *all* underdeveloped nations deserve aid equally. The chief limitation on this notion seems to be the "corruption" or "honesty" of the beneficiary government or its attitude to communism. But of course this is nonsense. Not only does a country like India have a well-trained civil service and corps of native engineers and scientists, the gift of the British, while Indonesia does not, in part the fault of the Dutch, but the pre-industrial civilizations of Afro-Asia on which the aid programs must build are anything but uniform in their attainments. This is not a racial argument. No one who is even slightly familiar with the achievements of Chinese civilization could deny the immense creativity and productivity of this nation (nor, on the record, the similar qualities of the neighboring Japanese), nor doubt the eventual success of China's transition to industrialism. But that Malay society, or Arabic society, can similarly absorb Western technology and strike an accommodation with the modernity *we* define as modernity, is less self-evident.

The very use of the terms "underdeveloped" or "developing" nations begs the question and ignores immense differences—as if all human societies were pointed on a single road, or ought to be. They cannot be lumped, as they are in our popular debates. Societies like China, Japan, Islam, and India are ancient and accomplished civilizations with a life-style and philosophy which, at least before they were fragmented by the impact of the modern industrial West, were valid alternatives, in some respects perhaps better alternatives, to our own. Latin America is something else. Very largely a backwater of the Western world, it is European in its origins, so that its problems today are largely economic and organizational and, measured by the immense problems of Afro-Asia, comparatively slight. Sub-Saharan Africa, whatever the historic and geographic reasons may be, was and largely remains a primitive continent—a land of tribal societies hardly beginning to cope with the problems of civilization, let alone with modern Western industrial civilization.

Within these regions there are further immense differences.

Ghana, however repressive its government, has been able to achieve internal order, and so absorb a modicum of technological aid; the Congo, on the other hand, is likely to exist in something like anarchy for many decades to come. The problem is a social and cultural one, not merely a problem of capital accumulation or literate manpower.

In effect, this is to say, at the most vulgar level, that some nations "have it," and others do not—whatever "it" may be. Private investors regularly make such distinctions: that the Japanese or German work force is disciplined and dependable and the Congolese is not is unquestionable. Whether, given some decades of social tranquillity, the Congolese work force might be transformed (the social problems are immense) is another question; but it is futile to pretend that what has convulsed the Congo since independence is mere economic deprivation. Congolese society is one of initially feeble attainments all but shattered in the nineteenth and twentieth centuries by the impact of a rapacious, contemptuous, and exploitative West. That this is so, and that the prospects for much of Africa in this century are exceedingly bleak, is an issue that needs to be squarely faced. It needs to be faced, not merely because Africa's condition limits the good we can expect our economic aid to do there, but because it limits the harm that we need to fear from communism, Soviet or Chinese, in Africa. In some sense tribal society south of the Sahara is not ready either for democracy or for communism, since both are austere and work-oriented systems unsuited to the Dionysian emotional climate of this region.

The problem of the "unthinkable." In common usage the problem of the "unthinkable" is limited to nuclear war. "Nuclear war is unthinkable," former President Dwight Eisenhower has said, while, it might be observed, he was acquiring the forces. More recently Herman Kahn has taken up the challenge and produced a book entitled *Thinking about the Unthinkable* which, its specific arguments aside, is unassailable in its central notion that to prepare nuclear forces and yet refuse to speculate on how they might be used is a sure way to court defeat, or national suicide.

But the problem of the unthinkable transcends nuclear war: it embraces all those situations in which the central fear is that to think about an issue is to advocate it, or by some implicitly magical process to bring it on. In addition, it embraces those situations in which a policy is so compromised by events, or so costly in its consequences, or so founded in illusion, that to question a single feature is to break the spell—and bring down the structure of illusion. More accurately, this latter is the problem of the unsayable.

Of the two, the second situation is the more important for policy, since it is precisely these fears that prevent such established policy structures as alliances from being renovated as conditions change. No one in NATO, for example, with the exception of the French, is willing to tell the West Germans that we do not know how to reunite their country within the framework of our present policy. Actually, it is worse than that. It is an open secret in Europe and America today that all nations, with the exception of Germany (and some Americans who have identified with the German interest), are happy with the present division of Germany. But the truth that there is such a fundamental conflict between Bonn and its NATO allies, in which Bonn must press for revisions of the European *status quo* while Bonn's allies prefer an emasculated Germany (so that NATO itself is built on a fundamental contradiction) is hardly ever voiced in public or private councils. Yet how is a realistic European policy to be framed if this division of interest is not faced?

Another clear case of the unsayable is the issue of Communist China's membership in the United Nations. The steadfast refusal of the American government to open the issue to public debate, or to consider alternatives to present policy if despite our best efforts the required majority votes China's admission to the U.N., is a prime example of the "unthinkable" in action. Equally "unthinkable" among some critics of American policy is the possibility that Communist China, once admitted to the United Nations, might not thereby be influenced to co-operative international behavior or to observe such agreements as the Nuclear Test Ban. In fact, it is likely to make very little practical or emotional difference to Communist China whether it is seated or not; it is not even certain that Peking wishes to join the U.N. China's role in the world as revolutionary is surely enhanced by its pariah status. Nevertheless, the whole issue of China remains beyond discussion: the United States magnifies the Chinese strength, promise, and danger, and debates China policy in such emotionally charged terms that there is more than a slight suspicion that present policy expresses attitudes that, in part at least, stem from irrational sources.

For years it was "unthinkable" that the United States should acquiesce in the Soviet domination of Eastern Europe. The satellites were to be "liberated," short of war perhaps, but in precise circumstances few cared to define. If illusion had remained illusion it would have been harmless enough. But the myth of liberation was allowed to dominate American policy-planning, though only in the unrealistic terms of a liberation to be accomplished through United States initiatives. When after Stalin's death the Soviet empire was shaken by revolt and dissidence, the Soviets might have welcomed a negotiated settlement in Central Europe as a way to withdraw. But all alternatives to the canonical American policy of liberation were rejected out of hand—mostly because few had been willing to give any thought to such possibilities. America talked liberation—and stood aside when the East European revolts were suppressed.

Similarly today, when analyzing Europe's security needs, it is inadmissible to suggest that the present American guarantee to use nuclear weapons to defend Western Europe is unwise, or even less than honest. Yet in the present balance of forces between the United States and the Russians an American strike on the Soviet homeland, to defend against a Soviet invasion of Europe, might cost between fifty and a hundred million American lives. Apart from the question of whether such a costly guarantee, steadfastly voiced in preference to other alternative means of maintaining West European security, is wise diplomacy, there is a question of *fact* to be ascertained. Faced with the actual challenge, would the United States—*could* any American President— honor the guarantee? It is at least arguable that the United States would not do so. The loss of life implied by such a policy, if it were confronted as a real possibility rather than an abstract one, might override our commitment. Yet these implications of American nuclear policy with respect to Europe are hardly ever discussed seriously.

The problem of "literalism." Literalism might be defined alternatively as simplicism—the failure to distinguish between what an enemy (or friend) *says* and *means; wants* and *can do; wants cheaply* and is prepared to *pay.* To make these distinctions may seem easy; yet in general discussion of the modern American dilemmas they are hardly ever made.

During the Congo's regional rebellion, Peking was loud in its support of the rebel leader Antoine Gizenga, and this support, coupled with evidence of minor arms shipments to the eastern Congo, raised the public specter of a Chinese military intervention in Africa. But the Chinese merchant fleet was rudimentary; the Chinese air transport capability was negligible. A major Chinese intervention, over many thousands of miles, even assuming the effort could have been mounted, would have proved painfully vulnerable to interdiction. (Indeed, as H. L. Mencken once wrote of panicky fears in 1917 of a German invasion of the eastern United States, how this invasion was to be accomplished in the absence of divine intervention was quite unclear.) But press accounts and official warnings hardly ever betrayed any awareness of these physical constraints on Chinese actions.

Comical examples of such literalism, or naïveté, are not difficult to come by—as for example the alleged intervention of Fidelistas in the Zanzibar rebellion of 1963, as if Castroite Cuba, balked in the Caribbean, could hope to intervene on the east coast of Africa, or as if verbal support for a distant revolution implied connivance or even a willingness to divert meager resources.

The problem is most serious in analyses of Soviet, and especially Chinese, behavior in the contemporary world. China's Marshal Lin Piao declared in the fall of 1965 that the "rural" world should by Maoist strategy encircle and overcome the imperialist "urban" nations. But what precisely does this mean? Modern China is in the process of distinguishing itself from the Soviet revolution. This is to say that the Chinese nation is searching for a revolutionary identity of its own. It is also attempting with mixed success to supplant Soviet influence, itself waning, in disturbed areas of Afro-Asia. One means to distinguish itself from the Soviets, and to supplant them as the new center of worldwide revolution, is to assert the reverse of the Soviet program, whatever that program may be. China since Stalin's death has consistently opposed the Soviet line. China is a zealot today because in 1966 the Soviet Union is moderate. A decade ago, when the Soviets were fighting to maintain their grip on the

European satellites, China drew close to "revisionist" Yugoslavia and Poland. The aim was to undercut the Soviets; and no doubt with a maximum of ideological "sincerity" and adroit self-deception the Chinese have tacked between liberalist and zealot winds. But their consistent course has been service to the interests, not of world revolution, but of China.

It is equally clear that there is a vast distinction between what might be called the Soviet Union's stump oratory and its real intentions. Once the Cold War developed in 1945–1947, Stalin was uncompromising in his doctrine of inevitable and total war between capitalism and socialism, between the United States and the U.S.S.R. On the occasion of his concluding speech to the 19th Party Congress in 1953, the Soviet theoretical journal *Kommunist* had this to say: "Leninism teaches that the imperialists cannot be 'appeased' by tiny concessions, as suggested by various liberals who have broken with the theory of the class struggle and descended into right-wing opportunism. Concessions and small concessions too in basic issues of principle weaken the positions of the socialist country and encourage the imperialists to increase the pressure . . . to put forward fresh and ever more insolent demands. *Plainly only people who break with Marxism can go along this path.* As Comrade Stalin teaches, the laws of the class struggle demand an intensification of the offensive against the positions of reaction, and not concessions. . . . Successes on the front of the class struggle are won in the course of a fierce struggle against the enemy."[2] Yet nothing was further from Stalin's intentions than a reckless offensive. Stalin was a cautious leader, albeit a cruel and cynical revolutionary. His business was not national suicide; nor is that the business of the Chinese today.

Apart from this distinction between declaratory policy and action policy, as the two are called in today's Washington, and apart from the problem of the practical limits which reality places on theoretical revolutionary doctrine and military action, there is a problem of costs which must be considered by Russians as well as by Chinese. No doubt, had Stalin been able to seize Western Europe in 1947 he would have done so; but the price —the obliteration of the Soviet homeland—was higher than he was willing to pay. No doubt today's Soviet leaders, for all their mellowing, would be glad to humble the United States and reassert a revolutionary supremacy if they were able. They are not yet so changed that they are friends of the United States. But they are unwilling to risk nuclear war, or even conventional war—or even, it sometimes seems, large-scale diplomatic unpleasantness between them and us. That being so, we need to learn to distinguish accurately between the bluster and insult hurled at us and our friends in today's world and what an enemy nation intends to do, and *can* do.

The problem of "parataxic distortion." As used by the American psychiatrist Harry Stack Sullivan, the term "parataxic distortion" was borrowed from ophthalmology to describe a range of emotional phenomena whose common denominator was that the disturbed patient mistook one object or situation for another and reacted in inappropriate ways.

In a certain sense the problem of parataxis sums up all the others we have listed. Its cumulative effect is to warp the political vision and induce us to mistake one revolutionary movement for another, to see threats where there are none, or conversely to perceive friendships or affinities where none exist, or reliable instruments of policy where there are only weak clients or cynical adulants. If the United States could consistently and accurately define the world within which it lives, and simultaneously define its national interest in that world, the task of devising viable policies for so powerful and well endowed a nation would be relatively simple. There is no case in history of a nation which possessed the power of the United States today; but it may also be that there are few cases in history of so great a state so prone to unreasonable fears and so fearful of change and of the unknown.

The last third of this century is clearly an age of revolutionary upheaval. Not only is the spread of modern technology and politics to once passive regions like Afro-Asia bringing new actors and new movements in bewildering combinations onto the international scene, but the evolution of military technology constantly alters the balance of forces. Each year introduces new instabilities and vulnerabilities. Yet the fundamental position of the United States in the midst of this revolutionary ferment is very strong. Ours is not a situation which requires a general decision *for* interventions and *for* speedy (or even panic) actions. The truth is that a crisis in Latin America or Afro-Asia would have to deteriorate very far indeed before the vital interests of the United States were fatally or even seriously compromised. Nor, despite much rhetoric to the contrary, is the drift of world politics actually unfavorable to the United States. It is the communist movement that has suffered most from time; it is not Russia that "has time," or China that "has time." It is they, and the new hysterical revolutionary movements in the world, nearly as alien to them as to us, which measure themselves against time. In Russia's case, for example, it has been only some twenty years since the end of World War II brought the Soviet empire into being, and only a little more than half that time has elapsed since Stalin's death began the process of that empire's disintegration. This is not an impressive record as history counts empires.

Whatever China's present strength may seem to be in Asia, Chinese communist diplomacy cannot be counted a success: less than two decades have brought China into fundamental conflict with the two most powerful nations in the world, and there is every prospect that further diplomatic errors will only serve to bring into the combination against her Japan—the greatest industrial power in Asia and one of the greatest in the world— a traditional rival.

It is tedious to cite the nightmares of the 1950's and 1960's which have not taken flesh, except that they have been forgotten so soon. Castroism has not swept Latin America. Gamal Nasser has not succeeded in uniting the Arab world against America, nor in leading it (assuming he ever wanted to) into an association with the Soviets. The Soviets have not breached the Middle Eastern tier, nor even penetrated Iraq, where all American aid and influence were expelled in 1958. Guinea, Zanzibar, Ghana, and Algeria have not swung to communism.

What has happened, of course, is something else; decolonization has left vast zones of chronic instability. In Afro-Asia and Latin America we have seen a proliferation of hysterical mass movements, each vaguely "left" in orientation, arbitrary, statist, chauvinist. What these movements are, in fact, and how they affect the American national interest, is a subject we will return to. But they are *not* communist movements; neither the Soviets nor the Chinese have achieved a secure lodgment in the Third World. It does not even seem as if they will.

It would be a great error to attribute this generally favorable configuration of world politics to American interventions. There have been American interventionist successes, notably in Europe after World War II; but only in the most general way has the United States exercised influence over the course of politics in Africa, the Middle East, or South Asia, and, it may be, of Latin America as well. Seldom has anything the United States has *done*—its gifts of arms and economic aid, say, or the construction of fragile regional alliances—served to make the difference. So far as the United States has affected these affairs, it has been by the fact that the United States simply *is:* a vast American power exists in the world, and the general interests of the United States are known. These two factors have been enough to constrain the actors and hold their policies within definite bounds.

The same report, however, cannot be made of American intervention against communism, or more accurately against what the United States has often fancied to be communism. Exaggerated American fears have often functioned as a self-fulfilling prophecy, making of political movements the very thing we have feared they would become. And where this has not been true, and the communists have not gained, the result of ill-considered interventionism has as often as not been a legacy of anti-Americanism, chronic social instability, or despotic rule (as in Santo Domingo, Laos, Iran, or Vietnam).

THE RUSSIAN CHALLENGE

"The power of the communist world is wielded by revolutionaries who take history as their frame and world domination as their goal. Ever since the Russian Revolution the world has had to reckon with an inner daemonic force which has left no corner of a continent untouched and has become the political climate of our time."[3] Max Lerner wrote these words, accurately transcribing what has been for nearly half a century the Soviet pretension. But we have entitled this section "The Russian Challenge" to underline a dissent. In 1917 it was Lenin's claim to open a new era of history and to forge a power which would transform the world by manipulating the science of history. A half-century later there is only Russia.

To say that there is "only" Russia is, of course, also to acknowledge that this Russia is the second industrial nation of the world and a military power whose presence is felt in outer space and along a vast arc from the Elbe to the Sea of Japan. But to be a large nation is not the same thing as to be a great one in history; and measured by the Soviets' own hopes and pretensions, it is far from clear that the state that Lenin founded is more than a qualified success.

The collapse of the Soviet dream, this humbling of what once purported to be not so much a state as the embodiment of a secular religion and transmundane conspiracy, is one of the great dramas of the twentieth century. It is also a telling demonstration of the futility of ideological politics. What we have seen in Russia since Stalin's death in 1953 has been a rapid and profound transformation; but the process has been more complex than the mere transformation of a Byzantine totalitarianism into a rudimentary constitutional state. Along with the undeniable bettering of living standards and the softening of autocracy presided over by Stalin's successors, there has been another parallel process. *Pari passu* there has been a catastrophic decline of Soviet foreign influence and prestige.

Why this should be so deserves attention for the light it throws on contemporary politics. The curious but undeniable truth is that the Soviets seem to have been loved best in the world when, objectively, they were their brutal worst. As they have mellowed they have gained respectability—and lost magic and authority, over their former satellites, over the international communist movement they once led, over the contemporary liberal imagination. "The great hopes and fears that Russia evoked a generation ago are forgotten," Max Beloff wrote in a nostalgic, and curiously bitter, passage. ". . . Lenin's mausoleum is no different from Napoleon's tomb at the Invalides—another sight to tick off in the guidebook. . . . For twenty years Russian history and politics have been a major academic interest of mine. . . . For me the great fact of modern history had been the Russian Revolution. . . . [Yet] a few tired slogans on the walls or building sites are all that attest the fact that one is present at the building of what was once heralded as a 'new civilization.' A tourist could easily forget that this is not just Russia but *Soviet* Russia. I now think that we shall have to consider the Russian present in quite a different way. We may have to demote the Revolution to yet another [Russian] 'Time of Troubles.' "[4]

The Soviet Union that confronts us today is an enemy vastly altered, in complex ways, from the enemy that confronted the world in 1945–1947 as the Cold War began. But before evaluating the present challenge of the Soviets we need to consider in what ways the situation and character of this enemy have changed, and in what ways they have not.

The first thing to be emphasized is that the Soviet Union which Stalin ruled was no normal state. It was a messianic state, infused by an ideology of power, whose purpose was not to pursue definable national interests within the inherited terms of traditional diplomacy, but to take, and transform, the world. With such a state no normal diplomacy was possible and no binding agreements could be struck. This is a point worth remembering if we hope to trace the distance Russia has come—and the distance it has not come—in recent years. The Soviets stemmed from an era of totalitarian and magical politics, an era which produced not only the political ideology of Leninism-Stalinism in Russia, but Hitlerism in Germany, fascism in Italy and the Balkans, and a feverish Bushido nationalism in Japan. These movements in effect derived from the collapse of the European and, ultimately, world order in 1914–1918. The irrationality of politics within the Soviet Union, from the 1917 Revolution forward, echoed and resounded with the collapse of rationalism and the rise of hysterical politics in a Europe which had plunged into a purposeless carnage between 1914 and 1918 and then, in the aftermath, saw the economic underpinnings of its society swept away. The effects were worldwide. Beyond Europe, even the United States, insulated in part by a general prosperity, felt the influence in new leftist radicalisms of the ideological sort—Stalinism and Trotskyism superseding the native populism and the anarchist tradition expressed by the "Wobblies." In Afro-Asia, World War I confounded the nineteenth-century political and moral verities—the beliefs in order and the superiority of European civilization—which the white colonialists had taught, and planted the seeds of irrationalism and political violence.

The Soviet Union was born in that era. How irrational and terrible the political structure of Stalinism was can easily be forgotten.* A "reversion to Stalinism" is still seriously discussed as a valid political possibility for the Soviets in the mid-1960's if the liberalizing and reformist wing of the Soviet Communist Party does not succeed in winning its way. Opponents of reform are still described in both the Western and Soviet press as Stalinists. Because Peking denounces "revisionism" and attacks the denigrators of Stalin's memory, the Chinese leaders, whose style is very different, are labeled "Stalinists" as well.

Nothing could be further from the truth, whatever unfortunate turn future politics in the U.S.S.R. or China may take. Obviously, there are die-hards in the Soviet Party leadership, men who believe in peremptory police methods, austere living standards, and the cult of state power. But Stalinism was more than that. Like Hitlerism it defies a wholly reasonable explanation. It was a political style out of Kafka. It is conservatively estimated that between 1925 and 1950 twenty million victims died in Stalin's sub-Arctic and Inner Asian death camps for crimes which often enough the victims, and the judges, did not know. We have forgotten the state-induced famine of the early 1930's when gangs of feral children roamed the Ukraine and the corpses of obdurate peasants were hauled off like cordwood; the blood purges of 1936–1938; the obliteration of whole nationalities like the Crimean Tartars.

The Great Purge of 1936–1938 claimed between seven and eight million victims, of whom more than half were murdered. A third of the membership of the Communist Party of the Soviet Union were purged—800,000 persons in all. The dead included six out of thirteen members of the Politburo; 1,109 out of 1,966 delegates to the 1934 Party Congress; more than one third of the elected deputies in the Supreme Soviet. Between 20,000 and 35,000 army officers were murdered; three out of five marshals; thirteen out of fifteen army commanders; fifty-seven out of eighty-five corps commanders; a hundred and ten out of a hundred and ninety-five

---

* Stalin, of course, inherited the Soviet Union from a dying Lenin in 1924. There has been, in recent years, some tendency to romanticize the figure of Lenin; but it should be remembered that the terror began with him, not with his successors, though he did not go so far as Stalin, was a far more sophisticated mind, and was able to gloss over the brutality of his methods. Stalin in any event inherited the revolution, and it is probable that he did not do so by accident. Had Lenin not died a natural death, no doubt within a year or two, as his powers failed, he would have been purged.

division commanders. The numbers of the nameless and faceless common people snatched up in this purge will never be known.[5]

Surveying this record, one might suppose that the Great Purge, and the postwar trials, left the fabric of Soviet society hopelessly weakened. One might suppose that the vast majority of the Soviet people would have been driven to desperate acts against a state that so misused them. One might also suppose that the sight of such massacre would have turned the whole body of mankind away from Stalin, the Soviet Union, and the worldwide political movement that was centered in Moscow. Again, nothing could be further from the truth. When all due allowance is made for the efficient police methods of modern totalitarianism and the lunacies of Hitler's war plan against the U.S.S.R. (most especially the desperate motive he gave the Russian people to fight on), the facts remain that from 1930 forward, there was no significant political protest against Stalin's rule, and between 1940 and 1945, when the German armies drove within sight of Moscow, the Soviet Army was prepared to lose more than eight million battle dead, and the U.S.S.R. as a whole to sustain losses, from all causes, of more than twenty million without giving way.

Twenty million dead for Russia was a loss of more than one in every ten; but Stalin's rule emerged unshaken from the national ordeal—even though it ought to have been clear enough to the Party and general population that Stalin's own political and military blunders in the months of 1939–1940 had very nearly cost the Soviets the war. With the expulsion of the Germans, the political terror began again. The odd feature of the story is that it was then, in the aftermath of a bloody war in which the Soviet leaders had convincingly demonstrated their political cynicism and brutality, and their weakness and latent power as well, that the reputation, influence, and prestige of the Soviet Union stood highest in the world. In the moral vacuum after World War II—in Western Europe, in Afro-Asia, in Latin America, and even in the United States—the Soviet Union was able to exercise a vast influence over the imaginations of men.

Stalin, by force but also by guile and the mere terror of his reputation, was able not only to garner a vast satellite empire in Eastern and Central Europe, but to annex part or all of the territories of Germany, Japan, Estonia, Latvia, Lithuania, Rumania, Czechoslovakia, and Finland. Only very late in the game, in Turkey and Iran, was he balked by the intervention of the United States. In Europe, in Greece, Yugoslavia, and Albania, and in Asia, in China and Indochina, revolutionary movements for which he had done virtually nothing willingly gave him their loyalty. Had he called for an armed uprising in postwar France and Italy it is almost certain that the mass communist parties that adulated him could have brought down the shaky structure of those postwar governments. His agents were at work throughout Afro-Asia; and in each of the European colonies the local communist parties, without exception, looked to Moscow for direction.

Stalin will undoubtedly remain one of the imposing figures of history, worthy to stand beside a Genghis Khan or Caligula. But while in 1945 it may have seemed that he had triumphed over Hitler and would far outclass his rival in the permanence and scale of his achievement, a little more than a decade after his death the structure of the satellite empire he put together, and especially the structure of the worldwide political movement he directed, is shaken. Two communist states, China and Albania, are schismatics of the Left; one, Yugoslavia, is a schismatic of the Right; a fourth, Rumania, cultivates a guarded neutrality, hinders Soviet foreign policy, and even goes so far as to claim the return of territories seized by the Soviets after World War II. Of the communist parties of the world, at least one third have broken away from Moscow; the remaining parties, as in France or Italy, while technically orthodox, no longer defer to Moscow's ideological leadership. The gross national product of the U.S.S.R. may be two or three times as great today as in Stalin's time; the Soviets may demonstrate an impressive space and military technology— but whereas Stalin's writ ran unquestioned from Canton to Prague, in the world today there is a quality to Soviet diplomacy and political action which can only be described as plaintive.

This is an imposing shift of fortunes, and one, it must seem in the Kremlin, that defies explanation. The problem lies in the notion of *rational*: the appeal of the Soviets in the world was never a rational one, and if the present Kremlin leaders believe, as Nikita Khrushchev put it in Budapest a few weeks before his fall, that "communism is goulash and ballet," they are very wrong.

The Bolshevik revolution was a titanic upheaval in a time of general political and moral collapse in Europe, and, by influence, beyond. What subterranean forces this revolution released, and

for a short time Stalin harnessed, we only touch on here.* But
the appeal of Stalinism in the world was indeed irrational. And
with the return to comparative political sanity in the U.S.S.R.,
with the breaking of the ideological fever, everything has changed
for the Kremlin leaders. It was not the open secret of Soviet
poverty, nor Stalin's grotesque boasts about the primacy of Soviet
technology, or Soviet "justice," that made men give themselves to
Stalin with a kind of joy. For the generation of the inter-war and
early postwar years, the Soviets functioned as a type of messianic
kingdom. The worse Soviet reality was, the more the true believers—disoriented and anxiety-ridden by the collapse about
them of the traditional political, economic, and moral order—were
able to summon up reserves of faith. Theirs was a faith that had
nothing to do with reason or evidence. And it was in this irrational quality, together with the inner violence of the Stalinist
ethos, that the great danger of communism, as an international
system, lay. As an economic system, Marxism hardly mattered at
all, and undoubtedly in the more sophisticated and technically
competent environment of Western Europe or America it could
have been made, within limits, to "work."

It is the achievement of Stalin's successors that inheriting a
political system that was, literally, more than a little mad, they
have been able to bring it to a kind of reason. But by curing the
irrationalism of Soviet society, by reducing the claims of the Communist Party from being the priesthood of a new messianic kingdom to a mere cadre of organizational and developmental
specialists (a claim itself doubtful), the new Kremlin leaders have
stripped themselves of glamour and, it may be, of ultimate influence in the world. By competing on the level of reality—caloric
intake, butterfat production, the availability of antibiotics—they
have submitted to a mundane standard. This is a standard by
which, as any open-minded visitor to the U.S.S.R. will confirm,
they must lose. Put simply, Soviet society without Stalin is a bore.

One suspects that the Soviet future is dark, or clouded at best.
The Soviet leaders are struggling with a difficult legacy, but it is
not enough that this society should make its uneasy peace with
the closing years of the twentieth century—the years of the end
of ideology. Tens of millions have died for the Soviet dream; it

* For a fuller discussion, see the authors' *The Politics of Hysteria: The
Sources of Twentieth Century Conflict*, New York, 1964, pp. 144–163.

was a messianic adventure which Lenin began in 1917, and a half-century later his successors, dim and undistinguished men, cannot simply say it has been a mistake and call it all off.

This is not to predict a new revolution of the masses in Russia, least of all a revolution of freedom. It is to say that in the years ahead there are some violent adjustments to be made in Russia; the process will not be an easy one—for Russia or the world. Whatever the Soviet Union is or is not, it is far too large and powerful a state to suffer shocks and upheavals without endangering the world.

No doubt it will be many years before the man in the street, *Homo Sovieticus*, is aware that the bloom is off. But the new intelligentsia is aware, and through them the ranks of the Party are being made aware, that after half a century of heroic effort the ultimate direction of Soviet society is no more clear than it was in the beginning. What may save the nation, and even the system, is the national sense. Russia is a nation of great pride.* It is frequently forgotten that the Bolshevik revolution stemmed not from economic oppression and collapse, as the official ideology would have it, but from a catastrophic defeat in war. The revolution of 1905, which first shook the structure of Tsarist society, came in the aftermath of a distant defeat by Japan in the Far East; the 1917 revolt came in the aftermath of the three years of humiliating defeat on the Ukrainian front against Germany. World War I discredited the Tsar and his generals, and similarly it revealed Tsarist society to be hollow. From Peter the Great's day in the seventeenth century forward, the Romanovs had made a

---

* National pride, and the special sense that Russia is a peculiar treasure whose mission is to convert the world, long antedate communism, and no doubt will last long beyond the breaking of the present ideological fever. As early as the fifteenth century a monk of Pskov expressed Russia's national mission in these words to the Grand Duke Basil II of Moscow: "The Church of Old Rome fell because of its heresy; the gates of the Second Rome, Constantinople, have been hewn down by the axes of the infidel Turks; but the Church of Moscow, the Church of the New Rome, shines brighter than the Sun in the whole Universe. . . . Two Romes have fallen, but the Third stands fast; a fourth there cannot be." This sense of imperial mission which is at bottom religious remained a powerful current in Russian thought to the eve of the revolution, and merely emerged in new form with the Third International. As the modern Russian philosopher Berdyaev has put it, instead of the old fantasy of a "Third Rome in Russia, the Third International was achieved, and [to it] many of the features of the Third Rome were transferred. . . ."[6]

signal effort to adapt the technology of war and the political organization of the advanced European states to Russia—a nation that was not Europe, but dwelt uneasily on the European borderlands. They failed. The revolution of 1917 was not so much an economic revolution—even though the ideology of the men who led it, or rode it, proclaimed it to be that—as it was a national and social revolution: one more effort in a long series of agonizing efforts by the Russian peple to assimilate and use the technology and organizational techniques of the Western world, to maintain the nation and preserve the national identity by adapting and using, to their own ends, the sources of strength of their foes.

This technology and politics have twice been adapted in Russia in novel ways: first when the early Romanovs like Peter the Great and Catherine built a centralized monarchical state that superficially resembled the France of Louis XIV or the Prussia of Frederick the Great; the second time when Lenin proclaimed that communism was "the Soviets plus electricity." But the Russian people are an original force in history, capable of immense and original achievements, and the Europe which most forcibly impressed itself on the men who made the Bolshevik revolution was the Europe of 1914–1918. This was not the Europe of parliamentarianism and social progress, but the quasi-totalitarian Europe of World War I which had instituted mass conscription and centralized economic planning for war, suppressed free speech, and manipulated the arts and public information media for purposes of the state. It was a Europe which casually resorted to violence as an instrument of policy.

The Romanovs had adapted what they believed to be the political and economic system of the *ancien régime* and then lived to see dynastic Europe evolve into the nineteenth-century Western Europe of mass politics, constitutionalism, social progress, science, and industrialism. In some similar sense the modern inheritors of the 1917 Revolution have seen its premises outmoded, for whatever Europe is today, or may be in process of becoming, it has left the experience of 1914–1918 behind it. The tone of the closing years of the twentieth century is different from the quality of the years of World Wars I and II. But like a biological organism which has adapted itself too closely to a single environment, the Soviet Union is increasingly ill at ease as the political climate of the world changes. To some degree it is challenged even to find a way to survive without once again changing itself out of all recognition.

Stalin's Russia was well suited to survive in the frenetic political environment of the 1930's, the years of totalitarian high tide, and in the demoralized and exhausted international climate that followed World War II. But the system Stalin constructed (for it was he, rather than Lenin, who put the essential stamp on the U.S.S.R.) is less well adapted to the conditions of the present day; and despite all that his successors have done, it is *Stalin's* Russia, in its essential forms of economic, political, and social organization, that they rule today.

This alteration of the world is a serious challenge to the Soviets. It is not merely that Europe and America have changed; it is that the political quality of Afro-Asia—the regions where Khrushchev sought to turn the flank of the West after the Soviets had been balked in Europe—has changed as well. As the Bolshevik revolution approaches the half-century mark it is now a middle-aged movement and its sober, work-oriented ideology is out of step with the newer and hysterical style of politics in much of Afro-Asia. The Soviets hardly understand the racist and national concerns of the newer revolutions. These are fundamentally incompatible with the class-oriented ideology of orthodox Marxism and its emphasis on proletarian internationalism.

However the Soviet leaders may bend the dialectic, they cannot account for their sudden obsolescence. The fragmentation of their empire, the appearance of Chinese, Albanian, Rumanian, Hungarian, Yugoslav, and Polish national discords within what was proclaimed as an over-arching proletarian "brotherhood," the rise of racist politics in Afro-Asia, especially as advocated by Peking, the stunning rise of the West European economy, the sustained prosperity of the American economy—all these things refute the dialectic, the so-called "science of history" which they pretended to understand. And compounding these foreign failures are the domestic ones: their recalcitrant agriculture, the slackening industrial growth rates, and, worst of all, the growing sense of alienation among the rising generation—an alienation not only of the intelligentsia, but also of the unintellectual young.

Some such perception of complexities and failure must account for the peculiar political diffidence of the new Soviet leaders. They seem like uncertain men, a little as if they were afraid to speak in a difficult, and only half-learned, foreign language. They may learn to speak out in time; the Soviets have confounded their critics before. But the prospects do not seem especially bright. At the very least it would seem that they have their work cut out merely to remake the Soviet Union at home and to retain some semblance of authority over the communist movement that today survives in Europe.

As the Soviets return to normalcy they must function within the realm of normal diplomacy—though they are not entirely reconciled to this. But while diplomacy and negotiation are now feasible with the U.S.S.R. in a way impossible in Stalin's day, the question still unanswered is what kind of "normalcy" the Soviet Union can know. At the very least, Russia is a nation with a long history of aggressiveness. The Russians are by inheritance a messianic people, in the national sense if not in the ideological, and they have habitually menaced their neighbors. Their style of politics is authoritarian, though a tradition of authoritarianism does not necessarily imply totalitarianism.

It would be wise to be wary of Russia for a good many years to come. The Western world should not be implacable and punitive in its dealings with the Soviets; but it would be prudent to expect sudden checks in the process of *embourgeoisement* and political melioration, to anticipate that conservative forces, or merely unpragmatic *idealists*, in the Soviet Union will try to prevent the loss of Russia's claim to a peculiar greatness—its claim to difference from the rest of the world.

A process of *embourgeoisement* in Russia, moreover, is no guarantor of peacefulness. That middle-class societies are peaceful is a tender-minded nineteenth-century notion that ought to have been blasted once and for all on the fields of the Marne and the Somme in 1914. Bourgeois nations do make war. The Kaiser's Germany had everything to gain from peace in 1914; it did not wait. The mere rise of living standards in Russia does not give any assurance of peace. Beyond this there is the caution that Russia as a nation is troubled in deeper ways than economics can cure, and its troubles are of such a kind that they are not easily accessible to exterior help. Russia is in no real need of money or of technical and cultural aid; the technology is formidable, and one might suspect that modern Russia has, for the moment, all in the way of "new thought" that the society can bear. Russia needs to know—still needs to know, after all this time and grief—what Russia's real identity and place in Europe may be. It has yet to find peace with the West, and thus with itself. Western contact with Russia is desirable, and initiatives on the Western side may sometimes be welcome. But it is Russia which must make the long journey to normalcy—and we must remember that "normalcy" is a state of mind which Russia, as a nation, has never quite experienced.

THE NEW CHINESE MENACE

It is a curious comment on the state of the contemporary world that the waning of ideological fervor in the Soviet Union and the parallel decline of Soviet aggressiveness have left the Western world nearly as disoriented as the Soviets. Certainly this is true in the United States, where, if the challenge of the Soviets was at first taken up reluctantly, twenty years of Cold War have instilled in us a persistent taste for political crisis. After twenty years of political combat Americans are a little like colonels of the British Indian Army who retire to Kensington, and after a lifetime of eating curries, find they cannot taste British food.

Some such inability to adjust must lie behind the exaggerated fears with which Communist China is viewed today by Americans. The Chinese communists assuredly are ill-disposed to the United States, malevolent, ideological, and on occasion ignorant and naïve. But there is a difference between hostile declaration and hostile intention, and between intention and capability. It is a very arguable proposition that China for many years to come will be seriously capable of damaging the interests of the United States, or even the interests of our friends, or that China is so given to irrationality that no intercourse with it is possible.

To say this may seem shocking, even irresponsible; but that it is so is a measure of the emotional charge we have invested in this whole question of China. Behind the American obsession with China there seems to lie a quality of unreasonable fear. The Yellow Peril is an old American bogey; one suspects that Communist China has emerged in Asia as the new incarnation of an old nightmare, the Yellow Peril fused with the Red.

Beyond this, in American attitudes to Peking there seems to be an element of bewilderment and hurt. For more than a century the United States had championed China's national cause. The policy of maintaining free access for all nations to China's trade was first embodied in the Treaty of Wangshia in 1844 and steadily expanded in the nineteenth century until it became a cardinal principle of the American government that Chinese territorial integrity was to be defended. As Tyler Dennett observed: "The spirit of the policy [of the Open Door] is as old as the Declaration of Independence"; or as Walter Lippmann put it in 1944: "The Open Door is at bottom a short name for the American way of life, projected abroad."[7] On the popular level, China became the great arena of American religious, educational, and medical missionary activity—the whole nation, in effect, a vast American philanthropy. In this process Chinese history and culture were sentimentalized out of all recognition. Because the warrior held low status in the Confucian social system, China, it came to be believed, was not warlike—as if there had never been the great empires of Han, T'ang, and Ming, each aggressive far beyond its inherited frontiers. Because urbane Canton and Shanghai merchants were polite to the foreign bankers who would not admit them to their clubs, the xenophobia in Chinese culture was ignored. Because traditional Chinese religion seemed more than a little cynical, the evidence of irrational and superstitious intensity that burst forth in the T'ai P'ing and Boxer rebellions of the nineteenth and early twentieth centuries, when millions perished, was brushed aside.

The two attitudes, the official espousal of Chinese territorial integrity and the American reforming religious mission, were nicely summed up by Woodrow Wilson in 1914. Hailing the Chinese revolution of 1911–1912, he declared: "The awakening of the people of China to a consciousness of their possibilities under free government is the most significant, if not the most momentous, event of our generation. With this aspiration the American people are in profound sympathy." His Secretary of State, William Jennings Bryan, thought the new Chinese political aspirations were deeply inspired by Christian example, and Wilson himself asserted that the American Minister to China should, as a matter of course, be an evangelical Christian.[8] Thus China was to be made both democratic and Christian and, as such, would exercise a stabilizing influence on Asian affairs. In less extreme form the fantasy persisted through World War II, when it was a cardinal principle of American policy that Chiang Kai-shek's China was to be treated as a great power. At American insistence Chinese became one of the four official languages of the United Nations. The conviction that an independent China would function as a progressive influence in Asia lay behind the remark in 1939 of Joseph E. Grew, our ambassador to Japan at the time of Pearl Harbor: "Once Japan is destroyed as an aggressive force we know of no other challenging power that can appear in the Pacific. . . . Japan is the one enemy, and the only enemy, of the peaceful peoples whose shores overlook the Pacific Ocean."[9] No better demonstration of the traditional hold of illusion over American Asian policy could be found. Yet having espoused China's cause for a century, and having fought a bloody war against Japan as much for China's sake as for any other, we emerge today in Chinese proclamations as the irredeemable enemy. The ingratitude may rankle; but resentment is a poor foundation for policy.

There are more than six hundred million Chinese. China has demonstrated the beginnings of a nuclear capability, and is attempting to build a modern industry. The nation is more than a fifth of the world's population, and no negligible fifth. Yet what is this China? One consequence of the Cold War—and the ideological habits of thought it has stimulated and strengthened —has been to focus attention on the *communist* character of China's rulers and ruling party. The notion that seems to underlie most American public discussions of China is that if we could substitute another government for the communists the result would be a peaceful China, once again grateful to the United States and a stabilizing factor in East Asia.

But what evidence is there for such a notion? Even the most cursory study of Chinese records will reveal that China is a great civilization—profound, original, technically competent. It is equally evident that Chinese civilization is autocratic in origin, placing small value on the individual—a nation which regards itself as the very center and norm of mankind and which has for more than two thousand years been accustomed to conduct diplomacy in terms of overlordship and vassalage. When China has been strong, it has acknowledged no equals, and certainly no superiors. The lordly-minded Chinese, when they first met the "South Sea barbarians," as they called the traders and emissaries of Western Europe who came to them in the sixteenth and seventeenth centuries, said of them that "of all nations the Chinese have two eyes; the Europeans one; all other nations of the earth are blind." As late as 1792, when Lord Macartney was appointed ambassador to China from the Court of Saint James's, he was escorted to Peking under banners marked "Tribute Bearers." Such was the habitual stance of China in foreign affairs, when China thought itself strong.

Thus the China into which Europe first broke four hundred years ago was a conceptual universe of its own. The Chinese name for their land was Chun-kuo, the "Middle Kingdom," which is to say the center of the world. China was guarded on the west by the barrier of the central Asian mountain ranges and on the south by the jungles of Cochin and Burma. Unlike Europe and the Middle East, which had existed in violent but creative interaction from early medieval times, or even India, which had suffered repeated invasions by barbarian Sakais and Huns but also by civilized Saracens and Englishmen, China knew nothing of an external world that was not her manifest inferior. The civilized kingdoms of Japan, Korea, and Annam, however they might struggle for a political independence, never aspired to supplant the parent Chinese culture.

China is poor today, and within the past century has suffered a succession of droughts, famines, and wars, and this blinds us to the fact that in the sixteenth, seventeenth, and eighteenth centuries this was the richest and, within its own terms, the happiest nation in the world. It was well governed. For nearly two thousand years the Chinese had governed themselves, not by a crude system of hereditary feudal overlordship, as for centuries was the case in Europe, but through the operations of a sophisticated civil service —entrance to this elite was gained by competitive examination in which merit played the decisive role. While China was a despotism, it was an egalitarian society in the sense that the principle of the *carrière ouverte aux talents* prevailed. A peasant boy became the Han emperor, and he was not the only such case in Chinese history. In eras of stable government, there were countless cases of humble men rising to great power as provincial governors or advisors to the court.

The Chinese governmental tradition thus was bureaucratic and centralized, as well as despotic, and except for interregna of "warlordism" between ruling dynasties, Chinese society has always been governed from the center and from above. There is no native democratic tradition. China is a highly cultivated nation; but civilization and democracy are not the same thing.

Nor, as we have remarked, is China a peaceful society. There have been great warrior dynasties in China. Most of Chinese history from the earliest times to the present has been a story of expansion. There has been an essentially peaceful expansion of peasant tillers into the neighboring steppes and arable bottom-lands; there have also been ambitious military expeditions against independent kingdoms. Dynasties like the Han and the Ching penetrated far into Central Asia. The fact that Soviet Russia has incorporated regions of Inner Asia, Manchuria, and Siberia that are "rightfully" Chinese is one of the major issues between Moscow and Peking. It is not even true that at the level of philosophy China's tradition is pacifist. The Confucian tradition gives little honor to the warrior; but the "Realist" tradition, the school of law and political philosophy that guided Chin-Shih-Huang-Ti, China's centralizer and "First Universal Emperor," was the reverse. "A people that looks to warfare as a ravening wolf looks at a piece of meat is a people than can be used," said Shang Tzu, a counselor to the emperor in the fourth century B.C.

Something very like this aggressive, centralizing spirit of old imperial China is alive in China today. And it is hardly open to question that the Kuomintang government, had it succeeded in bringing order to China after World War II, would have expressed the same impulse. Even today the Kuomintang government on Taiwan refrains from criticism of the communist capture of Tibet or the argument Peking makes with respect to the border between China and India. Where the national integrity of China is at issue, ideology takes second place.

There is another feature of native Chinese culture which must be understood in considering China today—the place of the individual and of private property in this society. The Confucian tradition itself tolerates mercantile activity but does not especially honor it. There is, however, another radical, egalitarian, and violent tradition in Chinese social thought which is represented by such revolutionary movements as the nineteenth-century T'ai P'ing, which preached a syncretist Christian doctrine fused with the social radicalism of such ancient books as the pre-Confucian Utopian classic *The Rites of Chou*. "These ancient texts called for a sort of primitive communism in which twenty-five households among the peasantry were to form one communal unit, each with its treasury and church and two superintendents," the modern historian Kenneth Scott Latourette has written of the movement. "In these communities the fields were to be tilled in common, as on a communist collective farm today. Food, clothing, and money were to be used in common. The surplus from the harvest was to revert to the communal treasury. . . . In other social teachings the T'ai P'ings advocated equality between the sexes. They inveighed against slavery, concubinage, foot-binding, arranged marriage, cruel punishments, and the use of opium." Their borrowings from Christianity were distorted, and selective. The T'ai P'ing emperor proclaimed himself the "Younger Brother of Christ" and the universal ruler of mankind, in keeping with Chinese egoism and ethnocentricity. "Rewards and punishments they borrowed from the New Testament, together with descriptions of heaven and hell. But they omitted distinctive Christian teachings concerning the spiritual power of love and forgiveness, and of humility."[10]

What is new in Chinese communism is not the notions of work and property held in common, nor the abolition of distinctions of privilege and sex; it is the scientism which it claims—its effort to banish superstition from political practice—as well as the fact that it is a wholly secular movement.

Unfortunately for China, the distinctions between the new political practice and the old are not always fundamental. Chinese communism makes use of native superstition where necessary—vide the rehabilitation of the traditional (and worthless) medical system of acupuncture. Modern China displays a considerable distortion in its perceptions of reality; the new ideology is certainly a melding of ancient Chinese traditions with the secularized religion of the twentieth century, Marxism, which entered China after World War I. Marxism in modern China is a revolutionary successor to the official (and ostensibly Christian) values of the old colonial powers, now discredited.

It is the chauvinist quality of modern Chinese revolutionary movements (even those like the nineteenth-century T'ai P'ing and twentieth-century communists that borrow from the Western world) that is most significant. The T'ai P'ing arose in the aftermath of China's humiliation by Britain in the Opium Wars, when fantastic stories of Western power swept China and the central government had been shown incompetent. Like the T'ai P'ing, Chinese communism arose in the aftermath of China's later degradations: the carving up of once inviolable territories of the Middle Kingdom into foreign concessions, China's defeat in the Sino-Japanese War of 1894, the suppression by foreign troops of the Boxer Rebellion in 1900 (whose slogan had been "Cherish the Dynasty, Expel the Foreigner").

Where the French, British, Russians, Germans, Americans, and aggressively Westernizing Japanese established territorial and commercial enclaves, the old mandarin tradition of the Chinese was affronted. For the China that had only a century earlier regarded itself as the norm of mankind, this was the ultimate crisis. It was not so much foreign economic exploitation that distressed the Chinese literatus, or even enraged those unemployable products of mission schools who drifted into revolution, though Marxism stressed exploitation and provided an economic rationale for nationalist sentiment. It was the invidious spectacle of a nation of ancient culture and vast attainments unaccountably brought low by foreigners.* In the nineteenth and early twentieth centuries China was treated with open contempt by every nation of the world, with the possible exception of the United States, and the United States subjected China to what was, perhaps, the final humiliation—pity.

Clearly, the victory of communism in China was not inevitable. Nor is communism a political system that has won the Chinese people's free consent. But the minimum that must be said about communism in China today is that it does not fit China so ill, as Stalin once put it of the Germans, "as a saddle fits a cow." Moreover, it must be said that as applied to China the notion of free political consent may be irrelevant: the Chinese in history have been used to granting political consent to that power which succeeds in establishing itself and in maintaining itself; this

---

* It might be objected that the fall of China was a political tragedy only to the elites, and that the Chinese coolie, that traditional pacifist who cares for nothing but the good earth, was unmoved by the political degradation of China. But the T'ai P'ing and Boxers—like the communists—enlisted the support of literally millions of Chinese peasants. Despite the intensive Christian missionary efforts, the Chinese converts to official Christianity were always few, so great was the native resistance to alien ways. The revolutionary lead against the West, of course, always came from the elites.

is the well-known "Mandate of Heaven." Until a government begins to fail, and the regime reveals itself as inept, the Mandate remains. The tradition in China is one of not initiating revolutionary action until the moment comes when the dynasty has demonstrated that it is no longer fit to rule. Then, with a push, it falls.

Barring a series of disasters, the Peking government is not likely to fall very soon, and we ought to admit, in any case, that the United States is afraid to overturn it. When in recent years exaggerated stories of Chinese famine and governmental weakness have circulated through Hong Kong and other watch posts, the chief care in Washington has been to ensure that Nationalist forces on Taiwan do *not* attack. Caution in such circumstances is obviously indicated; the consequences of a new Chinese civil war, both for Asia and for Soviet-American relations, would be most dangerous. But the truth is that we are the victims of cant with respect to Peking: we do not like the Chinese communists, but on the other hand we are not quite sure we want them to go away.

This doubt too conceals an inner wisdom. The truth is that the Chinese, for all their bluster, are a relatively weak state. China is not nearly so capable of action on the world scene as its leaders, or we, sometimes seem to think (it is the Soviets, after all, who could today ravage the United States with ICBM's); yet China has done vast damage to the international communist movement. Probably no other single factor has played so large a part in bringing the Soviet leaders up against reality, revealing the hollowness of their pretensions and the insufficiency of their vaunted science of history, than the defection of the Chinese from their Russian alliance. China is America's enemy; but the over-all effect of its enmity has been, by weakening Russia, to strengthen the United States position by and large and to increase United States security. Whatever China's role and gains may be in Southeast Asia, by weakening the unity of communism the Chinese have done inestimable service to mankind. That it is an involuntary service is beside the point. What the future holds may be something else; but let us remember that the danger that China poses is not merely to the United States. America, despite its present commitments in Southeast Asia and the Western Pacific, is not the proximate enemy—and neighbor—of the

Chinese. China's real threat is to the Soviet Union (more even than to India, which is largely protected by distance and a mountain barrier). Russia's border runs for more than three thousand miles with the Chinese.

In any case, Chinese diplomacy today can hardly be counted a success. Chinese self-assertion would have it that China is a claimant to world leadership. But while China's intellectual resources are very great, China is not a rich country like Russia; in Russia a government, barring great wars, must be inept indeed to starve and fail. But in China—such is the Malthusian situation—it may be that even the most devoted and astute government cannot win. It is a myth of the modern West, preserved virtually intact in America, that given intelligence and application, success is a certainty. But the world is more complex: there is death as well as life, failure in place of success.

At present, it seems, China is holding its own. But in the exaggerated Chinese ideological claims, and in the official hope to lead a worldwide revolution of the disinherited against the "cities" of the world—Western Europe, Russia, and America— there is more than a suggestion of compensatory fantasy. The political theories of Mao Tse-tung and his Defense Minister Lin Piao may make interesting reading, but they are not necessarily a blueprint for victory. "The countryside of the world [i.e., the underdeveloped nations], and the countryside alone, can provide the revolutionary bases from which the revolutionaries can go forward to final victory," they have asserted. ". . . The revolutionary people of the world will sweep away everything that stands in the way of their advance. . . . The imperialists, the reactionaries, and the communist revisionists, who have all set themselves against peoples' war, will be swept like dust from the stage of history by the mighty broom of revolutionary people."[11] This is heady stuff, though unspecific. How is this to be done?

Seven or eight hundred million people are not the same thing as wealth. Indeed, the great problem for China is to support its burgeoning population and find a surplus for its armed forces. Sheer population is not an easy weapon to use. War is still a matter of communications and logistics; even peasant armies, however devoted and austere, demand to be fed. Four destroyers, ten frigates, and a handful of submarines (the Chinese navy today), even supplemented by armed junks, are not an amphibious force. If an enemy were to oblige China by attacking in China, China's defensive power might prove formidable—though even this is not so certain.* Chinese capabilities for offensive action, certainly against serious enemies, are something else again.

But to stress the role of military action in Chinese policy is to miss an important point. The Chinese planners do not rely on war as a primary instrument of policy. Nothing is more glaring than the contradiction between the (qualified) bellicosity of Peking's pronouncements and the record of what the Chinese have done. As the Russians have sometimes noted in reply to Chinese polemics, Peking preaches a doctrine of inevitable conflict and uncompromising hostility—but Hong Kong and Macao, to say nothing of the offshore islands of Quemoy and Matsu, remain in "imperialist" hands. In today's world, the Chinese provide the clearest example of the distinction between ideological pronouncements, which are to be understood purely within the

---

* The record of the ground fighting in Korea is a good example of the difference between reality and its perception. It was commonly thought that China, at the least, held United States forces to a deadlock, and may have inflicted a defeat in 1951. But when the call for a cease-fire was issued by the Soviet delegate to the United Nations, Jacob A. Malik, in May, 1951, the Chinese and North Korean armies, since their entry into battle, had sustained battle losses of nearly a million men and were close to collapse. "In a year of combat in Korea and especially during April and May of 1951, the Communist armies in Korea had taken a blood-letting of tremendous proportions," the official United States Air Force history of the Korean War records. "In addition to the 163,130 enemy soldiers in the United Nations Command prisoner-of-war camps, United Nations intelligence estimated that the North Koreans and Chinese Communists had sustained 863,949 battle casualties. Altogether, the Communists had lost a total of some 1,191,422 soldiers through capture and battle and non-battle causes."[12] It was the initial entry of the Chinese into Korea that was a military success. But once the United Nations forces had regrouped, and air power was brought into play against the Chinese forces, the roles were reversed and the Chinese forces met disaster. "Free from the danger of hostile air attack, United Nations forces were able to maneuver as they wished during daylight hours. The Communists, on the other hand, were compelled to move and fight at night. Air-interdiction missions destroyed enemy troops, equipment, and supplies before they reached the battle zone. . . . In each offensive . . . the Reds took heavy losses, and each offensive dwindled for want of logistical support before it could bring decisive manpower to bear for lasting ground decision."[13] Even allowing for exaggerated claims of battle deaths, and for Air Force bias, the record of modern arms against underequipped Asian mass armies on moderately favorable ground, in Korea, is impressive.

declaratory or "magical" context, and those words, formulations of careful policy, that are meant to be believed.

China's true hopes center, it seems, on political warfare. We have seen the Chinese set themselves up as a rival center of world revolution with innovative theories. They have jettisoned classical Marxism, with its emphasis on the role of the urban proletariat, in favor of a peasant base. This is the Maoist innovation; it is far removed from classical communism, whose founders Marx and Engels could speak of the peasant as the "barbarian of civilization." And in this appeal of the Chinese to the downtrodden of Afro-Asia and Latin America there is, of course, the suggestion of an appeal to racism.

Such theorizing and such appeals contain what orthodox Marxists would term an "inner contradiction." For Marx and his successors, a class analysis of society and an appeal to proletarianism were consistent with claims to have founded a *universal* creed. The working class existed everywhere; if men could achieve a horizontal organization of society, founded on a single class, the barriers of nationality and race could not impede proletarian brotherhood. In more practical terms, for Lenin and Trotsky, who made the Russian revolution but intended it as the opening gun in a vast struggle against the capitalist strongholds of the West, an appeal to proletarian revolt meant a union between Russia's interests, and indeed its survival, and the interests of the industrial masses of Europe and America.

But national or racial appeals are intrinsically divisive, not universal. There is not even a "colored" four fifths of humanity who conceive of a common interest, to say nothing of a common hope to oppress and exterminate the remainder. When we in the West speak of the "colored" peoples of the world we reveal our innate racism. It is our own egoism which tells us that the world is divided between "whites" and "coloreds." The coloreds know better: an African is no Tamil; a Malay is not a Pathan. The cleavages between them are as deep as any in the world. If anyone doubts this, let him study the history of communal and racial tensions in Asia—or for that matter current race relations in East Africa, for example, where Hindu traders are regarded with approximately the warmth reserved in the last century for Jews in Ukrainian villages.

The sole real advantage the Chinese maintain over the Soviets in this struggle is that they are poor. It *is* possible for the poor and degraded of Afro-Asia to identify in this respect with China, as twenty or thirty years ago they could identify with the Soviets. But if the Chinese succeed in achieving even comparative wealth, they will find, as the Soviets have done, that they have forfeited submerged mankind's sympathy in the process. And in any event a common poverty is hardly enough, alone, to bring into being a disciplined international alliance committed to Peking's leadership.

IV

The Challenge to America,
Myth and Reality — II

It is one of the conventions of the Cold War that it is a contest
for the Third World—the belt of poor and backward states of
the Southern Hemisphere whose allegiance to communism or
adherence to the values of freedom will tip the balance of world
power. "The less-developed lands . . . promise to be the principal
battleground on which the forces of freedom and communism
compete—a battleground in which the future shape of society
may finally be tested and determined," John McCloy has written
in a statement of the case that will do duty for a vast public
literature.[1] On the communist side the belief is essentially the
same: balked in Europe after their initial postwar successes, the
Soviets after Stalin undertook a vast new diplomacy in Afro-Asia.
More recently the communist leaders in Peking, seeing the failures of the Soviets as a chance for themselves, have advanced
a novel ideological theory whereby Afro-Asia—the "rural" areas
of the world—can encircle Western Europe and North America
—the world's "cities"—and bring about the ultimate defeat of
the capitalism that flourishes there.[2]

But the proposition that the fate of the world will be decided
in this backward region is dubious in the extreme. Considered
in material terms, the region is not vital to Western—or to
Soviet—prosperity. As for its power, present or potential, this
too can be exaggerated. While it is true that the majority of
mankind inhabits the Afro-Asian world, effective power is
very slight; the region is barely self-sustaining in food production,
and elaborate foreign aid programs, funded at many billions of

dollars since 1945, have scarcely made a dent in the chronic miseries of overpopulation, undercapitalization, exhausted soils, one-crop economies, and rudimentary technical skills. In the mid-1960's the region, basically agricultural, needs to import $4 billion in foodstuffs each year. "At a growth rate of five per cent, the underdeveloped countries would, seventy-five years from now, reach the same average income a head as the countries of Western Europe were enjoying in 1960," the president of the World Bank, George D. Wood, has written. "That in itself would be a tremendous achievement. It would compress into less than a century an evolution that it took today's industrial nations three or four times as long to accomplish. But there can be no question of reaching such a goal quickly.

"In most of the underdeveloped countries the basic task is still to establish the preconditions of development, to reach a position which the industrial nations of today finally gained in the nineteenth century, when for the first time there became available the complex of factors needed to create a predominantly industrial society: among them an acquisitive outlook, technical capacity, adequate sources of energy, mobility in transportation, and adequate credit systems. . . . [P]roduction in the under-developed world is growing; but increasing output is having to be shared among more and more people. . . . In the underde-veloped world as a whole, the yearly addition of some fifty million people to the population may eat up half the gain in production in a single year."*

The extension of the Cold War from its beginnings in Europe to Asia, and then to Latin America and Africa, was a process roughly paralleling a basic change in the Soviet and American understanding of their struggle. The Cold War began in Europe with the meeting of Soviet and American armies on the Elbe in April, 1945, and rapidly developed as the Soviets incorporated Eastern Europe and the Balkans into a postwar empire. In effect, the early Cold War was a contest for the control of a prostrate, but fundamentally very rich, continent that had func-tioned as the center of world politics for three hundred years. Possession of the industrial resources and human skills of Western

* _The Times_ (London), September 16, 1965. Mr. Wood's article is candid in its discussion of the difficulties and it is only fair to record that he calls for greater effort rather than less.

Europe could plausibly have tipped the balance of world power in Russia's favor. This was what Stalin wanted and a disaster that the United States prevented.

The transformation of this battle for Europe into a worldwide struggle for ideological influence was perhaps inherent in the Soviet conception of their role as agents of a universal revolution. Yet to seek revolution in Afro-Asia before it was accomplished in Europe actually contradicted Marxist-Leninist doctrine, although the success of the revolution in Russia in 1918 had itself been such a contradiction. Marxist orthodoxy held that the advanced societies with large industrial proletariats would lead the way to communism. When the Bolshevik leaders found themselves in command in Russia in 1918 they were conscious of this anomaly: "Our backwardness has thrust us forward," Lenin wrote in the spring of that year; ". . . we shall perish if we are unable to hold out until we meet with the support of other [developed] countries."[3] But, supreme opportunists, the Bolsheviks disregarded the failure of revolution in Germany and industrial Central Europe after World War I, and their movement proved itself to be—despite its universal pretensions—a *national* movement.

Stalin directed an international organization—the Comintern —which professed to be an association of the fraternal communist parties of the world, but he used it wholly in the service of Soviet foreign policy. He was a realist, at least within a pathological conceptual scheme, and when in the late months of World War II his armies entered Central Europe, he acted to consolidate Soviet power within these contiguous territories —territories in which Russia itself could act with decisive force, territories which defended the western invasion approaches to Russia. He continued to use the Communist International (or, later, Cominform) for political warfare and intelligence purposes, but seldom if ever committed the Soviet Union to any enterprise beyond the reach of its military power. Even the attack on South Korea by the Soviet puppet government in Pyongyang was an effort to pick up a piece of undefended territory flanking the Soviet maritime provinces.

The real reason that Stalin's successors opened up the new Afro-Asian front after his death was simply that they did not know what else to do. In Europe, American economic aid, used to restore already developed economies, and the North Atlantic Alliance had re-created prosperity, social stability, and military security. After the Czechoslovak *coup d'état* in February, 1948, there were to be no more easy victories for the Soviets in Europe; and the lesson was driven home by the collapse of the Greek guerrilla movement later that same year and the failure of the Berlin blockade.

Following the development of a stalemate in Europe, Stalin, who had been shaken by the defection of the formerly loyal Yugoslav Communist Party, was content to consolidate his territorial gains and build up his military capacities. The challenge of Titoism was met by a new series of purges in Eastern Europe in which communist leaders and the rank and file in the slightest degree tainted by nationalism, or localism, were killed or jailed. The satellites, which until 1948 had at least preserved the fiction of local autonomy and innovation, were welded into an ideologically uniform and docile mass. The Soviets rapidly acquired nuclear and thermonuclear weapons to achieve a defensive preponderance in Europe. But clearly, by 1948 Stalinist foreign policy had exhausted its possibilities. Stalin, in any event, had been formed, and had functioned, in an essentially European age. Europe was not seen as "finished" until late in his lifetime.

It was left to Stalin's successors, checked in Europe, to undertake serious programs in Afro-Asia. Their horizons were broader because, as somewhat younger men who came to power after World War II, they were infected by the dream of the Soviet would-be successorship to Europe. Though their experience was the parochial one of the Soviet *apparatchik*, or Party functionary, they had a wider, though not necessarily more accurate, vision than Stalin of the postwar world. When they turned to Afro-Asia they largely made use of aid programs, attempts to secure diplomatic influence, adventures in subversion—measures in which the real factors of Soviet power could hardly be brought to bear. They acted out of frustration in Europe, but also out of ideology—out of their belief in the old universal mission of communism to world revolution. Their belief, though, was perhaps more sentimental than real, and was ill-adjusted to their simultaneous efforts to make post-Stalinist Russia itself "respectable," a sober Great Power in world affairs. In fact, they found themselves in more than one local dilemma, ideologically committed to support a subversive Communist Party's revolutionary action in the same country where they sought the good will of the non-communist government. Almost without exception— in Egypt, in India, in Burma, in the lesser Asian states—they sacrificed the local communists to the larger Russian diplomatic interest.

The parallel American ideologizing of the Cold War developed both in response to the new Soviet activities and out of that American taste for ideologizing and moralizing foreign policy that we have already discussed. The "realism" of early American Cold War policy in Europe—the Marshall Plan, the Truman Doctrine, and the creation of NATO—had responded to the equally "realistic" Soviet military and political pressure against Russia's peripheral areas. The transfer of the struggle to Asia and Africa marked a new stage not only in the scale of the Cold War but in its character. It now became not so much a political combat as a moral one—a campaign to convert allies, rather than to conquer or defend territories.

When Khrushchev and Bulganin toured Asia in the mid-1950's and made the first tentative beginnings in Soviet foreign aid to the underdeveloped countries, their effort was simultaneously to enhance the attractiveness of the Soviet Union as a nation while attempting to win the support of governments that the ideologically more uncompromising Stalin had regarded as bourgeois and corrupt. The Soviets, not a nation with vast sums of money to spare, did spend in the years that followed very large amounts in foreign aid—by 1965 they had spent $225 million in Indonesia alone. It is hardly an exaggeration to say that the result of this vast Soviet effort has been nil. Indonesia, Ghana, Iraq, Guinea, India, and Burma, to name only six favorite recipients of Soviet aid, do not today revolve in the Soviet orbit any more than do "enemy" Thailand or Formosa. And for the Soviets, even Cuba is at best an unearned and only qualified success.

Whatever its defects, the Stalinist method of acquiring empire, step by step within the shadow of Soviet military power, was the traditional and tested mode of the conqueror. Like so many other of Nikita Khrushchev's innovations, the ideological campaign of the Soviet Union in the Third World, calculated to undermine the strength of the West by indirection, has proved a costly failure.

THE CRISIS OF AFRO-ASIA

But to say that after two decades of Cold War the Soviet Union has no reliable friends among the underdeveloped nations, nor much hope of incorporating Afro-Asia into a centrally dominated power system, is not to say everything about the challenge of the Third World. Whether or not communism flourishes there as an ideology, there remains the basic question of the intrinsic instability of the region. The Third World has the ability to generate movements of its own, communist or non-communist, which can disturb the general peace.

That Afro-Asia (and to a lesser degree Latin America) is in a state of endemic disorder—that governments are overturned and new revolutionary movements spring up with bewildering speed —is self-evident. But how is the turmoil of the Third World to be dealt with? To answer this question we shall first have to answer another. What are the sources of this turmoil?

The Soviets argue that the Afro-Asian revolution derives from factors essentially related to their own revolution. The dialectic is such, in the Marxian scheme, that all revolutions are conceived as class movements, economically generated. But Louis Lomax has commented on the African scene: "Racism is the irritant on Africa's raw nerves—not colonialism, but that *white* people have colonized *black* people; not settler domination, but that *white* settlers have dominated indigenous *black* people; not social discrimination, but that the *white* power structure sets itself apart from the *black* masses; not denial of civil rights, but that *white* people deny *black* people their civil rights."[4]

This is exaggeration; given the shock of two world wars and the belief, widely accepted after 1945 even by the colonial nations, that imperialism was a moral outrage, the structure of the French or Belgian or British empires could hardly have endured in Africa or Asia. Racism is not the whole issue any more than economic exploitation. Afro-Asia is at fever heat over something a good deal more complex than poverty or the denial of human rights. But for Soviet policy, the result of ignoring such complexity, and attempting to force the new political movements of Afro-Asia into the inherited ideological mold, has been such lunatic and humiliating adventures as their abortive 1961 intervention in the Congo:

as if a secure, steady, planful, work-oriented Marxist order could have been built in a fractured Congolese tribal society driven to frenzy against the alien and hostile culture which had exploited it for a century.

On the other hand, the United States cannot claim much greater wisdom or understanding than the Soviets. Years of chronic violence and discord in the Congo have still not taught us that communism's prospects there are as meager as democracy's. The Congo, in its poignant upheaval, can no more convert itself to the austere politics of Marxism than to multi-party representative democracy. Yet there is scarcely an American newspaper, or scholar, that has not habitually related the Stanleyville insurrection of 1964 to the issue of communism and Soviet (or Chinese) intervention. How was a movement which killed its "intellectuals"—those who merely could read—to function within the communist imperial scheme? Where were the disciplined and indoctrinated cadres to seize this revolution? Of what materials could they have been made? The Christian missionary Martin Bormann has written of the "Simbas"—the Congolese rebels—at first hand, noting that they normally appeared on their raids "with a wild-looking witch-doctor at their head. They were shouting, 'Simba, Simba, Simba, mai, mai . . . Lumumba.' "[5]

Of this and other reports an able student of contemporary Africa, Roger Anstey, has commented: "The significance of the incantation reported by Bormann . . . has still been only partly elucidated. More especially the separate terms of 'Simba, simba, mai, mai, Lumumba,' as well as their linking together in an incantation, have a magical and psychological significance. The reason for bestowing on the soldier the term for a lion is presumably that 'simba' conjures up the stealth and sudden pounce of the attacking lion as well as its great strength. This identification would seem also to have a psychic dimension in a world-view in which the universe is made up of hierarchically arranged and interacting 'force-beings.' For, in such a world-view, the strengthening of the individual's *force vitale* is of major concern and is possible through magical means. Seen in this light, there is a supernatural significance in the incantation of 'simba' and 'Lumumba.' In regard to the second term of the incantation, 'mai,' [meaning water] Bormann has indicated that its significance was the Simba belief that this would turn the bullets of their op-

ponents to water. There is abundant evidence that rebels have
often believed that they possessed this kind of immunity. On a
study of psychological basis of these magical beliefs the present
writer has neither the space nor the competence to embark.
Fascinating comparisons with magical beliefs in other African
rebellions and particularly, perhaps, with Mannoni's observations
on the Madagascar rising cry out to be made. But it must here
suffice to say that a study of the rebellion which did not bear in
mind its psychological and magical aspects would be as meaning-
less as an explanation of the operation of a steam engine which
omitted all reference to the draughting arrangements."[6] This was
the movement so widely feared to be communist.

The spirit of the Stanleyville movement is far closer to the
hysteria and fantasy of China in the Boxer Rebellion than to any
"scientific socialism." To note that there was a magical element in
Lenin's thought in 1917, or to call attention to the irrational forces
that the Bolshevik revolution unleashed, is one thing. To confuse
an Antoine Gizenga or a Patrice Lumumba with a Lenin, or even
a Mao, is quite another. The Congo rebellion, of course, was an
extreme case of psychosocial disturbance finding a political outlet.
It is not the archetype of the Afro-Asian revolutions. But neither
are the Soviets or Communist Chinese.

What, then, is the real nature of these disturbances? For one
thing, there is no single Third World revolution, because there is
no single Third World—the phrase, along with the "underdeveloped," "developing," or "new" nations, is the product of
political rhetoric. Our habit of treating the disparate parts of the
non-European world as a unit is an expensive error, a kind of
political nominalism that leads us to ignore distinctions that make
all the difference. Asia is the domain of sophisticated and accomplished civilizations. Chinese culture, Indic culture, the Moslem
world—these are civilizations which have practiced the arts of
government, produced philosophies and science, developed an
individual sensibility, ordered human existence in complex ways.
The very brilliance of the past of these cultures is a bar to their
easy adaptation to modern Western technological society; not all
values are compatible. Hindu religiosity, a vision which sees the
material world as phantasm and rejects the very notion of reality,
let alone the possibility of rational and exploitative manipulation
of the material environment, cannot very well coexist undamaged

with blast furnaces and a centrally directed development plan. One or the other ethos must give way; and we of the West might beware of an arrogance which assumes to dictate which choice it is to be that others must make.*

The continent of Africa, south of the Sahara, has produced no cultures comparable to Asia's, though the anguish of its elites as they are required to give up ancestral ways is hardly less intense than the Brahmin's or the Buddhist scholar's. For Africa's backwardness, long isolation from the main currents of human civilization, a formidable physical environment, and a savage slave trade are largely responsible, but the fact remains that it is a gross oversimplification to speak of the problems of Africa in terms borrowed from Asian politics.†

---

* For the contrast between the Hindu spirit of worldly rejection, and the Western Faustian ethic of material manipulation and control, consider the following words of the Lord Gautuma Buddha to his disciples in the Diamond-Cutter Sutra: "By this wisdom shall enlightened disciples be enabled to bring into subjection every inordinate desire! Every species of life, whether hatched in the egg, formed in the womb, evolved from spawn . . . with or without form or intelligence, possessing or devoid of natural instinct—from these conditions of being, I command you to seek deliverance. And why? Because in the minds of enlightened disciples there have ceased to exist such arbitrary (and erroneous) concepts as a living being, or a personality."[7] The contrast with the Book of Genesis, ancestral to the Judaeo-Christian ethic at the root of Western culture, and thus of modern capitalism and industrialism, is stark: "And God blessed Adam and Eve, and God said unto them, 'Be fruitful and multiply, and replenish the earth, and subdue it: and have dominion over the fish of the sea, and over the fowl of the air, and over every living thing that moveth upon the earth.' "

If the West today were merely a social and economic order imposed on Asia, it would be easy enough for Asians to reject it. Unfortunately for the Asian intellectual, there is no aspiration of modern Asian politics which is not ultimately Western in origins or at least influence. Asia cannot longer define its ambitions without reference to the political and economic vocabulary of an intrusive Western world.

† Recently it has been pointed out that the history of sub-Saharan Africa is richer and more diverse than the Western stereotype of tribal savagery or barbarism would suggest. Undoubtedly this is true: there is a rich tradition of plastic art in West Africa and the Congo, and an imposing political tradition in the memory of such empires as Mali, Songhai, Mandingo, and Ghana in the African Middle Ages. Sensitive observers of the African scene like Laurens van der Post have, moreover, properly cautioned against depreciating the human values of traditional African society. The fact remains, however, that in Africa the roots of civilization are sketchy in the extreme, and the resources with which to construct the modern state are few. What aroused Africans' fury when the United States and Belgium intervened to save several hundred white hostages in Stanleyville during

THE IMPACT OF WESTERN CIVILIZATION

By contrast with Afro-Asia the problems of Latin America might seem simple ones: Latin America, after all, is a colonial offshoot of Europe, as authentic a child of Europe as are the United States and Canada. Its basic patterns of life are essentially the patterns of Latin Europe, though to say this is to ignore much detail. The Indian element aside, Latin America, unlike Sukarno's Indonesia or modern Japan, to say nothing of Mao's China, is thus essentially Western, not *Westernized*. And this is fundamentally true even in countries like Bolivia and Peru, with their oppressed Indian populations, or Brazil, where a large population of Negroes and mulattoes introduces social tensions and to some significant degree complicates the process of establishing a technological society.

Latin America's problem is not that it is non-Western but that it is an *archaic* Western society. The Europe from which Latin America stems is Iberia—an old province of Europe, but in history one that has been cut off from the mainstream of European development by mountain barriers, Islamic conquest, the establishment of a peculiarly centralized and authoritarian church after the expulsion of the Moors, and the tragedy of a self-ordained and grandiose political mission in the sixteenth and seventeenth centuries which proved beyond Spain's real strength and left her exhausted. Of all the major subcultures of Europe, the Iberian tradition is the least technological; Leibnitz and Einstein were Germans, Newton and Boyle were Englishmen, Pasteur and Lavoisier were Frenchmen, Galileo and da Vinci were Italians. Even the Russians, late converts to European civilization, produced the great Mendeleyev in the nineteenth century. But there is no Spanish name in such a list. Latin America's misfortune, as

---

the Congolese disorders of 1964 was not that it was an instance of neo-colonialism, but that chaos in the Congo—which was taken as a reproach to all Africa—clearly justified the move. It is no argument for a congenital inferiority or backwardness to say that the process of adaptation to the modern world, to say nothing of defining an "African soul" in that world, as the philosophers of *négritude* would wish, can be anything but a process of years. It is no favor to Africans to suggest the reverse. It may unfortunately be true, as Charles de Gaulle has remarked, that "this is not Africa's century."

it seeks to come to terms with twentieth-century technology, is that its inherited tradition is not the tradition of the *modern* West (though we must add that its tradition also stresses qualities that North America could well use—among them, solidity of family ties and a sense of geographical place and stability). It is not a technological tradition; nor is it an acquisitive tradition, at least in the sense that trade and production, rather than land, are understood as the sources of modern wealth.

That the modern tradition in the world is Western and technological, and in fundamental terms incompatible with the root traditions of the three great regions that go to make up the Third World, cannot be overemphasized. We in the West who have invented the modern tradition, and are even ourselves sometimes uneasy with it, should not underestimate the pain that any alien society must feel when called upon to join the West—to engraft itself onto the root stock of a culture whose values are bound to disrupt the religious, ethical, and social forms of the past. The modern West is not an easy culture to assimilate to. Its Faustianism and drive are disturbing enough; but not so disturbing as the intrusive power with which this culture breaks into other cultures, stripping the individual and leaving him to face the crises of life as an atomized unit. We in Europe and America are sentimental about ourselves, about the value of our individualist tradition, without appreciating its full costs, and more than that, in ignoring our habit of violence. In modern times Europe has originated wars of violence and crime almost without parallel in history. For us the Western tradition is rationalism and humanity.

This view has been summed up persuasively by a distinguished historian: "Modern Western civilization differs from older and contemporary dogmatic and authoritarian ways of life—in the broad sense of the word, including religions, ideologies, and social political structures—by its critical and practical approach. All others have stressed uniformity and have called upon, or forced, their adherents to follow an unequivocal path of life, the only one which promises salvation. Western civilization, on the other hand, emphasizes diversity. . . . It was a new and revolutionary civilization, based upon the belief in the equal rights of all, irrespective of religion, ancestry or class; upon the concern for the dignity and humanity of every individual; and upon the right to intellectual and political opposition and criticism. Such conditions did not exist in Greece or Rome, in Judaism or Christianity, or in any European country before the eighteenth century.

"Though modern civilization originated in northwestern Europe, it cannot be defined in a geographic way. . . . Some European areas have not accepted or do not presently accept modern Western civilization. In the early spring of 1941, by far the greatest part of Europe—under the then apparently closely allied dictatorships of Stalin, Hitler, Mussolini, and Franco—was confidently waging war on modern Western civilization and all its fundamental ideas."[8]

But it is possible to dissent: Germany and Italy cannot be written out of the Western experience. Nor can modern Russia be excluded: communism, certainly, is a product of the Western intellect. The Western tradition is not merely *habeas corpus,* representative government, and painless childbirth. It is also the legions of dead on the World War I battlefields of the Somme and the Marne, the butcheries of Hitlerism against the Jews, totalitarian government, the British fire raids on Dresden and Hamburg, the American fire raids on Tokyo, the fury of the atomic attacks at Hiroshima and Nagasaki. This too is the modern West. We cannot dismiss the dark side of our tradition. Like any other people, we of the West are a mixed proposition. European colonialism was a *mission civilisatrice* and the slave trade both; our powerful technology gives life and death. If there has never been a civilization to match the Western world's technical accomplishment and daring, that is not the whole story. There is a violence and exploitativeness in the West to which the Third World cannot be expected to give itself gladly.*

---

* See, for example, the remarks of Yen Fu, a modern Chinese intellectual who devoted the earlier years of his life to translating Adam Smith and John Stuart Mill into Chinese: "Western culture . . . has been corrupted utterly. It seems to me that in three centuries of progress the peoples of the West have achieved four principles: to be selfish, to kill others, to have little integrity, and to feel little shame."[9] There are many others. Consider these remarks by Jacques Rabemananjara, a poet and political leader from Madagascar: "The primacy of European values was . . . a thing which was taken for granted; one of the most remarkable consequences of the Second World War was that it shook confidence in the stability of this dogma. . . . Whence came the awakening? From a shock. The narcotic lost its effects once the duplicity of the West was made obvious to us, the contradiction between principle and conduct, between theory and practice, between words and deeds. We began to be uneasy. And we began to doubt. The jarring revelation was this: Europe had inherited the privilege of Janus; she had

But whatever the faults and virtues of our modern technological culture, one thing is clear: it is inundating the world. The fact that Afro-Asia has no alternative but to accept it, in some form, is one thing. "The old culture [of Asia] managed to live through many a fierce storm," Jawaharlal Nehru once put it, "but though it kept its outer form, it lost its real content. Today it is fighting silently and desperately against a new and all-powerful opponent, the *bania* [merchant] civilization of the capitalist West. It will succumb to this newcomer, for the West brings science, and science brings food for the hungry millions. . . . When India puts on her new garment [it is because] she must. The old is torn and tattered."[11] Inevitably the feelings of modern Asian and African elites, even while they are forced to transform their fragmented and technologically weak traditional societies, are mixed: they are being asked, or asking themselves, to accept an alien and often repugnant patterns of life. This means, in their terms, not merely that they are going to "better" themselves, but to surrender.

Writing in the nineteenth century as a foe of unfettered industrial civilization, Karl Marx observed: "The bourgeoisie cannot exist without constantly revolutionizing the instruments of production, and thereby the relations of production and with them the whole relations of society. Conservation of the old modes of production in unaltered form was, on the contrary, the first condition of existence for all earlier industrial classes. Constant revolutionizing of production, uninterrupted disturbance of all social conditions, everlasting uncertainty and agitation distinguish the bourgeois epoch from all earlier ones. All fixed, fast-frozen relations, with their train of ancient and venerable prej-

---

two faces. On one side, a face of stone, of death, a grimacing face, Gorgon's face, of unequalled cruelty, cynicism, rascality, and self-satisfaction, the face incarnated by our inventors of Negro barbarism, of the experts in supplying human flesh for the cremation furnace. On the other side, a face of lilies—one kingdom has even made them the symbol of its arms—a face of purity, of spring water and dawn, the marvellous imprint of the mask of Venus, so beautiful that she seems to have embodied in herself the sum of all human perfection, in being the first to call forth from the limbo of our consciousness all the luminous principles of the Rights of Man. . . . It is true that there exists a Europe which we do not love, which we cannot love, which we shall never love; there are too many lies, too many injustices, too much blood and dirt between her and us."[10] Jacques Rabemananjara is a Malagaysan intellectual, but his attitude is typical of modern Africa and Asia.

udices and opinions, are swept away, all newly formed ones
become antiquated before they can ossify. All that is solid melts
into air, all that is holy is profaned, and man is at last compelled
to face with sober senses, his real conditions of life, and his relations with his kind. . . ."[12]

But the effects that Marx attributed to the bourgeoisie were,
in fact, inherent in modern industrial civilization itself—as the
bleak record of social alienation within the "socialist" states of
the Sovet sphere attests. The process of detribalization is inherent
in modern life; and if the ferocity of the process has, in the mid-
twentieth century, been somewhat mitigated in the West, it is
only recently that some new balance has begun to emerge. And
even this remark must remain qualified hope: the record so far is
an inconclusive one. The modern West, though—that society
Marx deplores—was the result of an earlier Western system's
having outmoded itself. The Western world generated within itself the forces that destroyed its traditional agrarian and status
culture. Afro-Asia is not so lucky. The technology and modern
political ideologies that come to Afro-Asians, and outmode their
past, are the white man's ambiguous gift.

THE ORDEAL OF MODERNIZATION

For Americans the most convenient means of grasping the
dilemma of the Afro-Asian modernizers might be to borrow a lesson from race relations at home. Negro society in America is a
society of the poor and oppressed. Power, privilege, and glamour
all belong to the white society that discriminates against the
Negro. Thus every Negro, whether he wishes to or not, is forced
to define his relationship to the exploitative society of the masters,
and decide how he will come to terms.

A Negro may submit; but the disparity between the privileges
of the white man and the Negro is invidious. If the Negro were
merely poor, that would be one thing; but the white men are, by
and large, rich. Besides, white society itself has circulated slogans
of universal freedom and dignity—and these stimulate the Negro's
own demand for justice. If white society were single-minded in
its exploitative relationship to the Negro, the colored man might
submit, feeling rage all the while on dulling himself; he might
also rebel. But this situation would essentially be a simple one,

calling for straightforward emotional responses. The element of neurotic ambiguity, and harm, would not come into play.

Integration in modern America makes more complex demands. If the Negro elects to join white society, one thing becomes clear immediately. If white society will have him at all—and this is rare —he must give up nearly all those qualities which are peculiar to him as a Negro. The special characteristics of the Negro family, the Negro love relationship, the Negro attitude toward labor—qualities which have grown up within the subculture for some two centuries—will have to be expunged: he will be required to discard his past. If he chooses to join white society by "passing" and is able to because his skin is light, he capitulates— in effect surrenders all claim to dignity as a Negro. But even if he chooses the more self-respecting path of integration, the arduous process of schooling in the conventions and customs of American white society—in order to end up, eventually, a teller in an integrated bank—is at some level a self-denial. Given this dilemma, it is hardly surprising that Negro reactions vary along a wide spectrum: there are the capitulationists—the "Uncle Toms" and those who pass; and there are the militant and alienated anti-whites—the Muslim movements which reject the notion of integration altogether (but which still pay a covert homage to white society by their defensive pose). The reactions are infinite, and some are bizarre. (Some of the splinter sects of Negro Christianity, with their strong emphasis on messianic deliverance, clearly function as "religions of the oppressed.")

Whatever the outcome of America's racial dilemma, at this point the notion to bear in mind is the agonizing quality of the Negro's psychic situation: faced by a white world that both attracts and repels, and with alternatives largely obliterated (those American Negroes who have gone to modern Africa to identify themselves with the African struggle nearly always find in the end that—to Africans and even to themselves—they are "white" Americans), psychic disturbance is what any sensitive Negro must feel.

A similar dilemma confronts Afro-Asia: to borrow the culture of the West is to save the nation; but to do so is to lose it in the process anyway. Certainly, to cite only one case, the history of Japan since the mid-nineteenth century suggests that even a brilliantly successful process of adaptation cannot be accomplished without very considerable psychic stress, and possibly damage. There is little in Japan's story to support the notion that economic development in Afro-Asia leads to social peace. Indeed, as Walt W. Rostow has pointed out, there is a repetitive pattern to the histories of newly industrialized nations—a tendency to turn their initial industrial superiority against weaker neighbors, as Japan did against China and Korea, as Germany did against the backward Slav regions of Eastern Europe and the Balkans in the nineteenth and twentieth centuries, or, for that matter, as the young United States did against Mexico in 1846.

Psychic and social damage aside, the material difficulties are enormous. Some of the less well endowed nations may never complete (or even seriously begin) the process of modernization. To say "never" is, of course, to use the term in a metaphorical sense only; but there is no inevitability about industrialization. There are regions of the world—the Solomon Islands, say—still fixed in an essentially neolithic economy, that is, a level of society that is centered in small villages, practices a rudimentary agriculture, and uses no metal tools. There are marginal tribes in Australia and southern Africa that in the midst of twentieth-century affluence inhabit the world of the Old Stone Age. The shift from a hunting and scavenging economy to agriculture is at least seven or eight thousand years old; and the shift from village agriculture to an urban trading economy dates at least from 4000–3000 B.C. in the Middle East. Granting that the tempo of the modern world is more rapid, that communications are efficient, that the process of development has become the subject of rational study, and that the Faustian idea of manipulation of the physical and social environment is now loose in the world, we still had better not exaggerate the speed with which societies change, or ignore the truth that some will fail in "modernization."

Faced with such problems, it is hardly surprising that the political ideologies of modern Afro-Asia are often shrill, hysterical, and bizarre, or that the Afro-Asian elites often exhibit acute signs of personal disturbance. Men like Ahmed Sukarno in Indonesia or Norodum Sihanouk in Cambodia are a fascinating study in contrasts—at once brilliant and naïve, ambitious for their nations but self-indulgent in personal style, vulgar, charismatic, calculating, and simple. For the leaders of Afro-Asia compensatory fantasy is a common device, perhaps a necessity, with political relevance. Fantasy affects the nature of the political response to the "revolution of hunger," or the "revolution of rising expectations" that is shaking our world. And there is still another danger: that political fantasy in Afro-Asia may stimulate the Western world to vengeful fantasies of its own.

No aspect of Cold War politics has been more disturbing to Americans than the penchant these Afro-Asian leaders display for "socialism"—for planned economies and societies. There is no new state of the many dozens freed since the last war that is not contemptuous of the economic system that has given America and Europe their vast wealth. But to see in their pronouncements, as we and the Russians have done, a real affinity for Marxism, or even an understanding of its workings, would be naïve. Colonel Nasser's Egypt may qualify as a planned society, in the sense that there is a government sector of the economy and a bureaucratic elite to schedule and oversee investment priorities; but to suggest that Egypt controls its internal economy, let alone its relationship to the world economy, is something else again. And in the case of nations like Guinea and Indonesia, which are virtual bankrupts, the claim is absurd.

For Afro-Asia, socialism and "planning" are badges of modernity—a hypermodernism which is not without magical overtones, given the domestic reality. And, in any case, socialism is not less attractive because it annoys the United States. But the invidious motive is minor; it is the claim to a pseudo-modernity that dominates the imagination of the new Afro-Asian elites. It is, in essence, a rejoinder to the old colonial powers: a declaration that Afro-Asia, by going socialist, is going modern, and passing "old" Europe and "old" America by.

But socialism, in the Afro-Asian imagination, is also something else. "It is easier," as Eric Hoffer has remarked, "for the advanced to imitate the backward than the other way around. The backward and weak see in imitation an act of submission and a proof of their inadequacy. They must rid themselves of their sense of inferiority, must demonstrate their prowess, before they will open their minds and hearts to all that the world can teach them. . . . Thus the grotesque truculence, posturing, conceit, brazenness, and defiance which usually assail our senses whenever a backward country sets out to modernize itself. . . . Imita-

tion is least impeded when we are made to feel that our act of imitation is actually an act of becoming the opposite of that which
we imitate. A religion or civilization is most easily transmitted
to alien societies by its heretical offspring which come into
being as a protest and challenge."[13] For Afro-Asia to carry on
the economic system inherited from the old colonial powers
would be to carry on the colonial fealty in new form. But Afro-
Asia is in process of defining itself *against* the West; it is striving
for a new personality. That its successes to date have been few
is beside the point. Indeed, the very feebleness of Afro-Asia,
its discouraging reality, coupled with its rancor against the West,
provides powerful motives to adopt, on the declaratory level
at least, an ideology which is at least quasi-Marxist. Marxism
is simultaneously a critique of capitalism, and thus by extension
of the old exploitative and intrusive "West," and a distillation of
the nineteenth-century Western belief in mechanical progress
and perfectability. By adopting the West in this variant form,
Afro-Asia "modernizes" but saves its soul.

But Afro-Asia is not really Marxist at all. If anything, in real
spirit the revolutionary movements of Afro-Asia are nearer to
the social fascism of the post-World War I years (in Italy, say,
and the Balkans) than to communism. The spirit of Soviet and
Chinese communism is austere; it has nothing in common with
the national mood expressed by Indonesia's President Sukarno,
who can ask his people to give themselves "like dry logs" to the
fires of a national redemptive revolution. The ideologies of Afro-
Asia are authoritarian and anti-capitalist, but, with few exceptions, they are hypernationalist, even racist, as well. "Unity,
solidarity, and cooperation of all elements of the nation, and
self-denial and self-sacrifice on the part of the individual to
ensure the safety, prosperity, and integrity of the motherland,
are the fundamental factors for the success of a political revolution," Gamal Nasser has asserted. ". . . The disintegration of
values, disruption of principles, dissension and discord among
both classes and individuals, and domination of corruption, suspicion, and perversion of egoism form the foundation of social
upheaval."[14] There is not much resemblance here to the proletarianism, class-warfare doctrines, and proclaimed internationalism of Soviet and Chinese communism. But neither is there a
kinship to capitalism. Capitalism stems from the Protestant,

acquisitive spirit of Northern Europe, and while greed is perhaps universal in men, the free-enterprise system is not. There is a vast difference between the notion of "making" money and "earning" money. The latter spirit is the spirit of the United States, and we cannot expect to see it widely shared; it is not even shared by such kindred societies as those of Latin America and Spain. But Americans who are able to coexist on easy terms with the practice of polygamy in Indonesia or Nigeria ought not be roused to moral fury by the notion of state ownership of rubber plantations and oil. If we are going to confront the Afro-Asian revolution successfully, or even learn to live with it, we will have to learn the difference between what is an affront to the American national interest and what is not.

THE LATIN AMERICAN CRISIS OF IDENTITY

For Latin America the problem is different. Latin America is the West, though an archaic West—where *pre*-industrial and *pre*-capitalist economic and social patterns linger on. Latin America, for one thing, is very nearly the only part of the Western world where the nineteenth-century controversies between clericalism and anti-clericalism, reform and reaction, classical liberalism and classical communism, live on. Thus it is the only corner of the Western world where Marx is esteemed by intellectuals as a social philosopher *and* as an economist with something new to say. Latin American intellectuals are *Marxisant* because, naïvely, they believe Marxism is *à la mode*.

Once again, of course, to typify a vast region in such terms is to indulge in a gross oversimplification. There is, after all, Hispano-Indo-America—countries like Mexico, Guatemala, Bolivia, Peru—as well as the "pure" Iberianism of Argentina, Colombia and Uruguay. Traditionally, "Latin America" extends from the Rio Grande to Tierra del Fuego, but as a culture area it encompasses not only Portuguese-speaking and mulatto Brazil but, by extension, French or Creole-speaking Haiti, and even, it may be, French Canada. The distinction lies in the term *Latin*: North America is, at bottom, Protestant *Anglo*-America. Its habits and concerns are alien to the Iberian-Mediterranean tradition from which Latin America ultimately derives. That modern young businessmen in Caracas and Buenos Aires speak English and send their children North to study engineering does not conceal a vast difference of ethos. The "Americanization" that takes place is at the most superficial level, as the frequently disastrous cross-culture marriages attest. Buenos Aires and New York are perhaps twice as far apart as New York and Paris, and the archaicism and deliberate formalism of Latin America is such that the differences in time, and dimension, are greater still. It is only a geographical convention that describes North and South America as inhabiting the same hemisphere.

To note the archaicisms of Latin America is, of course, to note too that Latin America assiduously preserves these archaicisms— differences which divide and distinguish it from the North. This is no historical accident. A small power or insecure culture in the shadow of a large and energetic state must accentuate the differences that define and distinguish it if it is to survive at all. It is a fact of Western Hemisphere politics that for Latin America, preserving the differences between *Latin* and *Anglo*-America de-mands attention; they are a condition of existence.

Some such phenomenon seems to lie at the roots of Castroism —a political movement whose main thrust seems not to be the drive for social justice or modernization so much as a simple political defiance of the United States. The conventional economic, ultimately Marxist, notions of the motivation of revolution will not explain Castro's Cuba: living standards in Cuba, even in the Battista era, were well in the vanguard of the Caribbean and of Latin America as a whole. What not many seem to have noticed about Cuba is not so much that it was poor, but that for more than half a century it was a dumping ground for North American moral filth (a convenient locus of gambling casinos, brothels, and cheap abortions), a dependent, and later subsidized, one-crop economy, and the repeated victim of thoughtless and casual polit-ical interventions. Viewed dispassionately, Castro's Cuba is not very different politically from the kind of revolutionary movement we might expect to see established by the socially pulverized proletariat of the slum districts of Spanish Harlem in New York. There is no Cuba in fact; it is an island without a real identity —short of the political movement that keeps its name in the news.

That this revolution has moved "leftward" is only a convention of modern power politics. Cuba's ideology is diffuse. As the historian John Lukacs has observed, if Hitler's Germany were now, as in the 1930's, the strongest anti-American power in the world, and seeking to penetrate the hemisphere, we could expect Castro's Cuba, as Peron's Argentina once did, to take on an avowed fascist stamp.

Beyond that, Castroism is an undisciplined and romantic movement—rhetorical but not intellectual. The association between Castro and the Soviets is not much more than an accident of history; and it might be added, when the risks incurred by Moscow in the Cuban missile crisis of 1962 are weighed, Cuba's adherence to the socialist camp has availed the Soviets precisely nothing. Havana is an unreliable partner (*vide* the constant diplomatic and ideological teetering between Peking and Moscow). It is no real base for the penetration of Latin America, for the simple reason that since the Cubans have given themselves to the Soviets, they have compromised the real source of their appeal to other Latin Americans. Their image, as a small and lonely power defying the North American giant, is now a tarnished one. Behind Castro stands the U.S.S.R. that subsidizes him. Thus the real political importance of Cuba consists chiefly in the importance most Americans insist, blindly and obsessively, in giving this unhappy Caribbean dictatorship. And the real appeal of communism to Cubans is that it places them among the world host of revolutionary nations opposed to the United States. Communism gives power and "legitimacy" to Cuba's defiance of the United States. For an American President to debate and slang with Castro and Castroism is for America to give Fidel Castro's movement a solid meaning.

Castroism is not the wave of the future in Latin America. But however alleviated by the political rhetoric and thinly disguised bribes of the *Allianza para Progresso* (and exacerbated by panicky military interventions like Santo Domingo), anti-*yanquismo* is likely to endure in Latin America, whatever the United States does, for a good many years to come. It will endure as long as Latin America is weak and North America is strong. Like the anti-Americanism of early postwar Western Europe, it is not so much a reflection of American diplomatic errors (though these can be costly) as a reflection of a nation's or region's own sense of helplessness and discontent with itself.

The challenge of Latin America is therefore not the challenge of world communism, or even the challenge of the revolution of rising expectations. It is a crisis of identity in which a backward region of the Western world must teach itself what the rest of the Western world has learned. It is Latin America, however much the world helps it, that will have to satisfy its rising expectations. The intellectual and cultural resources are there, for Latin America is the Western world. Its elites have the intellectual means, though, it may be, not the social conscience, to work the transformation for themselves. Viewed against the somber background of Afro-Asia, Latin America is a fortunate continent. It is possible to predict how it might succeed, even if it may not.

But for most of the poor and backward states of Afro-Asia the future is exceedingly somber. There is no denying this: there are formidable problems of depleted resources and rising population pressures; there is a vast illiteracy to be overcome; but even more, there is the simple problem of cultural shock. Afro-Asia is in shock because the modern world—our West—has broken in on it and invalidated the old assumptions by which Afro-Asians once ordered their lives. The reflex notion in the modern West is that therefore Afro-Asia needs aid; it does. But in these conditions, we must beware of simplistic intermeddlings. The economic transfusion that brought the patient back to health in postwar Europe was one thing; in Afro-Asia massive doses of "aid" may only be poison in the blood. In these conditions, aid will have to be longer in term and more subtle in its workings, more temperate in its expectations and means than the methods we have devised to date. We need to reflect on what this century has done to Afro-Asia, and define a good deal better what it is we hope to see in the next.

In any case, given aid or not, wisely or unwisely, for many decades to come the Afro-Asian future will be one of greater or lesser degrees of political and social distress. Turmoil and, it may be, violence are inevitable. What is not inevitable is how we shall react—with dispassion and charity, if we are wise; with panic and cruelty, if we are not. And as we shall see, panic and cruelty are no idle possibilities for America, given our distortions of diplomatic reality today.

THE RETURN OF EUROPE

The Cold War began in Europe, we have said, as the inevitable outcome of the destruction of German power in the heart of the

Continent. With the collapse of Hitler's empire, there was no native force in Europe to stop the westward thrust of the Red Army. "Rarely can hostility have been so predictable," Raymond Aron has written of the break-up of the wartime alliance between the Western democracies and Russia. "The Germans never ceased to proclaim its inevitability . . . and Goebbels was unable to understand that the more he insisted the more he forced the Americans to camouflage it. Not for a moment, of course, did the Russian authorities forget, but the Anglo-Saxons, and particularly the Americans, often acted as if they did not regard the hostility as fundamental."[15]

The Soviets soon proved that it was a fundamental hostility. Soviet acts against the spirit, as well as the letter, of the wartime alliance had begun even before the German collapse—and had reached a climax when in August, 1944, the Red Army halted in the suburbs of Warsaw and for sixty-three days acquiesced in the destruction of the Polish resistance, which had responded to the Soviets' own signal to rise against the Germans. By 1946 Stalin had abandoned even the pretense of great power unity. His lieutenant, Andrei Zhdanov, announced a new foreign policy in November of that year with a speech that proclaimed a dichotomy between a group of "democratic" states, led by the Soviet Union, and "reactionary circles" in Britain and America. The Cominform, successor to the Comintern, was established the next year.

However limited Stalin's wartime goals may have been—perhaps to expel the Germans, regain the territories won by the Nazi-Soviet Pact, and possibly establish hegemony over Poland and the Balkans—the conditions of postwar Europe were such that inevitably they led him on, more or less in accord with the Leninist political maxim: "If the bayonet strikes bone, withdraw; if mush, push on." There was little bone in Europe itself. The Continent was not merely ravaged by a war that had cost the European allies and the defeated Axis countries some thirteen million dead alone, but it was in a state of moral collapse. The experience of occupation, and too often of acquiescence in a neo-barbarism, had left Europe psychologically incapable of resisting the vigorous new offensive from the East. For Europe the advance of the Red Army seemed yet another plague in what seemed a twentieth-century political apocalypse.

The British had attempted to check the Soviets in the Balkans during the final stages of the war, but had been rebuked by the Americans. Then, in the aftermath of the war, the British supported the Greek monarchist government when the left wing of the wartime resistance, with guarded Soviet support, opened up a civil war in Greece. But Britain, a technical victor in the war (as well as the one nation which made victory possible), no longer had the resources to maintain its old Mediterranean role. The United States, after intense domestic controversy, took over the effort. With the Truman Doctrine's guarantees to Greece (and to Turkey and Iran, who were directly under Russian pressure) and the Marshall Plan to rebuild the West European economies, the United States committed itself to a major role in the affairs of Europe. And with the hardening of the Cold War came the formation of NATO and, eventually, the rearmament of Germany under American sponsorship.

The new American policies were intelligent and effective; but they responded to something more than the Soviet threat alone. They expressed as well an American sense of successorship to Europe—to that Europe which before the war had dominated the world but also had thrown it into great crises twice in twenty-five years. Moreover, America's belief in the passing of Europe's primacy was not ours alone. The Soviets as well regarded themselves as inheritors of power from a discredited Europe; even Afro-Asians sensed the emergence of a post-European civilization, and believed that they would create societies that transcended the old West. As Christopher Dawson put it: "Not only is Europe reduced to insignificance by the giant powers to which she has given birth, but it is difficult to find any people, however weak and backward, who will admit her claim to cultural superiority. . . ."[16]

Certainly Europe's autonomous political dominance was believed finished—for good. The postwar plans in the West for European unification and renewal were largely economic in scope, and their political significance was defined (by Americans, but also by most of the Europeans associated with the Monnet group and the Council of Europe) in an Atlantic context. While the opinion that Europe might reconstitute itself as a balancing "Third Force" between America and Russia was also influential from the war's end onward, its effective expression did not come until the late 1950's, with the success of Gaullism in France. And it today remains a controversial proposition in Europe—and even in France.

The European ambition to play a "third" role between East and West is, of course, even more controversial in the United States. Our postwar assumption of leadership in Europe is now largely taken by Americans to have constituted an irreversible step in the evolution of European-American relations. Europe is held to be materially incompetent for a major world role—as well as being politically discredited, by its imperialist past and record of instability and war. One of the axioms of the classical Cold War (and now an axiom of those who would "end" the Cold War by striking a bargain between Washington and Moscow) was that Europe, at least in its form of nation-states, was "finished." Under Secretary of State George Ball once put the argument this way: "The attainment of a minimum size or scale—the possession of a minimum volume of resources of material, of technology and manpower—is an essential element in determining the role of nations. . . . It is, therefore, no accident that in recent years the predominant leadership roles have been played in large measure by two states, each organized on a continent-wide basis, and that there has been a *de facto* polarization between the two great centers of power—Moscow and Washington."[17]*

Yet Europe today seems anything but "finished." Today the Continent is again prosperous and stable, enjoying a degree of political and social peace unknown since 1914. The physical scars of World Wars I and II have nearly all been eradicated. What lingers is a kind of psychic wound; there is a political diffidence in Europe only now beginning to give way. At bottom, one suspects, Europe fears itself. This fear is especially strong among

---

* The substance of Mr. Ball's remarks—which argue against French nuclear ambitions—cannot be dealt with adequately without resort to technical argumentation, but two comments are in order. First, the French nuclear force has proved to be a slighter financial burden than France's foreign aid program; it costs appreciably less than France spends each year on its former African colonies, less than it once spent on the Algerian war. It is, moreover, technically competent and, as the French orbiting of space satellites suggests, likely to result within ten years' time in a most formidable force—one, certainly, that would distress the United States were it in the hands of North Vietnam or Castro's Cuba. Second, the degree of polarization of power between Moscow and Washington is not as great today as a mere half-decade ago. The 1960's have seen the relatively swift decline of both American and Soviet prestige and influence abroad.

liberal elements in West Germany, but it is not a German fear alone.

There is reason for fear: the Continental European record in politics is not a good one. It is a record of ideological extremism and excess, a habitual turning to violence on a mass scale. This is true even in France, where the rationalist tradition is strongest. Given its past, Europe does not seem to trust itself to experiment on the world scene, or even to speak out. This diffidence, which contrasts with its great economic power, is similar to the postwar diffidence of Japan and is markedly different in spirit from the political assertions of the comparatively weak "new" states. France and England aside, for a continent which has been the center of the world, Europe's concerns today seem oddly parochial. But after two decades the old dependency on American power and policy is coming to an end. It is ending because whatever Europe's fears of itself, the old fears of Soviet invasion are now dismissed; and the United States no longer, by its qualities and demeanor, quite shows itself fit to lead in the same way.

To say that Europe stirs is not to imply that this is wholly a good thing, merely that it is inevitable. What precisely is reanimating Europe is not so clear. There is something daring and glamorous in the Gaullist vision of a reborn Europe, with its ideological divisions healed, returning to action on the world scene. But there is also a more sinister side to the picture. For France to refurbish Paris, or to begin again to give special honor to her war dead of 1914–1918, is one thing. To reignite European chauvinism is quite another. But this has been one political consequence of Franco-American diplomatic clashes since 1958.

AMERICA'S EUROPEAN POLICY TODAY

Washington today still seeks to "maintain, strengthen, and devise new tasks for NATO"—or, conversely, it plans the relocation of lines of supply as France "defects" from the alliance. But the problem is that the assumptions of that alliance are fragmented. The reasons are deeper than mere French "archaicism" or Gaullist pique. America's historic mission in Europe has been fulfilled. Europe has been saved, and it may be that the overwhelming American presence has begun to damage prospects for further progress. Europe does not need America any more, either for defense or as an economic prop. It is not surprising that the alliance has begun to chafe.

This is true not merely for France, where the alliance hinders not only French hopes for a predominance in Europe but the more defensible French ambitions for an independent diplomacy cut loose from the Cold War and giving some promise of healing the breach in Europe—bringing Germany firmly into the mainstream of Europe and eradicating the Iron Curtain. It is true in Germany, where the inner contradictions and ultimate helplessness of America's policy with respect to Germany's unification are painfully obvious. So far Germany seems to fear striking out on an independent course; but it is becoming widely understood in West Germany that America has no theory by which the Cold War—Germany's cold war, the reunion of the country—can be won. So long as West Germany is tied to America, German policy —still formally predicated on "liberation"—is at a dead end.

Yet residual American fears about the military security of Europe and anxiety to preserve American authority have led to an increasing emphasis on the German alliance, within NATO, to the exclusion of other concerns. Britain is so vulnerable economically, and currently so diffident in the political-military sphere, that Washington has tended to dismiss it from its calculations. Italy is an unstable base for a military operation in Europe. The result is that as France has more and more struck out on independent lines, Washington has relied on the German link.

The German orientation of present American policy in Europe hardly springs from rightist sentiments in the Pentagon. The prevailing intellectual notions of the Pentagon are the unanalyzed, conventional political notions of the great American consensus. It has come about by a process of political subtraction, as one by one the other partners of American policy in Europe have proved themselves unsuitable. It has come about as well by a process of uncritical generalization from the fact of our military alliance with West Germany. We have come to believe that because there is total congruence of American and West German interests on the single issue of the territorial integrity and security of West Germany against Soviet attack, there is a similar identity of interests on German reunification, or Germany's ultimate role in world affairs.

But the purpose of the postwar American intervention in Europe was to restore security and balance in Europe, not to eradicate Germany's World War II defeat. It is true that the United States has pledged itself to seek German reunification; but the United States has other obligations as well, as solemnly uttered, and earlier in time—obligations to the peoples of Eastern-Central Europe, for one thing.* The fact is that contemporary German national aspirations (and they are by no means all illegitimate) cannot be satisfied within any presently identifiable pattern of European settlement. And the ultimate aim of diplomatic and military policy in Europe should be European settlement. The present *status quo* in Europe is abnormal—it rests on a suspension of political action. Germany is divided; Europe is divided; the balance which was maintained for ninety-nine years in Europe, between the Napoleonic Wars and 1914, and broken in two world wars, is maintained by the American presence in Western Europe and the Soviet presence in Eastern Europe. But the Soviet grip in the East is weakened, and nothing holds the Warsaw Pact together more than the perceived threat of Germany—of a reunited Germany which could once again threaten the East. The American grip is weakened as well, and the American purpose ought to be to seek conditions under which we can safely withdraw. Instead, we today resist the signs of the restoration of self-confidence in Europe and hinder the conditions within which Europe might, with some safety, be left to itself.

* A European policy that does not at least include some theory as to how these East European regions are to be reintegrated with the admittedly now secularized but, at bottom, Catholic Europe that lies behind the present reality of "The Six," can hardly be dignified with the name of policy. (The Common Market comprises France, West Germany, Benelux, and Italy. Of these six, five are predominantly Catholic, as well as "Elitist" and "Positivist." By tradition, only The Netherlands has strong affinities with maritime and Northern Europe, and there the native Catholic population has nearly reached a majority. It is East Germany that is Protestant.) In viewing the problems of Europe, Americans, whose dominant governmental and cultural tradition stems from Northern Europe, tend to overemphasize the "Atlantic" orientation of West Europe and to ignore its affinities with Central and Eastern Europe. But the Thirty Years' War, perhaps the decisive event of modern German history, determining the course of events for nearly three centuries afterward, was a Central European war. Poland, Bohemia (now Czechoslovakia), and Hungary were intimately bound up with the Renaissance and with the subsequent wars of the Reformation and Counter-Reformation.

It is no Gaullist argument to say that American efforts, deliberate or merely unthinking, to drive a wedge between France and West Germany have been a tragedy. That the American response to the Gaullist challenge, and to France's bid to lead a European coalition based on the Franco-German Treaty of Cooperation, was to demand a choice from Bonn—follow them or us—is natural enough. But that it was natural does not prevent the policy from being one of dreadful risk. What may emerge is not merely the collapse of America's grandiose designs for Europe (which, being American, could never have taken shape in Europe), but the re-emergence of Europe on the worst possible terms: a Europe divided and estranged from itself, in which old animosities, and new ones, threaten new conflict.

American policy today reflects a failure to understand that the United States cannot be permanently in Europe—though after the experience of two world wars neither can we accept the Gaullist notion that Europe's destiny is no business of ours. By confusing the "grand designs" which characterize our isolationist-interventionist notions about political progress with those less grandiose possibilities which reality allows, we obscure, and even check, that humbler process which lies at the root of all peace—the process of political reconciliation. European reconciliation does not of necessity imply European unification; for France and Germany to quiet the hatred that has divided them since Louis XIV and Napoleon, and twice ignited world wars, would of itself be a great and historic achievement. It would be equivalent to the reconciliation of France and England in 1904—the framing of the *Entente Cordiale,* or even perhaps the reconciliation between America and England after the Civil War. To make such friendships is no small thing.

But the United States, along with France and West Germany, must bear blame for the present bitterness of Franco-German-American relations and the futility of alliance politics among the three nations. What is more, the United States and West Germany bear more than their share of responsibility for the fact that Gaullist policy increasingly looks toward the East. If there is a chronic overestimation of the American role in the world, it nowhere is more glaring than in Europe. America is a great power, and no doubt there could have been no victory in two world wars without us. But it does not lie with the United States to forgive Ger-

many, or to lead it back into the community of Europe. We have
not suffered enough from Germany. For us to give charity, in this
instance surely, is too easy. For more than three hundred years
Germany has gone a deviant course in European politics, and thus
in the politics of the world. It should have been the cardinal purpose of longer-range American policy in Europe to foster a return
of Germany to the better tradition of Europe. Instead, the effect
of our *ad hoc* policies has been to separate it once again from
Europe, drawing it into a transatlantic association that is distant
and, because it is unnatural, must eventually break. When that
happens, Germany will be left with its old problem—to define
its relationship to the peoples to its south and east.

To say that American policy has supported the notion of European unity—and that we have proved it by our record of dealings
with the Common Market, and that it is France which hinders
economic and political integration in Europe—is to miss the point.
The United States has insisted on treating the issue of European
political *reconciliation* and *pacification* as if it were identical with
unification. Even more, we have complicated the issue by mixing
in the purely extraneous issue of Europe's relationship to America.
We have made European unification largely synonymous with a
continued American presence in Europe; we have done this by
insisting on a dominant voice in NATO, a dominant voice in the
politics and economics of Europe, by tying the problem of the
Common Market to the problem of the membership of Britain
(conceived of as our instrument) in that community, and to the
problem of Germany's loyalty to us.

We shall return to the alternatives of European policy in a later
chapter. But the costs of present policy are worth noting. They
are the costs of identifying uncritically with the German interest
and confusing that interest with the West's, or NATO's, or our
own. They are the costs of pursuing policies of *détente* with the
Soviets, of East-West reconciliation, while simultaneously striving for a West Germany tightly integrated into NATO, a united
West European Six or Atlantic Union, and German nuclear sharing, all of which presuppose, if they are to have any logical consistency, an almost unlimited vista of Cold War. They include the
risks of a nuclear guarantee which we have given in full sincerity
yet without considering its real implications—that the United
States might suffer as many as a hundred and fifty million dead
in the event it were invoked.

Most important, United States foreign policy is guilty of an archaicism: we have accepted the myth of post-European successorship, which has led us to magnify a world role which once was a pragmatic and reluctant intervention, and to resist the political processes by which a balance of power might be restored in the world. The dangers of this are nowhere more glaring than in Europe, because the twentieth century, as Americans have never tired of saying, is the age of decolonization. And the dilemma of Russia and America is essentially the same: how to relax their grip on this dynamic European continent without being destroyed in the process of letting go.

WORLD PLURALISM AS THE CONTEXT OF POLICY

The significance of all we have said thus far about the contemporary political arena might be stated in a single word—variety. There can be no realistic or effective United States policy that does not take the political pluralism and ideological variety of the world as its starting point. To object that the United States, certainly from the Kennedy Administration on, has publicly welcomed this pluralism misses the point—the distinction between the declaratory and the real.

Faced with this trend to variety, there have in fact been two official reactions. The first has been to assert that pluralism is an illusion, that the fundamental components of American national power—wealth, technology, population, productivity—remain intact, and that the communist threat is unchanged in intensity. This is to assert that nothing essential has changed in the world, only that we must try harder, and more subtly, or more earnestly, to accomplish our purposes within the Western alliance, say, or Latin America, or in the larger world. This was Mr. Ball's reaction, we have seen, to the return of Europe. The second reaction is to salute the growth of political pluralism and yet ignore its implications. This, by and large, is what the United States does today. Policy, in reality, remains much as before.*

* In the era of John Foster Dulles, an era characterized by a high degree of actual polarization of power between Washington and Moscow, the Secretary of State's abrasive style of diplomacy was such that he tended to ignore the sensitivities of allies and to issue policy unilaterally. In 1961 with the Kennedy Administration there was a marked change of verbal style. On the declaratory level, the Kennedy Administration welcomed the growth of pluralism, and even sought it as an end—for example, the return of Europe as an actor in world affairs. But actual American assertions of

Nevertheless, the power blocs in the world are inexorably fragmenting. The war in Vietnam aside, the major unrest and conflict of recent years have reflected causes largely remote from the rivalry of Russia and America—or America and China. The irrelevance of the Congo rebellion, or the Indo-Pakistan war of 1965, or the Rhodesian secession, to the issue of communism or anti-communism is glaring. The process of ideological diversification, innovation, and assertion of national difference continues with increasing speed. The process can hardly be checked. Why should we try?

Obviously many of these new trends and movements are unwelcome. A good many of these new political assertions and ideas are detestable in their own terms—despotic, anarchic, antirational, incompetent, cruel. Beyond question they hinder any movement of the world toward international order, conciliation, higher living standards, and "progress." It does not follow, therefore, that a plural world is a world of peace. The reverse may be true: the United Nations is weakening; the once powerful trend toward regional units and co-operation is slowing, or may have even reversed; European Common Market integration has ground to a halt; the East African Common Market has splintered; the notion of British Commonwealth political and economic co-operation is virtually dead; pan-Arabism has foundered; CENTO and SEATO are fictions; NATO is strained; the Warsaw Pact is strained. Thus, to say that we should not resist political variety

---

authority in NATO grew more insistent, and this was equally true in Latin America and Southeast Asia. "It is not in our interest to try to dominate the European councils of decision," said the late President on the occasion of his European tour in 1963. "If that were our objective, we would prefer to see Europe divided and weak. . . ." But the issue of European "equality" was tied to the issue of "Atlanticism"—in short, an American orientation. American military policy in NATO, for example, was to seek an American monopoly of nuclear weapons (and sole decision on where, when, and how they should be used)—a policy which led to the gratuitous affront offered the United Kingdom with the cancellation without adequate warning of the Skybolt missile on which the RAF had virtually staked its future, the collision with France over sharing nuclear information, and the ultimate debacle of the mixed-manned nuclear force (which was in effect rejected by Western Europe because it was an open secret among the military that the force was not, and by implication was not meant to be, a "credible" one, lest it frighten the Soviets and encourage nuclear proliferation). In the present Administration of President Johnson, the tendency to unilateral assertion of what is fancied to be the American interest has, if anything, grown.

and pluralism is not to assert that in a plural world we in the United States "win." It is a sentimental notion that once freed from the communist menace, the trend of the world will be up.

For America to welcome variety in the world, to sustain it and work within its terms, would simply be to translate to the larger world environment the American belief in domestic diversity—diversity of power, but of interest and style as well. It would be to assert a belief in tolerance—for what is not our own; it is to demonstrate a practical tolerance for social movements that are repugnant to us, so long as they do not, coolly assessed, harm our definable and vital interests.

It is the Soviet messianists, or the Chinese, or any other would-be universalists who will break themselves by fighting for a unitary political or social order. No lesson of history is surer than that. The collapse of the Soviet messianic dream—an undertaking begun with unparalleled imagination, application, and political ruthlessness, harnessing a vast national base and the talents of a gifted and devoted people—is reason enough for much faith in that lesson. What Russia, with its advantages, could not accomplish in the tortured climate of the mid-twentieth century, exploiting the opportunities presented by two world wars, will surely not be accomplished by incomparably weaker states in today's world.

For America to welcome variety would mean to abandon the universalism, the messianism, which has overtaken us in recent years and given us that sense of total involvement and responsibility which today results in a global American interventionism. It would mean welcoming those changes in the world which have inconvenienced our established beliefs and political investments, but which have in fact very often benefited us. A dichotomy of world power, the condition of the polar Cold War of the later 1940's and early 1950's, was intellectually easy to grasp and flattering to us—but it was fraught with perils for the world, and for us.

Our dangers today are different, although we are reluctant to acknowledge them. Our new dangers are as much our own creation as threats from abroad; they are more subtle, more insidious in their consequences for us. These new dangers now need discussion, for if the United States in the first decade of the Cold War won for itself a real honor, we today risk dishonoring that accomplishment.

V

Toward a New
Foreign Policy

The contrast between our interpretation of the international challenges to America and the view held by the globalists is clearly very great. To summarize the differences in gross terms, we would hold that Russia today is an insecure and troubled nation, uncertain of the way its inherited doctrines of Marxist-Leninism are to be matched to the conditions in which it now lives, inadequately equipped to understand the full reality of modern politics yet unable to abandon its formal doctrines without abandoning the means by which Russia has brought itself out of impotence to the status of a great power—without, in effect, abandoning the identity which Russia has taken for itself in the twentieth century.

The interventionist, on the other hand, sees Russia as a self-confident nation—and because of its maturity and new restraint, an even more serious threat to America today than ever before. Or, conversely, he sees a moderated Russia, nearer to our way of life, nearer to making compromises with the United States, which might allow the two of us, as kindred "superpowers," to preserve world pre-eminence, to check not only China but the restless Europe that twice in the past has drawn us into world war, to contain together the potential violence and irresponsibility of the Afro-Asian revolutions that threaten us both. Or, in fact, interventionism may simultaneously see both these Russias; and this is possible because both visions articulate a deep American impulse to believe that a single crucial challenge confronts America, and that this challenge is not really definable in national terms but in historical and even quasi-theological terms. The interventionist's view of Russia, then, for all its ambiguity and ambivalence, is not so different from the Soviets' own view of themselves and of their relationship to the United States—that "leader of the imperialist camp," embodiment of the historical "thesis" to which a worker's Soviet Russia is the triumphant antithesis, with worldwide communism the inevitable next stage in the dialectical fulfillment of history.

We would hold, too, that Communist China is an exaggerated threat to America: inimical but for a long time to come materially weak; a serious nation and perhaps eventually (much longer than ten or fifteen years) able to become strong, but deeply rooted in the perceptions and traditions—and arrogance—of Old China. We see China as thus limited in political as well as military competence, ineradicably Asian, fixed in a place and tradition, no less but no more than a great nation—which is to say a good deal—but no potential "Fourth Rome" of proletarian revolution, certainly no successful leader of a worldwide union of the oppressed of Afro-Asia. We see it as limited in its opportunities: an enemy to the two most powerful nations in the world and adjacent to Asia's true sleeping giant—the third largest industrial power in the world, a rapidly expanding and sophisticated economy, Japan. We have described communism in China as primarily a rationale by which Chinese civilization has structured itself to confront the powerful and destructive intrusion of Western industrial culture. For China, Marxism is simultaneously a means for condemning the West as evil and obsolete and a "scientific" method for seizing the techniques which have given the West its power.

The interventionist, though, sees China as the true successor to Stalin's Russia, as the embodiment of aggression and unrestrained ambition—a vast people disciplined to alien doctrine by fanatical leaders, potentially able to inspire a racial-ideological alliance of the world's dispossessed. The interventionist holds that unless China is checked militarily, the poor of the world will follow it into ever-enlarging revolutionary warfare; and that unless our own version of meliorist reform and constitutional progress can compete with China's violent doctrines in the Third World, the decades to come may bring deepening and spreading "North-South" war. The interventionist's belief about China is summarized—and, as interventionism's advocates have argued,

"proved"—by the Maoist thesis of inevitable struggle by the revolutionary "rural" world against the isolated "urban" nations of
Europe and North America.

The interventionist sees Europe as a continent whose day in
history is over. Gifted, resourceful, brilliant, but dangerous and,
so long as it remains disunited, hopelessly outmatched by the
superpowers, vulnerable to conquest unless protected. The interventionist seeks a united Europe, but ambivalently wants that
union only under conditions which effectively institutionalize a
predominant American influence over European external policy
and military action. This desire to check Europe, even while defending it, has comprehensible sources in the experience of two
world wars caused by European states; but the interventionist
theory defines Europe's future in the language of a vague altruism,
in schemes for a federal European community established on the
American precedent which would function as an element in a
larger association envisaged as a kind of next higher stage in the
evolution of the American-led free world. Europe's dangers would
then be ended by its assimilation to the larger grouping—in
short, by its fundamental Americanization.

But this, we argue, is no serious response to the real issue of
Europe's future. There is no actual federation of the free world—
or the West—in sight, whatever the theoretical merits of such a
possible development in international relations might be. And the
American obsession with "Atlanticism" obscures, for Washington
more than for Europe, the real and particular interests of the
European nations, Eastern as well as Western. European reconciliation is thus confused with European unification. Military
security is confused with political integration. The German problem of national division is not adequately positioned within the
larger European (and Soviet-American) interest in political settlement and the re-establishment in Eastern Europe of autonomous nations. The result is a foreclosure of real opportunities for
contributing to European stability (and to America's own European interests as well) in a period when the Soviet threat has
changed and new political opportunities exist.

We have described the Third World as a zone of discrete and
separate nations, very different in prospects, but all in some measure confronting the profound problem of coping with the intellectual, technological, and economic challenge of the industrial

West. We see aid to these states as wholly warranted on humane grounds, and hardly refusable on any grounds, but as affording mixed prospects at best for changing—quickly—the condition of most of the Third World. We see foreign aid to industrialize and urbanize these states as tending actually to enlarge and accelerate the disruptive trends which are responsible for throwing them into their present crisis. We see foreign aid and advice, in any case, as in a significant respect irrelevant to the "development" of the Third World, since the means for resolving the crisis of "development" must primarily arise out of the courage, inner temper, and discipline of each of these states—as was the case in the only truly successful great state of Asia to Westernize, Japan. We see the separate nations of the Third World as largely immune—and as a whole, wholly immune—to any single internationalist political doctrine or mobilization, certainly immune to communism as a recognizable Marxist (or Maoist) doctrine. The Third World is revolutionary in political style, but actually it gropes for help—for friends, precedents, support—in dealing with a radical crisis whose essential terms are cultural and social rather than merely material and political.

The interventionist tends to see the Third World as an interrelated zone of states, all at one or another point on a road of development—a process understood as development toward us: toward the model of the urban-industrial and parliamentary West (or, if we fail, toward our antithesis, communism). The interventionist thus regards the development process as posing a choice between communism and us, a choice fateful in its consequences for centuries to come and continually jeopardized by communist lies and subversion. We and the communists, in this view, struggle over the soul of the Third World—a struggle of freedom with unfreedom, with history believed to be in the balance. Interventionism holds that foreign aid can speed development, popular betterment, and prosperity; and it holds, moreover, that prosperity will then create order and an international consensus sustaining world peace. It (implicitly) foresees the eventual graduation of the Third World nations into an orderly and wealthy world civilization—a civilization very much like that of the contemporary West, or perhaps, even, an idealized America.

The interventionist, finally, regards the Cold War as fundamentally an ideological struggle, a struggle of values, rather than as a national struggle between states. In this view Russia might be defeated—or converted—tomorrow, and the Cold War would not be over. If the true battle is between freedom and unfreedom, then while unfreedom may rule Russia today, and have conquered China and Cuba, unchecked, it can tomorrow take life in still other countries. No *national* victory can end the Cold War. In some sense, then, only a moral conquest of mankind will solve the crisis. "Freedom is indivisible . . . as the area of freedom shrinks under aggression's blows, our own security and our own freedom are threatened."[1] These are the words of Assistant Secretary of State Douglas MacArthur II. Mr. Humphrey declares that we seek "a peaceful revolution against world poverty and the chaos that follows from it . . . a world civilization in which both persons and nations find their individuality enhanced, find their mutual dependence and mutual fate a condition to be welcomed rather than a threat to be feared."[2] The battle is worldwide. The prize is man's condition.

This Cold War, interpreted as essentially a value struggle, a moral contest, seems to offer endless struggle. And this accounts for the apparent "realism" of the repeated warnings that there are to be no easy victories in this war and that the struggle is long. It is reminiscent of the "realism" of fundamentalist sermonizing: the devil is wily and persistent, God's forces are too few, sin is multiform. Yet the power this vision holds over our imagination is that it really promises an endless peace as the reward for struggle. When unfreedom *is* finally defeated, the world will enjoy that new condition which is the ultimate goal of American policy—a world of legalism, prosperity, consensus, a just ordering of society, the suppression of outlawry; in other words, that "progressive international community based on common interest" (in Vice-President Humphrey's words)[3] toward which, Mr. Rostow adds, both American policies and "the prevailing currents of world history" direct us.[4]

Interpreting the Cold War as a value struggle thus gratifies the old American belief in the United States as above the corruption and compromise of other nations. Wilson thought us chosen by God for a crucial world mission, that the world "will turn to America for those moral inspirations which lie at the basis of all freedom . . . that . . . all shall know that she puts human rights above all other rights, and that her flag is the flag not only of America, but of humanity."[5] Today Mr. Johnson is faithful to this tradition in his earnest identification of America's goals as only what others "want for themselves—liberty, justice, dignity, a better life for all."[6] Mr. Ball can add that "we find ourselves in a position unique in world history. Over the centuries a number of nations have exercised world power, and many have accepted at least some of the responsibilities that go with power. But never before in human history has a nation undertaken to play a role of world responsibility except in defense and support of a world empire." The European nations—logical candidates to share responsibility— are not qualified for such a role, for, as Mr. Ball goes on, they "have had little experience in the exercise of responsibility divorced from the defense of territories of the advancement of quite narrow and specific national interests. To undertake—alongside the United States—to play a role of responsibility in a world where colonial empires have largely disappeared would require them to develop a whole new set of attitudes towards world affairs." In the language of the Pharisee who thanks God that he is not as other men, the other nations are told they may qualify themselves by joining in a "generalized common effort" with the United States, yet that this would require them to think in a new way, sharing "with us a role that is something new and unique in history."[7] They would, in short, have to assimilate themselves to us, abandoning their traditions of self-interested policy.

INTERVENTIONISM AND ILLUSION

Interventionism, we have argued, thus rests on illusory judgments of the world abroad, but it also expresses that judgment of America, that sense of American separateness, mission, and moral supremacy which we have already identified as an expression of the basic American temper—the parochialism and provincialism that give rise in other times to isolationism.

In both respects interventionism rests on a high degree of self-deception; the world is not the way the interventionist sees it, nor is America. Interventionism reflects a flight from politics— a rejection of the understanding of world affairs and history as an endless human process with crucial but complex moral content and without predictable fulfillment or temporal resolution. For realism about man and history, interventionism substitutes elements of progressivist historicism, naïve moralism, and national messianism. It projects onto world politics attitudes which at the level of serious intellectual analysis are thoroughly discredited. No modern philosopher, psychologist, or theologian at work in his own field would dare speak like Mr. Ball. While many political scientists and members of the community of foreign policy studies may reflect these attitudes, the attitudes are also almost without exception rejected by serious political philosophers and historians. There is a surprising intellectual lag between the beliefs of this latter class of scholars and the largely unanalyzed assumptions of the officers of government and the political specialists who serve them.

The interventionist projects attitudes which are by no means inevitable American attitudes; this country has in the past rejected them—in our domestic affairs, as we have noted, but sometimes also in foreign policy. As a counterpoint to our isolationist temper, there has been in this country a contrary minority tradition of political restraint. This realism dominated American foreign policy in the early years of the Cold War. Indeed, the success of a bold realism in 1947 and 1948 was so great as to overshadow our policy ever since, and our subsequent programs have attempted, with steadily diminishing success, to emulate those early achievements, repeatedly copying the forms of past policy in wholly new conditions while distorting the substance and purpose.

The Truman Doctrine, the Marshall Plan, and the organization of NATO have become so familiar and celebrated a part of recent American diplomacy that nearly everything we have done since 1947–1948 in the Cold War has been patterned on them; but the later schemes have ignored the limited purposes and restraint of our seminal Cold War programs.

No doubt the fall of China to the communists and the experience of the Korean War was the watershed. Even in the last years of the Truman Administration the original sense of the classical containment policy as defined by George Kennan began to be distorted as attention shifted from what had been very largely a European confrontation to a struggle with communism on a world scale. The Eisenhower programs of the mid-1950's, embodied in the Baghdad Pact, the SEATO Pact, the unilateral American guarantees to Laos and Vietnam, repeated the Truman Doctrine's pattern of American military guarantees to threatened states—but in wholly new conditions. In the case of the Baghdad and SEATO arrangements, there were attempts to establish joint staffs on the pattern of NATO, although without allocated troops. Each of our later alliances was accompanied by an aid program intended to build up the logistical infra-structure of the alliance or to subsidize allied troops, but also intended to reproduce the Marshall Plan achievement of economic reconstruction—now understood as economic development. The whole process took on a quality of automism: we had patented a policy, applicable to any situation, requiring modification only in detail to fit the Moslem Middle East, Southeast Asia, or the Caribbean.

Because Europe, the most intensely industrialized area in the world, had needed and been able to use capital funds for postwar reconstruction, we concluded that a "Marshall Plan for Asia" could create the conditions of social peace and economic prosperity for that area and secure it against communist subversion. Because territorial guarantees and the organization of an alliance were successful in thwarting Soviet claims on Iran and Turkey and in establishing military strength to block the Soviets in Western Europe and Greece, we generalized these as well. From such essentially simple and traditional acts of "power politics," recognizable to a Canning, a Metternich, or for that matter to any capable Roman proconsul, we came to imagine that military guarantees and the technique of alliance were appropriate to secure any state—however small and unstable—from communist-inspired or communist-influenced subversion, or even from internally sponsored civil war and communal turmoil.

The unthinking reiteration of old policy formulas has provided the appearance of continuity in United States policy while its inner spirit has radically changed. Our original purpose toward Russia, according to the principal author of our policy of the time, George Kennan, was simply to oppose "Russian expansive tendencies." We would do this by establishing countervailing military and political power at the points of explicit Russian threat. The moral distinction between communism and the parliamentary politics of the West was clearly understood, but the danger of communism was seen to be serious only when it was supported by—and served the interests of—the powerful Russian nation. We anticipated, as eventually ending the conflict with Russia, either a crisis in Moscow which would cause the Soviet regime to falter, or an evolutionary moderation in the Soviet government which would make pragmatic dealings again possible: such a restoration of the conditions of reasonable international relations was the goal, and only goal, of our policy.* The ideological warfare— organization work, the struggle to control international groups, the radio transmissions and clandestine political propaganda— which we inaugurated in the European countries that had sizable communist minorities and directed against Eastern Europe to discredit their communist regimes was in those early years understood to be an essential part of the political campaign to check the Soviet Union and its influence. Our concern over the Chinese civil war was explicitly motivated by our fear that Moscow dominated, or would dominate, the Chinese communist movement.

Today, as we know, our concern is no longer really with the Soviets, for in a sense we have come to terms with them, though the process is not yet by any means complete as long as Europe— especially Germany—remains divided and thus inherently unstable. Our concern is not even with China, although China bulks largest in our concerns of the moment. Our anxiety is almost universal: it is with events in the Dominican Republic, Rhodesia, Venezuela, Colombia, Brazil, Thailand, Laos, Okinawa, the two Congos, Zambia, Tanzania, Kenya, and Chad, to name a few among many. Our attention is not merely on Soviet activities— or Chinese—but with native leftism and revolution, with the radicalism of students and trade unionists, with organizing "responsible" groups to oppose "extremists," with "nation-building," articulating the aspirations of the peasantry, refining and transforming the goals of elites. The continuity with the containment policy of the 1940's is nominal only. Our new spirit is the spirit

---

* The formulative statement of the "containment" policy, George Kennan's "The Sources of Soviet Conduct," may be found in his *American Diplomacy: 1900–1950*, Chicago, 1951.

Our public men now instruct the peoples of foreign countries in how to be good citizens. Senator Robert Kennedy, during his Latin American tour in the fall of 1965, for example, exhorted Venezuelan students not to drop out of school, told Brazilian sugar company executives that they should pay higher wages, and chided the administrators of a Brazilian university for not recruiting more students of Indian and Negro blood, making his theme everywhere that "we are in the middle of a revolution here; it can be violent or not. It depends on what we make it."[8] The advice was obviously all good; the passion and moral involvement admirable. But the political

of globalism; our commitment is to worldwide ideological and moral combat. And our private disputes over policy are now largely tactical. Today we merely argue the merits of coercion and violence as against programs of reform, but the goal—an implicitly historical goal—is one which, itself, few will challenge.

THE DANGER OF SELF-FULFILLING PROPHECIES

If a foreign policy does not take account of the reality of the world abroad, and does not express the reality of a nation's situation and needs, it fails. Such a policy becomes a program of contradiction and futility—whatever its transient successes may be (and there will be apparent successes; no policy is without effect). Conceived in illusion and folly, it risks national humiliation, coarsening, and ultimately even defeat. This is the risk today. The assumptions of interventionism, because they are wrong, damage America's interests abroad and our own national life.

Conceiving politics as a universalized struggle of values with an anticipated conclusion in a new kind of world, the globalists combat communism by defiantly taking up their role as universal communism's universal enemy—thus lending support to the old Marxist claim that the forces of progress and of reaction have gathered around opposite poles in an ultimate struggle for the future of man. The effect of this, of course, is to reinforce communist megalomania, and the claim that communism on the one hand and capitalism or "imperialism" on the other provide the only significant modes of national organization and life: that they are the only choices for mankind. Skepticism about communism, pluralism and eclecticism in politics—attitudes which we should welcome—are accordingly undermined.

To deal with communism as a *national* phenomenon in Russia or China, and as only one (and not the most plausible) among the political and economic ideologies thrown up in the nineteenth century, would be to act upon a valid, if a less dramatic, judgment than the globalist's assumption. But to act on such a

---

involvement and the appropriateness of Americans' speaking out on the internal affairs of other nations in such terms were questionable. The asumption that the Latin American revolution is "ours" clearly expresses a Cold War universalism which identifies the interests of the United States with the social peace of all countries.

judgment would also serve to place communism in a realistic perspective for those nations and peoples who are the objects of communism's propaganda and intellectual claims. By treating communism as the only serious alternative to our own form of government and society, the globalist enhances communism's importance far beyond any serious historical assessment. Moreover, the effect is to press toward communism all those who—for whatever reason—react against the United States, or against the West, or who fear our influence, or rebel against the *status quo*—which by and large is a *status quo* congenial to us. Indeed, it is to say with Mao Tse-tung: "There can be no exception. There can be no sitting on the fence; there is no third road. . . . We . . . oppose illusions about a third road. Not only in China but throughout the world, one must lean either to imperialism or to socialism. There is no exception. Neutrality is merely a camouflage; a third road does not exist."[9]

Such an American endorsement of the importance of communism in the world cannot, of course, actually sustain the momentum of this dated and badly fragmented movement, with its pseudo-scientific claims to historical truth. The communists claim a role beyond their real qualities and competence. Communism today is a fading force in human affairs. But American interventionism obliquely identifies our own claim to national significance with communism's success or failure—defining us as communism's scourge. Yet this, surely, is not only an unworthy self-definition for a would-be great nation, but a petty one. Interventionism accepts many fictions about America and the world, and chief among them we find the fictions of the communists. The result is not only to make the United States' purpose oddly trivial, but it has produced a series of practical setbacks—worsenings in our international situation directly caused by actions based on our acceptance of globalist illusions.

The most dramatic recent examples of such worsenings of our situation include the bloody and expensive near-disaster we have incurred in Southeast Asia. For the first time we may realistically fear a "domino effect" in the politics of the region, resulting from an all too possible American failure in Vietnam, the ensuing collapse of our influence, and the parallel strengthening of our enemies. The consequences of the Vietnamese adventure already have included serious strains within our European alliance, a halting of progress toward achieving a political settlement with the Soviets in Central Europe, and a maldeployment of United States armed forces. Repeated on a larger scale, this Vietnam folly could produce even more devastating consequences for our world position. And this Asian confrontation largely results, in its inception, from our too literal acceptance of China's boasts of inspiring and leading an anti-Western revolution. Yet these Chinese boasts have—from the beginning—been directly contradicted by the record of China's cautious tactics. That record is one of failure except within China itself—and the communist success within China, the success of "Maoist revolutionary warfare," was no success against the West but against a rival (and weak) Chinese Nationalist movement.

The truth about Mao Tse-tung's revolutionary tactics is that China's national struggle against European political control was largely won in the 1920's and 1930's, *before* the communists became a major force in China. The war to expel the Japanese, who replaced the Europeans as China's main oppressor, was not won by the communists—or by the Chinese Nationalists, for that matter —but primarily by the United States' Western Pacific campaigns of World War II, which destroyed the Japanese empire. At war's end the Japanese were still dominant in China, and the communists were not their most serious threat. As the historian of America's wartime and postwar China policy, Tang Tsou, writes: "If [the communists] had been as strong as they claimed and if they had actively used their armies against Japan, they could have effectively tied down the Japanese forces, which in 1945 numbered 1,050,000 men in China proper. . . . But the Chinese communists obviously were not actively engaged in aggressive actions against Japan's occupation forces. . . . In 1944 and 1945 the Japanese largely left them alone. Like Chiang, the Chinese communists were actively expanding and preserving their forces in preparation for the postwar struggle for power in China. They undoubtedly exaggerated their military strength for political and propaganda purposes to a degree difficult to determine."[10]

The communist postwar victory over the Nationalists was victory in a civil war; it was a conquest of "imperialism" only within the distorted political conceptions of communism. Whatever America's generous supply of matériel to the Kuomintang, the Nationalists' political and military support from the United States was hesitant and qualified. (Hence the "Who lost China?" controversies in the United States in the late 1940's and 1950's; there would have been no need to argue the matter if the American commitment to Chiang Kai-shek had been whole-hearted.) Postwar American policy toward the Kuomintang may fairly be described as "passive" and our military assistance as "limited"; Tang Tsou adds that "after the breakdown of the Marshall mission, American officials felt that conditions necessary for the efficient use of American aid and effective Sino-American co-operation did not obtain in China." (At the time the Gallup Poll found, as well, that the majority of the American public was not in favor of strong measures to block the communists in China.)[11] Mao's conquest of China was an accomplishment in civil war, not in international struggle.*

We have today seen that whatever the grandiose claims of

---

* Mao Tse-tung's real accomplishment was to create an alliance of intellectuals (scholars and members of the administrative classes) and peasants. As C. P. Fitzgerald writes, these are "the two classes upon which all Chinese government must rest. The first by virtue of their education are essential to the workings of the government. The second must give their consent to be governed; if they withhold it no regime can stand, if the scholars—the educated—withdraw, no system can work."[12] Only two of China's many great peasant risings achieved this alliance; the first drove out the Mongols and founded the Ming Dynasty, the second was Mao Tse-tung's. China's other successful rebellions were the uprisings of generals. The Kuomintang had held the intellectuals from Sun Yat-sen's day early in this century until after World War II. By the late 1940's its incompetence and corruption had forfeited their support, and the peasant-based communist movement—even then an unorthodox communism by virtue of Mao's reliance on the peasantry instead of the urban proletariat of classic Marxist and Soviet doctrine—achieved the status of a genuine national rising. The Kuomintang, China's first serious political attempt to come to terms with the modern world and end China's humiliations and disorder, had at various times attempted to draw its organizational rationale from widely divergent sources: from Soviet communism (Sun ended his days a bitter observer of the modern West and an admirer of the Russian revolution, and Russian agents and the Comintern worked with the Kuomintang for a period); from fascism when fascism was the dominant European mode of national renaissance; and from the Protestant missionary Christianity which several of the principal Kuomintang leaders (including Chiang and his wife) professed. None had proved adequate; all had been foreign grafts onto the Chinese body politic and eventually were sloughed off. Mao's genius was to adapt the "modern" doctrine of communism as developed in the U.S.S.R. to powerful and persisting social currents in China—communalism, reliance on the peasant, rule by a selfless administrative elite, and xenophobia. Thus he created a *Chinese* communism. And because it is *Chinese* communism it is not compatible with Vietnamese or Thai or Congolese or Cuban society, whatever Chinese aspirations to lead Afro-Asia and Latin America may be.

Maoist international strategy, China's communism is not capable of sweeping Indonesia, even though the alternative political movements there—native Indonesian "socialism" and the Moslem and Christian political groups—are feeble. The North Vietnamese, beneficiaries of China's verbal and political sympathies, fight by their own tactics and their own revolutionary self-definition; the Viet Minh movement was well established and at war with France for three years when the Chinese communist offensives first reached the South China areas bordering Indochina. Ho Chi Minh's earlier wartime support and supply, as he launched his movement (initially against the Japanese), had come from the Chinese Nationalists and the American O.S.S. Moreover, the Vietnamese communists have consistently shown themselves anxious to balance the influence of China with that of Russia.

Chinese communism appeals to the Third World only in its rhetorical radicalism. It is attractive because it is unqualified—because it verbalizes that loathing of imperialism and the intrusive and powerful West which almost any Asian or African, at one or another time, must feel. But to rejoice, publicly or secretly, at China's verbal violence is not the same thing as to align oneself with China; and certainly it is very different from handing oneself over to Chinese imperial direction or domination. Thus the paradox that the only two groups which insist on the universality of the Chinese example are the Chinese—and in this, surely, it is China's deep sense of cultural primacy speaking, of being the "Middle Kingdom" at the center of civilization—and the American globalists who foresee a vast alliance of yellow men and black, directed by Peking, marching against the West. But such Chinese claims or American fears can hardly bring such an implausible alliance into being. Only a few years ago precisely this nightmare alliance against the West was to be led by the Soviets. Yet what Soviet Russia was unable to accomplish, with incomparably greater military power and economic resources (to say nothing of the advantage of novelty), is not likely to be accomplished by the far less well endowed Chinese—people who do not even have the advantage of remoteness on their side. The Chinese in Asia are not loved by those who have felt the imperialist pressures of successive Chinese governments or the economic pressures of the overseas Chinese.

The passionate American desire to "contain" China, so that we now attempt to draft our NATO allies into an association with us in Southeast Asia, suggests that the lesson of the inter-war years, of Hitler's aggressions, has been learned too well. In official pronouncements and in the daily press the dangers of appeasement are reiterated over and over again, without regard to the fact that the analogy of Communist China and Hitler's Germany is a forced one. The difference is simply that Hitler, by a strategy of intimidation, was able to throw off a series of treaty limitations on German power and then to begin a career of territorial aggressions which successively incorporated Austria, the Sudetenland, then the remainder of Czechoslovakia into the *Reich*. When it appeared at last that Hitler demanded a fourth partition of Poland, the weary democracies, having waited too late, went to war.

In such circumstances, when Neville Chamberlain, the British Prime Minister at the time of Munich, maintained that Czechoslovakia was a far-off country "of whom we know nothing," it was a kind of idiot recklessness. That allegedly "far-off country" lay on the eastern border of Germany, which abutted Britain's major ally France in the west and faced Britain itself across the North Sea; and in European terms of the 1930's, Czechoslovakia brought important industrial potential to the German war machine. The danger of appeasement was that successive additions to Hitler's power could serve to tip the balance against the democracies by directly contributing to the military potential of the enemy. It has never been maintained, however, that Chamberlain and his French counterpart Daladier were remiss in standing by while a host of minor fascist states, imitating Nazi Germany but often hostile to it, proliferated in Eastern and Central Europe. Appeasement was never a question of tolerating Admiral Horthy's Hungary, or King Carol's Rumania, or Tsar Boris' Bulgaria, or Ridz-Smigly's Poland, or Prince Paul's Yugoslavia, as they toyed with the modish notion of fascism; appeasement lay in refusing to see military aggression as Hitler's chosen mode and in failing to support those threatened directly by German territorial demands. To allow a potentially crucial state or geographical zone to be conquered by one's enemy is folly. But however true it may have been that the swing to fascism in the 1930's in Eastern and Central Europe corrupted the quality of international life, it would have been a rash and futile foreign policy for Britain and France to have embarked on a crusade against these petty fascisms. The Allies' greatest error was to play their cards (initially good ones) so badly that the latent tensions between the two largest fascist states, Germany and Italy, were not converted to a full-fledged rivalry. Italian-German tensions were acute through the period of the Austrian crisis of 1938, and Italian ambitions in the Balkans were an irritant to Hitler until midway in the war.

It is with the so-called lesson of Munich, therefore, that the process we have called paratactic distortion comes powerfully into play. Conceivably the Chinese invasion of Tibet corresponds to Hitler's reoccupation of the Rhineland in 1936—a zone demilitarized by the Versailles Treaty—but it certainly does not correspond to the bloodless conquest of Czechoslovakia or the attack on Poland in 1939. Tibet may have yearned to be free, and for that reason may deserve the sympathy of free men; but in a world where distinctions make all the difference, it is also true that Tibet, perhaps the most formidable mountain region in the world, is not a good logistic route to anywhere and that for many hundreds of years Tibet had been a part of the Chinese empire. (It broke away only after the republican revolution of 1911, when China was weak.) China's border war with India in 1962 was a minor political skirmish designed to chasten and humiliate the Indian government. It is not pleasant to say so, since India, whatever its defects, is a democracy, but the truth is that the Indian claim in the Himalayas rests on shaky legal grounds: the Chinese argument (accepted in Formosa by the government of Chiang Kai-shek as well) is that the boundary was imposed unilaterally on China by the British *raj.* The McMahon Line is a boundary which China has never accepted. Thus an effort to redress the issue cannot be taken entirely as a breach of faith. Burma and Pakistan managed to negotiate the issue with the Chinese. While it would be rash on this basis to assert that China intends to abide by such settlements, it cannot accurately be determined at this time just what China wants. The point, then, is not whether China is a tough, truculent, and dangerous nation within its logistic and military capabilities. It is. The point is not whether India deserves our help; as a friend standing against a potential enemy, whatever the legalisms of the case, it clearly does (though this does not mean that we serve India best by accepting all her claims). The point at issue is whether there is good evidence that China's aims are insatiable and universal *in fact,* whatever its truculent stance in international affairs.

Chinese propaganda and ideological claims are one thing. China's true intentions are another—and they are unknown, mutable, and too often the subject of dogmatic and unproved assertions. China's competence is still another thing, and this is the factor with which Western policy must chiefly deal. Thus far China has proved incapable of leading a worldwide revolutionary movement. The Indonesian reaction against China in 1965 reinforces the skepticism which is an appropriate response to claims as grandiose as those of Mao Tse-tung and Lin Piao. China has not even acquired satellites on its borders. North Korea is not a Chinese satellite, nor is North Vietnam. They are communist states independent of Peking, allied with China on some issues, at odds with her on others. Nor are they helpless; against the Chinese they have a powerful ally, if needed, in Moscow, which would no doubt dearly love to have the Chinese offer a clear-cut pretext for disciplinary action—which is what Chinese military moves against sister communist states unwilling to take her dictation would constitute.

In the end it comes to this: there is a radical discrepancy between the power and threat which the American interventionist assigns to China, and the real competence and success—and prospects of success—which China has thus far demonstrated. This overestimation serves to advance China's interests and to harm our own. What our illusionism accomplishes is to provoke American policies which do practical damage to our position in the world, and damage those people who find themselves the subjects of China's and our competition.

INTERVENTIONS IN THE THIRD WORLD

Another example of the consequences of this American endorsement of communist ideological themes is provided by Cuba today. The Cuban revolution was initially indigenous, radical, and anti-*yanqui.* It has since declared itself a communist revolution, and the Cuban regime has undertaken a self-conscious part in the counsels and controversies between China and the Soviet Union. It does so mainly because the United States itself has made it plain that a communist role is the one an anti-*yanqui* Latin American state is expected to play—and because this is the only role Cuba can play if it expects *safely* to defy the United States. "Safely" is exactly the word. A non-communist but aggressively anti-*yanqui* Cuba might expect to share the fate Nicaragua or Panama suffered in this century and the last, the fate Cuba itself experienced in 1898, 1906, and 1917, the fate of Guatemala and the Dominican Republic in recent years and months when they proclaimed, or ostensibly threatened to proclaim, a leftism that was distinct from communism. When Cuba was a radical state standing against the United States, it had to deal with the Bay of Pigs invasion; but since its open alignment with the Soviet Union, and its acceptance by Soviet Russia and China, it is in the unique position in the Americas of both defying the United States and remaining safe. It is now a member of that world-historical host which challenges the free world; and the United States must deal *seriously* with it. It is no longer merely a petty—and tragic —sugar republic. Such is the outcome of an American diplomacy of self-conscious "realism."

In the Dominican Republic—and elsewhere in Latin America— the effect of interventionist doctrine and action is an equivalent polarization of anti-*yanqui* forces around Chinese or Soviet communists (and most Latin communists would prefer not to choose between the two because their motivating interest is not in ideology but in the generalized power and mystique of communism; the Sino-Soviet split is an embarrassing diversion to them). This is of major consequence because, as we have seen, in the present and foreseeable relationship of North and South America, anti-United States sentiments will continue to be a major force in Latin America. Things can hardly be otherwise so long as the discrepancy of power and success, and the difference of outlook, between the two Americas, endures. It would be true regardless of the wisdom or generosity of United States policy, or the success of Latin American development; it is a fact of continental American political life, just as tension between Russia, Poland, and Germany is a fact of European politics, or tension between China and the Southeast Asian states is a fact of Asian affairs.

The interventionist's identification of communism as the one effective and powerful mode of challenge to the United States— the legitimate mode of defiance—can have no other effect ultimately than to recruit to communism Latin American rebels and dissidents, patriots, and idealists of the most widely divergent types. There is a poignancy in this—and an irony. The reputation that the United States once enjoyed for its championing of the rights of man—that idealized reputation which nevertheless was not unearned—has, we know, substantially disappeared in the course of the Cold War. But it is not entirely gone, and there still are many who want to believe in the United States. There are many in Latin America who would like to check their resentment of America's past interventions, make sensible allowances for well-intentioned error and private greed, believe in the fruitfulness of relations across the cultural barrier of the Latin tradition and the North American. Yet these men too often are the victims of the political polarization which continued American interventionism promotes. We embrace as our own those Latin leaders who attempt to define national courses of reform which are not communist—Rómulo Betancourt of Venezuela in the recent past, Eduardo Frei in Chile today—but the weight of our endorsement actually tends to undermine democratic socialism and Christian democracy as legitimate forces of national reform and identity in Latin America.

A too close American involvement with reforming or liberal circles in Latin America is the kiss of death. Political polarization destroys the autonomous middle ground where leaders who are moderate but nationalist can stand—sure enough of their nationalism both to stand against us, the Americans, on occasion and stand with us at other times. Anti-*yanquismo*, after all, is more than an emotional element in Latin America (and elsewhere); it is also legitimate. It is sometimes a politically deserved response to our actions. It is also inevitable in terms deeper than politics— in terms of the cultural and intellectual experience of small countries which must coexist with culturally different but powerful, ambitious, self-confident, and successful nations nearby. The fate of Juan Bosch in the Dominican Republic—whatever his failings, a Latin political figure who belonged to the serious middle ground and one who wanted to believe the best of the United

States—is likely to be the fate of others so long as the interventionists chop and fit the politics of Latin America and the world to fit the polar categories of communism/pro-Americanism.

Such effects on Latin American politics are the result of the general political polarization which the interventionist would sustain. Comparable practical judgments can be made on America's specific acts of worldwide intervention. In the late 1950's, for example, the United States supported an unsuccessful rebellion in Indonesia against President Sukarno, and the effect was to provide gratuitous grounds for anti-American sentiments and pro-communist political policies in Indonesia for years following. Indonesia did not "go communist" as a result; it still possessed that sense of national identity and national needs which would ultimately, in the autumn of 1965, lead it to reject the Chinese communists as it had rejected the United States. But we and China, by our abortive revolutionary interventions, only harmed ourselves—and harmed Indonesia too by contributing to conspiracy and violence in that country, further disrupting a political society of initially weak attainments and insecure prospects.

Similarly, the United States has given some support and sympathy to dissident elements in Cambodia who oppose that government's studied neutralism, yet Cambodia is one of the few small South Asian states with effective political leadership (despite, or perhaps partially because of, the personal eccentricities of Prince Sihanouk's political style and rhetoric). We have done this because Sihanouk has pursued a course of guarded compromise between China and ourselves, visiting Peking, expressing friendship for China (and Hanoi), chiding America (sometimes with justice and sometimes not), tolerating (because he must) North Vietnamese military activity in his country. Most of all he has been hostile toward the Thais and South Vietnamese, traditional enemies of the Cambodians, but our allies. Sihanouk is a riddle and his policy is far from certain to succeed, especially now if South Vietnam falls to the North; but whatever the particular merits of his policies and language, his course of action was comprehensible in terms of Cambodia's painful present situation and past experiences; and the actual harm he has done the United States is slight. Nor are we on the basis of our record in Laos or

South Vietnam able to offer a real alternative. Our interventions can only weaken Cambodia's independence; there is so far no realistic prospect of true national security in Southeast Asia based on an American military guarantee. Whatever may be said of America's brave efforts in the war against the Viet Cong, clearly we have not so far succeeded in giving South Vietnam any greater security than "neutralized" Laos and "self-neutralized" Cambodia now enjoy. We are even beginning now to fear for the Thais, whose clear choice of America has apparently not been enough to win them a secure political peace. By posing polar choices in Southeast Asia, by echoing Mao's condemnation of "Third Ways," we in fact have reduced the possibilities of reasonable choice for Cambodia and the rest.

In Cambodia today the consequences are a nation frankly hostile to us—although still not yet a communist state or even a true Chinese client. Even poor Laos is not yet communist despite the bungling American interventions since the mid-1950's. That feeble state has still managed to resist the total political polarization which we attempted to impose by thoughtlessly intervening to overturn the first neutralist government proclaimed in 1958 by the present premier, Souvanna Phouma, to whom we turned once again four years later when our own choice, "strong man" Phoumi Nosovan, proved hopelessly weak. We tacitly admitted a defeat in 1962 when President Kennedy reversed the policies of the Eisenhower Administration and negotiated a new agreement, in effect a partition of Laos, and gave belated American support to the new Souvanna Phouma government. The communist Pathet Lao movement, largely ethnic in origin and popular following, like many Asian communist movements,* did not end its pressure on the central government with this neutralization, and the conflict in Laos has become more and more closely bound up with the Vietnam war. (It is, of course, a legacy of the first Indochina war;

* The *political* content of much Asian communism is rather slighter than many American observers will acknowledge. The communist movements not only in Laos but in India's Kerala, Andhra, and Bengal states, in Indonesia and Ceylon, in Burma and Thailand, in Malaya, all in varying degree have been based in, or framed their appeals in terms of, old ethnic or communal conflicts. Today for one side to proclaim itself communist and the other non-communist in a traditional rivalry is a way of gaining external support as well as a talismanic modernity. But the old rivalries will outlast communism in these regions. Moreover the rivals may usually be relied on to expel communist activists when the ethnic or communal needs

Laos and Cambodia were both part of France's Indochina empire and were involved with the Viet Minh rebellion of 1946–1954, becoming independent states only as a result of the Geneva Agreement of 1954.) Yet the situation of the communist movement in Laos today is generally less favorable than at any time since the American overthrow of the first neutralist government in 1958. It will most probably be in the context of a lost war in Vietnam that Laos will be lost, if it is lost.

Even our "successful" interventions—sponsoring a military uprising in Guatemala in 1954 to overthrow a leftist government, acting in Iran in 1953 to overturn the Mossadeq government and re-establish the Shah, lending political support to the conservative Castelo Branco military take-over in Brazil in 1964, sending troops into the Dominican Republic in 1965—can be described as successes only in immediate, narrow, and expedient terms, and by disregarding both the legacy of hostility to the United States such interventions create among opposition elements, the support they lend to distorted communist explanations of an incorrigible American imperialism, and the precedent of internal disorder and violent dissent we help establish or maintain in countries with initially weak political institutions.

And to call them successes is, moreover, to disregard the irrelevance of most such interventions, even judged by the measures of expediency. Were they necessary? In the last ten years there has been a score of other such situations in which we might have intervened on equally plausible or implausible grounds but did not—whether out of wisdom or mere lack of opportunity. Algeria under Ben Bella conceived of itself as a revolutionary society akin to China's, and it co-operated with China; Guinea in 1958 angrily cut itself off entirely from the West; Iraq under General Kassim was aggressively anti-Western; Nasser's Egypt, Burma since 1962, even the Pakistan which has recently entered into an alliance with China, all have denounced us at one time or another and sought advantages from the communist powers. Yet not one has joined the enemy camp. Not one has more than mildly inconvenienced

---

of the group come into conflict with strictly communist interests. Thus, to treat them as if the issues really were those which we understand as political —as meaningfully communist in conflict with political anti-communism—can not only be misleading but can perpetuate and enlarge what otherwise is a transient alliance.

us. Not one *could* do more than inconvenience us. Our restraint has served our own practical interest—and indeed the interest of international stability and order.*

The argument that interventions in these situations would have improved things is untenable. The argument that our interventions elsewhere have made matters worse is in strict terms unprovable (we cannot know the alternatives), but it is perfectly tenable—and the damaging side effects can be calculated. Chief among these are the contributions we have made to an international precedent of expedient action, our endorsement of ideological conflict, our active sponsorship of civil violence and conspiratorial politics. These actions are not only wrong, they are mistakes that in the long run will hurt us.

ALLIANCE INTERVENTIONS

When the Cold War was extended in the early 1950's from Europe to larger international fronts, the initial American response was to organize a series of alliances modeled on the successful NATO alliance in Europe. The inadequacies of this policy as a means for organizing an effective anti-communist coalition are by now

* The American failures in Cuba and Vietnam should be contrasted with the success of French policy in Guinea and Algeria in recent years. When Guinea achieved independence in the late 1950's it began an assiduous courtship of the Soviet bloc, as did Algeria after achieving independence some years later. Since the fixed object of French policy has been to maintain an influence in the former territories of sub-Saharan Africa (France spends per capita more on foreign aid, largely funneled to these countries, than the United States) and the Maghreb, one might have expected, on the American analogy, a hysterical dialogue to ensue between the government in Paris and the governments in Conakry and Algiers. Nothing could be further from the truth. The government of Charles de Gaulle maintained a studied aloofness. Eventually an abortive Soviet political scheme in Guinea chastened Sekou Touré, and eventually nationalist forces in Algeria overturned Ben Bella. The French silence deprived Touré of the chance of playing a role as an African political messiah, as it deprived Ben Bella of a heroic role in the Arab world.

The closest analogy to American experience, of course, was the challenge of Ben Bella, who led a country formerly an important factor in the French economy and linked to France by the closest cultural ties. But while the United States by slanging with Castro has dignified him, the French policy in Algeria was exactly the reverse. Consider, too, the error that Stalin made in 1948–1953 by slanging with Tito; the effect was to raise the nationalist defection of a petty Balkan dictator to a major international challenge, making possible a Titoist ideology—an error for which the Soviets later paid dearly.

widely understood (though under the pressures of the crisis in Southeast Asia, there is a new emphasis in Washington on the SEATO alliance). But there is a further and less well understood point that needs to be made about alliances. The Asian alliances of the United States in the 1950's furnished us with the initial commitments that were to affect the internal affairs of the countries in these regions. These treaties were the vehicles for an involvement (as in Thailand today) which came to extend not only to advice and aid in military organization and strategy but in the employment of police, the use of domestic propaganda and indoctrination, the employment of economic aid, and on methods of domestic finance and trade. Yet there is imposing evidence that this kind of detailed involvement—this benign intervention, to say nothing of the military interventions which the alliances imply—in fact damages the legitimacy and autonomy of our allies, and thus damages our own interests, our purported interests as well as our real ones.

NATO, the first of our alliances, sprang from reality. Perhaps the West overestimated the imminence of the Soviet threat in 1949, but the impulse to defend Europe stemmed from a perception of threat which we and the Europeans shared; and the threat was real. CENTO—the Baghdad Alliance—was another matter. It purported to unite the "Northern Tier" of anti-communist states in the Middle East—Turkey, Iran, Iraq, and Pakistan—and may have been important to two of these states, Turkey and Iran, both of which had been threatened at the war's close by direct Soviet territorial demands. The alliance was not only useless to Iraq and Pakistan, but from the standpoint of their national interests, may have been positively injurious. A territorial guarantee of these states against Soviet invasion might have been relevant, but American diplomats wanted more—alliance and political association, including frequent public reassurances of anti-communism and pro-Americanism. In the event, as the overthrow of the Nuri-es-Said regime in 1958 demonstrated (as well as the success of subsequent Iraqi regimes in excluding communism), American stewardship in Iraq was both unable to assure political stability and unnecessary to exclude communism.

In Pakistan the attention of the country was fixed on the issue of the frontier with India, particularly in the disputed territory of Kashmir. What America constructed as an anti-communist alliance against the threat from the north, the Pakistanis hoped to exploit as a means of achieving American backing for their claims in Kashmir against a neutralist India. The result was that Pakistan gained little from CENTO (except the arms it used against India in 1965). The United States gained only reproaches —and the embarrassment of having supplied the munitions for a war against another friendly state. The United States demonstrated as well that it is neither a good friend nor a loyal ally where its own contrary interests are at stake. The American interest in the Indian subcontinent and the Arab Middle East is in peace and the exclusion of Soviet and Chinese power, and with little else.

While alliances are often necessary, they are never without their costs to the parties—and this is true, though in unequal degree, of both great powers and small. Alliances inevitably involve some measure of the surrender of sovereignty. When a state contracts an alliance it loses freedom of international action. It makes this surrender because it believes it gains in other important ways. Guarantees to national security, the provision of military aid, economic aid, and political support for certain international objectives are common reasons in today's world for contracting alliances, together with intimidation in the less pleasant cases. But while a large state in some sense puts itself into bondage to the interests of a small one when it concludes an alliance, the large state may denounce the treaty at will and without paying much of a price. Alliances between large and small states are thus inherently unequal and therefore unstable. They are sometimes gratifying to the *amour-propre* of the large state; but to the small one they are nearly always irksome. Thus the small state will tend to denounce the treaty as soon as the external threat or other condition that motivated the alliance is seen to fade, or as other more favorable opportunities for political action present themselves.

There should be nothing shocking in all this. It is an axiom of international politics that gratitude is ephemeral, if real, and that it is seldom real. It is a frequent charge against French policy in NATO that it is ungrateful; no doubt it is. The United States has done much for France—and for Europe. But there is no good purpose served by stating the problems of the American alliance in Europe in moralistic terms. The United States has gained from the past adherence of France to NATO. The present security of Western Europe is our payment, since the fall of Europe to the Soviets would have been a disaster not only to Europe but to the United States. That Europe should today want NATO to be re-formed should be no surprise. An alliance is an instrument of rational policy and as such should reflect changing conditions.

Granting that the United States for many years to come will retain interests in such regions as the Middle East and South Asia, and important interests in the security of Europe and the Western Pacific, it does not follow that alliances can best secure these interests. The real needs of the United States are two. The first is the territorial integrity of these regions against the incursion of major hostile powers—the Soviet Union or China (or some other nation in the future). The second is their political stability and freedom from internal disorders. The rationale of the first need is that these regions cannot be allowed to add their resources to the strength of a major enemy. The rationale of the second need is more complex. The internal stability of a region, or the form of government that prevails there, is primarily important to us only when the region is of sufficient intrinsic importance to constitute a potential major threat to peace in its own right. There are few such places. Western Europe is such a region, capable in its own terms of threatening the security of the United States (as it has done twice in this century). In alliance with the Soviets, Europe would tip the scale of world power disastrously against us. Japan is another such region. Perhaps the Indian subcontinent may be a third. But the three cases may exhaust the list.

The internal stability of sub-Saharan Africa or of the Middle East or Southeast Asia must, politically speaking, be a matter of comparative indifference to the United States. Turmoil in such regions may be a human tragedy, but the narrowly defined security of the United States is not likely to be seriously affected. For the Soviets to annex the Middle East or for the Chinese to annex Southeast Asia might, on the other hand, be exceedingly dangerous. So long as the U.S.S.R. or Communist China is a hostile power, their acquisition of local resources and bases could be a major factor in a struggle against the United States. It is, therefore, a matter of importance that the United States deny these regions to the Soviets or Chinese—that is, prevent a military conquest. On this point there is little argument.*

This is not the same as to assert—as the interventionist does —that the United States has an important national interest in Middle Eastern or Southeast Asian affairs *as such*. There is not sufficient power in the two regions, even if united under a single native leader such as Gamal Nasser or Ho Chi Minh, to constitute a serious military or diplomatic threat to the United States and its allies. Nor, in any event, is Middle Eastern unity likely—by consent or by conquest, as the record of rivalry and discord since 1945 attests. Arab unity remains a slogan, increasingly so as the Egyptians bend the slogan to their own national ends. A Southeast Asia wholly under North Vietnamese rule is equally implausible. For once the Vietnamese were fighting beyond their frontiers, they would collide with the same nationalism that makes them such formidable opponents on their home ground.

The largely theoretical possibility remains, of course, that a region, or a major state in a region, might ally itself voluntarily to the Soviets or the Chinese and so subordinate itself that it would be the equivalent of a conquered territory. Might not Egypt, or Iraq, or Iran ally itself to the U.S.S.R., or Cambodia or Indonesia to the Chinese, and hand over to Moscow or Peking peacefully what might otherwise have had to be won by conquest?

Again the question demands an empirical answer; no state has done so, not even Cuba, since whatever Castroism in Havana may or may not be, Cuba is far from Moscow, and Cuban independence is safe from the Soviets. Cuba is no abject Soviet satellite; and no state abutting the Soviets has shown even a guarded will-

---

* It is not, however, true that such a conquest, unfortunate as that might be and unwise to permit, would necessarily prove disastrous to the United States. The Soviet conquest of Eastern Europe did not prove such a disaster, nor the communist "conquest" of mainland China. Neither acquisition tipped the balance of world power against the United States. Indeed, two decades after the fall of Eastern Europe to Soviet conquest and a decade and a half after the fall of China to the native communists, it is not certain that Soviet national interests, narrowly considered, were served by the control of these territories. Eastern Europe, especially Yugoslavia, Albania, and Rumania, now mounts dangerous challenges to Soviet hegemony, and Poland, Czechoslovakia, and Hungary are sources of ideological contamination. The communist Chinese clearly are no help to the Soviets. Where World War II destroyed one threat on the Soviet eastern flank—Japan— the communization of China has merely called another into being.

ingness to put its head in the lion's jaws. Indonesia is no Chinese
puppet. Cambodia, too, plays a complex international game, but
it does so to maintain its independence, not to serve Chinese
interests.

Could not the Soviets or the Chinese foment a rebellion in the
Middle East or Southeast Asia? The problem of so-called wars
of national liberation is central to the interventionist argument;
but the truth is that the fear of foreign-inspired guerrilla wars is
exaggerated. The Soviets have not fomented rebellions in other
nations because they have not been able to. (The Greek guerrilla
war was not begun by Stalin, and as the Yugoslav communist
dissident Milovan Djilas has testified in his memoirs, it frightened
Stalin; he feared a military clash with the United States as a
result of helping the Greek rebels.) The Chinese talk as if they
could inspire rebellions at will, and we have credited them with
this ability, but there is no evidence that they have ever really
initiated such a guerrilla war, unless they are responsible (which
is by no means certain) for the guerrilla violence in Malaya in the
1950's (and that was a matter solely involving the overseas
Chinese in Malaya, not the Malayans themselves). The Chinese
incursion into Tibet was an old-fashioned military conquest, as
their probe into Assam in 1962 was a straightforward military
operation. The Indochinese rebellion against the French long
antedated the triumph of communism in China itself: Ho Chi
Minh was in the field against the Japanese as early as 1942 and
against the French in 1946, while Mao Tse-tung did not win his
victory until 1949 and was not until then in a position to "foment"
anything at all beyond China's own borders. Whatever the outcome of the present Vietnamese war, which now pits United
States troops against Viet Cong and North Vietnamese regulars,
it is not *China* that is likely to be the real beneficiary—unless
we insist on crediting the Chinese with an unearned victory.

The conclusion that must be drawn is that where old-fashioned
aggression by the Soviets and the Chinese is the issue, an alliance
with the threatened victim is not really essential to deter attack.
A unilateral guarantee by the United States, either tacit or explicit, will serve as well and does not have the effect of involving
the United States in the internal politics of states. Such a guarantee, provided in a situation of danger, does not, moreover, compromise the standing of the threatened government, rob it of

authenticity, and subject it to the charge of being a satellite or
puppet of the United States. It is also possible to give military
advice or matériel without an alliance.* The alliance tactic is
valid only when the objective threat is such as to demand pains-
taking advance preparation and integrated military plans. There
are not many such places: Europe in 1945–1953 was one such
place, an area which could not be lost without incurring the risk
of disaster and which faced a major Soviet threat. Along the
Chinese periphery there is hardly a comparable place. Chinese
military power, while relatively formidable in the defense of the
mainland, is comparatively immobile. Chinese logistic constraints
are serious; Peking's army cannot easily fight large-scale foreign
wars—which is one reason for the limited nature of Chinese action
in Assam in 1963 and the explanation of China's setbacks in Korea
a decade earlier.

As for NATO—the prototype alliance of modern American
foreign policy—in the conditions of the 1960's its reorganization
is overdue. It is a fact that Western Europe is relatively secure
against post-Stalinist Russia. It may well be that the overwhelming presence of American power in NATO today forecloses
promising avenues of European development. Certainly, it is

---

* In the case of India in 1962–1963 our interest in India's territorial
integrity was effectively expressed without an alliance. As a threat develops,
as it did in Assam in 1963, the United States can move accordingly. At such
a point, the threatened state will welcome either formal or *ad hoc* alliance.
In especially troubled regions, the United States can issue its territorial
guarantee long in advance of an immediate threat, or it can seek to cordon
off an area from hostile intervention. This last is to establish a kind of
regional quarantine, a tactic well within the capacities of mobile American
power.

It has been argued to the French, who sought a looser organization of
NATO, that France twice has come close to losing wars because no such
integrated alliance as NATO guaranteed her security in 1914 and 1939.
Such an argument avoids the issue of the scale and imminence of the
military threat; no doubt a larger and integrated British contingent in France
in 1914 would have been useful, but the British, as a political matter, were
not willing to commit themselves in all circumstances to joint military action
against the Kaiser's Germany, nor in the event is it certain that from the
point of view of British interests they were wise to join in the hostilities.
Hitler's threat was another matter, but it is not likely that an integrated
British-French force in 1939–1940 could have withstood the Nazi attack. The
Soviets managed to do so after 1941 without such an alliance and without
accepting close co-operation with the Western allies. The necessity for
integrated alliances is an open question.

difficult to see how the reintegration of the former Soviet satellites into Europe is to be achieved within present American concepts.*

THE CONTEXT OF INTERVENTION

In a region troubled by hypernationalism, alliance with a major foreign power may affect political stability adversely. The pro-Western Iraqi government of Nuri-es-Said in the 1950's lost indigenous support in part precisely because it had committed Iraq to a Western alliance. In Vietnam the overthrow of Ngo Dinh Diem in 1963 worsened the Saigon regime's struggle against the Viet Cong in part because Diem, whatever his reactionary and dictatorial methods and sectarianism, was at least perceived as a *native* leader, one who did not subordinate Vietnam to American power. The American insensitivity to these political consequences of our interventions stems from an unwillingness to understand the modern revolutions of Afro-Asia and Latin America; we insist on interpreting them as if they were revolutions essentially related to our own—mere searches for social dignity, or rational material satisfactions. They are not; they are, as we have seen, at bottom reactive, nationalist, even anti-rational movements.

Thus, to land American troops, or to assert American power in more subtle political ways, may foreclose military victory to

* While the United States continues to talk about the reintegration of the satellites into the Western world, or into a larger "Europe," its actual policies are predicated on an indefinite continuation of the division between East and West. The German problem provides the clearest example of this sort of schizoid thinking: in recent years West Germany has been asked to join in a variety of integrated nuclear schemes like the Multilateral Nuclear Force or the Atlantic Nuclear Force, which presuppose as an overriding problem the task of defending Western Germany (and Europe) from Soviet attack, rather than the overriding problem of seeking a settlement—that is to say, a "normalization"—in Europe based on the new diplomatic and military realities. Since Stalin's death in 1953 there has been a slow waning of the Cold War, a perceptible slackening of the Soviet threat, a decline of the numbers of usable Warsaw Pact ground forces, so that as a military matter it is chiefly the Soviet *nuclear* force (of which the Soviets themselves are afraid) that is the main Soviet military instrument in Europe. Moreover, there has begun to appear a possibility of new bargaining with the Soviets. Much United States policy, in the area of arms control particularly, is predicated on the possibility of striking self-policing or enforceable bargains with Moscow. Such arms-control bargains have the attraction of preserving the United States–Soviet duopoly and, therefore, tend to seize the imagination of American policy planners. The notion of a

an enemy movement—as we have "foreclosed" a communist seizure of power in Santo Domingo or may, in fact, have foreclosed a Viet Cong military victory in Vietnam. But this is not the same thing as achieving political and social stability. And while it is true enough that there cannot be any free politics in the event of victory by a communist enemy, it does not follow that the American victory, military or diplomatic, necessarily establishes the pre-conditions for social pacification. It may do the opposite. The one thing that can be said with confidence about the American military intervention in Santo Domingo is that among the Dominican people—the ordinary people and, curiously too, among the rich who have clearly benefited from our intervention—the resentment runs deep. If it will take some years for this resentment to find political expression, it is worth remembering that the visceral anguish of the Cuban people at their handling by the United States took more than sixty years to find a political expression in Castroism—sixty years of habitual political and military intervention by Americans that bespoke an attitude of the deepest contempt, whatever the rhetoric of any specific intervention may have been. Cuba and the Dominican Republic are small countries; their rage at the United States cannot really hurt us today (though the Cuban invitation to the Soviets to install missiles on the island in the autumn of 1962 gives some inkling of the ultimate risks we run). But Cuba and the Dominican Republic are the prototypes of other interventions whose consequences may one day be larger. It is a good admonitory phrase—to sow the wind and reap the whirlwind.

If these things are so, the inclination of United States policy ought to be *against* military interventions, all other things being

---

political-military settlement in Europe—the long-delayed end to World War II that would reunite Germany and leave the satellites freer to approach the West by expediting the withdrawal of Soviet forces to the U.S.S.R.—does not. The problem is that the normalization of Europe, if it could be achieved, would reduce the American world role rather than maximize it.

This dichotomy of interest between the superpowers and their allies has begun to be noticed in Europe: in France, in the satellites, and more recently in West Germany, where there is a growing unhappiness at the abnormality of a situation that a fifth of a century after the World War II armistice still perpetuates the division of the country. Europe—West Germany, especially, and the satellites—now seeks a solution to its own problems; it has little interest in America's involvements elsewhere in the world—or Russia's.

equal. The importance to the United States of a rebellion in Latin America, to take one example, is usually exaggerated. Mexico and the Caribbean may be close to the United States; Latin America as a whole is not. It is a statement of geography to say that Latin America and North America share a common hemisphere; but Africa and Brazil are closer than Brazil and the United States. The notion of geographical spheres of influence or vital interest is antiquated in any event. A political catastrophe in Europe could drag the world down with it. If Australia were to fall by internal revolt to communism, fascism, or some new aggressive ideology, it would be a grievous moral blow—the loss of an integral portion of the English-speaking and democratic world. But Latin American domestic political events are something else. There is, over all, no real history of democracy in Latin America, and for the next few decades surely, the region is likely to remain too weak to alter the balance of world power. Nor, in any event, is any single political movement likely to dominate such a vast continent whose extremes of culture, in Uruguay or Argentina, say, in contrast to Paraguay or Bolivia or Cuba, can be reduced to a sameness only by insensitive alien eyes. Latin Americans know very well the difference between the problems of Havana and the problems of Montevideo; it is only in their common suspicion of the United States that the two capitals join hands.

As for the seemingly chronic disorders of Afro-Asia, this "revolution" is hardly less sensitive to the American military and political presence than to that of the European colonial powers. In Afro-Asian eyes there is not much difference between the United States and the old colonial exploiters. To believe this is not so, as many Americans do, is to generalize from a sentimental image of ourselves—to impute our self-image to others. The truth may be that such a distinction exists in reality: the United States has not oppressed Asia or Africa (though it has oppressed Africans). But the distinction is lost on most Afro-Asians. It is white men who are invidious to Asia and Africa—and America is a white nation even when, on the diplomatic plane, it sends a Negro ambassador to a "colored" nation, or a Negro paratrooper to hunt down a native guerrilla. This is a truth we might have learned from our experience with China. It is America, the century-long defender of Chinese territorial integrity and sovereignty, that has become for China the incarnation of exploitative evil—and this image of America is shared by more than the professional propagandists in Peking. To the degree that the Afro-Asian revolution is anti-Western and anti-white, it may be that the introduction of American military power into these regions is a new infusion of poison, bound to stimulate new antibodies. The American military forces in Vietnam may stamp out the Viet Cong, or eventually hold it within fixed bounds. But it is difficult to believe that the American intervention will leave a legacy of political stability and order.

For America to intervene in such situations means to win military victories that are, at bottom, even a little unwelcome to those who benefit most; no Asian, or African, seeing a native guerrilla movement beaten in battle by United States Marines, can take more than an ambivalent comfort from the victory. At bottom such battles are merely an extension of Europe's old domination over Asia, the white man's domination over the yellow man and the black. And for native armies to be advised by Americans on how to win victories against such guerrilla forces is a small improvement. The issue, then, is not really whether in a direct trial of strength, in favorable or unfavorable circumstances, American military power can meet the test of winning a fight with the enemy. The United States is an exceedingly powerful nation, and if we bring our strength to bear in the narrow military arena we are almost certain to win (for the foreseeable future at least). The issue is rather what such military interventions accomplish.

It is perfectly true that military conquest supplemented by long-term military occupation can take and hold a given region. But is it the aim of American action to maintain a permanent military guardianship over such areas as the Dominican Republic, South Vietnam, Columbia, Peru, the Philippines, Paraguay, Burma, Jordan, Ruanda, the Congo, and the Sudan—to name only a few of the present and potential danger zones of the world? Is there no better way? The tragedy of recent American foreign policy is that we have consistently underestimated the range of alternatives open to us. One thing is clear: the record in Iraq, Egypt, Syria, the Congo, Zanzibar, Guinea, Algeria, Indonesia, Burma, Cambodia, and even Laos conclusively demonstrates that beyond the range of effective Soviet or Chinese military intervention, communism is no unstoppable force. All these nations, at one time or another, were unequivocally written off to communism, both by the popular press and by academics who ought to have known better. But native communism is no wave of the future. Where nationalism and communism collide, it is communism that loses and nationalism that wins.

The truth is that as between nationalism and communism, communism does not win, even on its home ground. In the Soviet Union, in the satellites, in China, the old Marxist-Leninist ideology has increasingly become contaminated by nationalism. The old internationalist phase of communism is ended. The interesting point is that nationalism has eroded communism, or compromised it, both where the Soviets have used force and where they have not. Communism has been less reluctant to use force as an instrument of policy than the West; but ten years after the Hungarian revolt, for example, the use of force in meeting the challenge of nationalism has hardly proved itself a success.

Since the Soviets are usually credited with political and military realism, their record in Eastern Europe since World War II is worth comment for the light it throws on the limits of force. It is difficult to believe that any area of the world could have been more thoroughly conquered and intimidated than Eastern and Central Europe was by the Red Army. By a process of military conquest and political intimidation by the secret police, the way was prepared for communist governments in Warsaw, Prague, Budapest, Bucharest, and Sofia. (In Yugoslavia and Albania the native communist parties installed themselves in power largely through their own efforts.) Yet the result has been no genuine acceptance of Soviet communism by the local populations—for the simple reason that the Soviet *idea* has been too weak to eradicate the idea of Polish, Czechoslovak, Hungarian, Rumanian, Bulgarian (to say nothing of Yugoslav and Albanian) *nationhood*. This sense of difference has little or nothing to do with the idea of democracy as against communism. Wartime and Cold War propaganda to the contrary, democratic habits are not well developed in Eastern Europe, not even in Czechoslovakia, the most "advanced" of the prewar states of the region. The contrast with the European conquest of Afro-Asia in the eighteenth and nineteenth centuries is glaring: in India, Britain was able to win and hold a subcontinent of more than two hundred millions with a handful of troops. At no time could the British have held India, or the French Indochina, against the kind of anti-colonial resistance we see in Afro-Asia today. But Afro-Asia, for nearly two centuries, accepted its fate, and was "Europeanized," at least among its elites, as much by the force of the European *idea* as by British or French power. In the Soviet case, the military power has been overwhelming, and remains so; but the force of the idea was and is not. Such considerations suggest that the United States should utilize the military-political interventions with the greatest caution. What may seem in the short run to be a success may turn out in the long run to be a disaster.

No real consensus of American opinion stands behind such moves as the interventions in Santo Domingo and Vietnam. (There is not even real support, it sometimes seems, for an indefinitely protracted American "leadership" in Europe.) Yet an intervention that does not command the solid support of a large majority of the American people is a dangerous gambit—and not only because of the divisive efforts of such interventions at home. In Santo Domingo the United States intervention was too small in scale and brief in duration to generate much disturbance at home; given its terms, it was an intervention within available American power. But the verdict on Vietnam is by no means in, and may not be for months and years to come. As casualties mount, domestic support, or acquiescence, in the military intervention may crumble. The result could be a replica of the Korean tragedy: a military victory won in the field, in which the American people did not believe, and since they did not believe in it, forced to be thrown away.

The failure of the American people in 1950–1952 to persevere in Korea may be read two ways: as a warning against a domestic retreat from military victory, or as a warning against committing American military power in a situation where the nation will not sustain the effort. But to meet a naked military aggression is one thing; to intervene in an endemic civil turmoil in Southeast Asia in which the interests of the United States and its allies are only problematically engaged is another. Initially, in such a situation, a presidential proclamation of national danger or commitment will be enough to give a semblance of national unity to the undertaking. But how enduring such a unity will prove to be is something else. Where a foreign war drags on for years without clear evidence of victory, or even progress, the ostensible national commitment is likely to erode. Bargaining for a settlement, with an exhausted or indifferent or impatient nation at one's back, is a bad recipe for advantageous peace terms. In Algeria, for example, it was not the military situation which defeated the French, but a national withdrawal of commitment. The result in Vietnam may be not only a settlement that is no better than could have been attained before the spilling of blood, but a settlement much worse.

INTERVENTIONISM AND MORALITY

Political evangelism is a dangerous calling in a world of proliferating nuclear systems. And that may be the least of the objections to it. It is the Marxists' claim to understand—and manipulate—history. Traditionally the United States has been more modest. Yet America, pragmatic and skeptical at home, has today embarked on a vast program of social engineering abroad. Is there such a thing as the "peaceful revolution" we hold up as a model to the world? There can be evolutions where a society holds within itself the capacity for continuous growth and the parts are essentially sound and harmoniously bound to one another. But revolution is something else. It stems from discord—a clash between the needs of one vigorous social class or interest against the constraints imposed by a dominant but antiquated or feeble class or institution. If the vigor of the revolutionaries is sufficient, the constraints will break. But revolution is an uncertain process. There is no guarantee in history that a new equilibrium will emerge from disorder, Marxism to the contrary. In any case, the process consists of violence. Even the American Revolution, that model of political "reason," was vindictive and cruel to the defeated—nor was it even a revolution made with the consent of the majority. Like any other revolution, the American rebellion was the work of a believing minority. That the revolutionaries were, by and large, led by wise men, and sought a compromise instead of a fanatical new order, is a separate issue; the reasons for the political moderation of men like Washington, Franklin, Hamilton, and Jefferson lay not only in their own wisdom but in the lucky accident of a favorable tradition of common law, parliamentarianism, and free speech in America. The wisdom of the American revolutionaries could not have been given to them solely, or even largely, by foreign example. Yet it is just this which the United States has attempted to do in recent years. We have set ourselves the task of defeating violence in vast regions of Afro-Asia and Latin America, pledging ourselves to remake societies wholly alien to ours. The result has been a predictable futility. Revolutionary violence, social warfare, nationalism, petty aggressions are with us still. There have been few victories for recent American foreign policy—because victory in the terms we have lately used to define victory is hardly possible. We cannot even claim that the general peace in the world—the absence of big wars—is really our doing; propaganda and political bluster aside, there is no one in this world who has any real wish to fight us. That the Russians have mellowed is not really our doing; and the prudence of the Chinese was learned in Korea in 1950—or centuries before.

The seventeenth-century French quietist Lallemant once remarked that "the more inward we are, the more we may undertake outward activities; the less inward, the more we should refrain from trying to do good."[13] Perhaps it is not reasonable to prescribe quietism for Americans—we are an active people, committed to the belief in intervention against evil—but some scaling down of the American lust for foreign action ought to be possible. It is long overdue, in fact, because the interrelationship between an individual, or a state, and reality is a two-sided process: the issue is not merely what sort of world confronts America, but also what sort of American attitudes confront the world. The simplicity of Lallemant's formula should not blind us. What is at issue is something Aldous Huxley has put in more somber form: "The effects which follow too constant and intense a concentration upon evil are always disastrous. Those who crusade, not *for* God in themselves, but *against* the devil in others, never succeed in making the world better, but leave it either as it was, or sometimes even perceptibly worse than it was, before the crusade began. By thinking primarily of evil we tend, however excellent our intentions, to create occasions for evil to manifest itself."[14]

If there is a moral component in a nation's policy, that morality rests in action rather than in the profession of remote, if highminded, goals. The sincerity of the American commitment to moral objectives—a peaceful world, a world of opportunity and human decency—is beyond question. But the influence of the interventionist's naïve historicism is so large today that we are increasingly ruthless with the obstacles we see as standing in the way of our irreproachable but distant goals. This is a dangerous trend—and it is primarily dangerous for us. Ideas do have consequences, and irresponsibility in thought produces irresponsibility of action. If we posit a high objective, it is easy enough to fall into the belief that the eventual attainment of that objective will redeem anything we find it necessary to do today; and that is what is happening in the United States.

Such rationalization, of course, constitutes ideological reasoning—ideological politics. There is a sense in which the United States, in its domestic affairs the least ideological of nations, is in its modern foreign policy faithful to the most pernicious tradition in modern Western politics. An obvious, if superficial, example of an expediency justified by high purpose is the interventionist's treatment of that very international law which it is his proclaimed objective to extend to the relations of all nations. Our intervention in Vietnam, one might think self-evidently, violates the letter and spirit of the Geneva agreements of 1954 and 1962.* Our air war against North Vietnam is undeclared international war—a frank violation of established law. Our intervention in the Dominican Republic in 1965 violated the charter of the Organization of American States, which was our creation, even though we sought *post hoc* legal justification for our violation. These actions have all been justified by the United States at two levels: first, that communist interventions have provoked us,

---

* The argument that the war in Vietnam stems from the invasion of one sovereign state—South Vietnam—by another—North Vietnam—is hardly tenable. The division between the two countries dates only from 1954, and the regional differences between Annamites and Cochins to which the line of demarcation roughly corresponds are no greater than the differences within South Vietnam between Buddhists and Catholics, and are less than those between the Vietnamese and the aboriginal Montagnards, or the surviving earlier settlers of the region, the Cham peoples, or the ethnic Cambodians who live in the area.

The 1954 Geneva Accord clearly assured the country's unity:

"The Conference recognizes that the essential purpose of the Agreement relating to Vietnam is to settle military questions with a view to ending hostilities and that the military demarcation line is provisional and should not in any way be interpreted as constituting a political or territorial boundary. . . ."

—Declaration of the Conference, Article 6

which, *legally* speaking, is not a defense, and second, that our actions were necessary because of the inadequacy of existing law and in pursuit of our larger goals of full freedom for these states and the subsequent establishment of international legality.* Whatever the specific merits of the arguments made in each of these cases, they are, from the narrow standpoint of our professed defense of international legality, sins committed in order to stop the world from sinning.

But there is another indictment of our policy that needs to be made, and it takes us into the deepest waters of morality and self-deception. In Vietnam we have entered into a war which steadily has widened, involving not merely troops but—as both combatants and victims—a major segment of the civil population of that country. We have killed civilians and hardly have an alternative to killing more if our goal is to destroy a guerrilla movement which conceals itself among civilians and—however much we may think them deluded—clearly commands the active support of at least a sizable minority of Vietnamese. We have acquiesced in our ally's assiduous use of terror, assassination, and torture, and we ourselves practice an air warfare which—whatever our intentions—must in some measure be indiscriminate. We have also entered into the practice of terror ourselves. One American officer, frankly described as a "counter-terrorist" in an American newspaper interview, explained: "Terror is terror. Murder is murder. Counter-terror is a word used by Americans because it sounds clean. The important thing is not the degree of cleanliness of the war but the degree of necessity. Let's not kid ourselves. . . . Wars are basically insane. We are trying to kill each other. But I also believe in Mao's distinction between just wars and unjust wars. If you believe this is an unjust war, then you've got to get out. . . ."[16]

Such a statement frankly poses the issue: if a war is just, the "necessity" great, are we justified in *any* "necessary" measures?

---

* The legal advisor to the Department of State, Leonard C. Meeker, characterizes such objections to these American actions as a "fundamentalist view of international law." Citing the danger to American citizens in the Dominican Republic and "the grave risk [that] a communist take-over of the revolt would fasten a new totalitarianism on the Dominican Republic which could not easily be dislodged," he says that "international law which cannot deal with facts such as these, and in a way that has some hope of setting a troubled nation on the path of peace and reconstruction, is not the kind of law I believe in."[15]

This American, and the others who take part in the "black" operations in Vietnam (and in the conventional military operations
which are indiscriminate in their effects), find much horror in
what they do since they are fundamentally good men raised
in a humane political tradition; they act out of "necessity." But
what is the necessity? It is not to be found in strict American
strategic or material needs in Vietnam, in proximate threats to the
United States as a nation, in attacks upon us. It derives from that
interventionist historicism which identifies the war in Vietnam as
an axial challenge in the combat of freedom with communist
unfreedom. The suspicion must be that Vietnam as a place, as
a testing ground of American will, is incidental. An accident of
history has struck that country.

AMERICA AND VIETNAM

Our dominating impulse in Vietnam is ideological; the conventional political and strategic justifications for the American involvement in Vietnam seem peripheral, and even doubtful. No
one seriously argues that Vietnam's domination by Ho Chi Minh
would of itself pose a material threat to the United States. Some
argue that its domination by China would jeopardize our allies
and our Western Pacific interests. But there is a gap in the argument here. The Hanoi government is not today directed by China;
that it, and its putative conquests, would be ruled by China in
the future is unproven, to say the least.

If—to take the serious possibility rather than the fantasy—
Vietnam (and Cambodia, Laos, and Thailand, for that matter)
were ruled by governments which practiced a version of communism and deferred to China, or acknowledged a suzerainty on the
pattern of certain past periods of Chinese imperial strength, the
consequences for American prestige would today be serious; but
again the material damage is hard to define. The situation is not
at all the same thing as a Chinese military drive to seize border
provinces of India, or dominate Pakistan or other areas beyond its
traditional influence. Were some other ideology involved, and
such a renewed China governed by the old Kuomintang, or any
other non-communist Chinese movement, we might be uneasy
at the Chinese renaissance (even though such a renewal was
ostensibly one of our wartime objectives), but it is hard to believe

that we would fight wars on the Chinese periphery to block China's mainland influence (and it is important to remember that China is a land power, not the maritime power we are, or that Japan was before 1945 and could become again).* The source of our hostility to China is ideological. We hold that we must resist China because China propagates an international system which is intrinsically evil and which we see as a world-historical challenge to ourselves.

In Vietnam the two great consequences of the globalist-isolationist perception of politics have come crucially together. First we have interpreted the initial events of the Vietnam war in largely superficial and ideological—polar—terms, and have failed to grasp the real tangle of nationalist and factionalist emotion, allegiance, and socio-cultural hysteria which lay at the roots of that terrible struggle. And we set—for ourselves and for our Vietnamese clients—an imposing (and in the practical terms of contemporary Vietnam, unachievable) goal: a military stalemate or even victory which would make possible there the creation of a liberal social and political "revolution," a revolution able successfully to compete with communism, outdoing Ho Chi Minh in revolution, demonstrating the superiority of free institutions over communism. We have read this terrible and essentially private Asian upheaval as a clearly defined manifestation of an ever-expanding communist drive for world power (even though the world unity of the communist world is demonstrably broken). The Platonic abstractions of Cold War geopolitics have been

---

* To say this is not to acquiesce in all of China's old political claims (which are both large and vague). There are excellent reasons for the United States to be hostile to China so long as China is hostile to us, to support a separatist government on Taiwan, to give sympathetic support to independent governments in Thailand and Cambodia, to support India against China (even if India's border claims are not all well founded). These reasons are *political* and *strategic* reasons—reasons of practical advantage in checking and embarrassing a government which proclaims hostility to us. They are not ideological reasons—based on a fancied American mission to redeem Asia from the moral evil of communism and lead it peaceably into the twentieth century, or to win a worldwide struggle to determine the political character of the next age of human history. There is a difference, and it is very important. It is important because material and political objectives are limited and attainable. Ideological goals are unlimited and unattainable. Taken seriously, the logic of ideological politics (although not its reality; there are, happily, practical constraints on the logic of ideology) is perpetual conflict and unrestrained action.

materialized and given concrete embodiment in the Viet Cong, Ho Chi Minh, and North Vietnamese infiltrators. But the Platonic shadows summoned from the cave have taken on a frightening life. The Vietnamese whom we have fought have themselves fought back savagely, and skillfully, and with an unexpected tenacity. The Chinese, attributed by us against all credible evidence with the ultimate direction of this war, have profited inordinately from America's frustration. Implicitly they have been credited with the zeal and courage of the National Liberation Front and North Vietnamese troops—which they do not deserve. The escalations, the greater American commitments—designed to intimidate the North Vietnamese—have merely deepened and hardened the crisis, and raised the risk of national humiliation for the United States. The men dying now are Americans, and it is a bitter war with no end in sight.

There is entirely too much truth in the repeated American assertions that we seek no advantage, no territory, no bases, no clients, from this war. It might have been better if we did. As it is, we are left with a war of belief—a war that is therefore inherently without limit. Terrible things are to be done in such a war. The enemy is uncompromising and brutal. Torture, assassination, impalings, intimidation, and kidnapings are among his methods. We, in turn, are implicated in the destruction of villages, in civilians killed because they cannot be distinguished from combatants; we acquiesce in brutalities and torture by allies and mercenaries, in "free zone" bombings—the bitter catalogue hardly needs recapitulation. Americans—American troops—may be uneasy about all of this; yet we go on. The dilemma is this: if this war is as we have described it to ourselves, it must be pressed on despite all brutality; if it is not as we have believed it to be, the brutalities might then be transformed from justifiable expedients into American crimes.

The moral dilemma is profound; and as we go on with the war the qualities of national courage and humility needed to make a general change in our policy possible become ever more difficult. It even becomes hardly admissible to contemplate an alternative, since now our moral investments are as large as our material and political commitments. We are morally committed to those who have stood by us in Vietnam. We are morally committed because all the deaths and all the horror must be vindicated by an outcome that can conceivably justify the interpretations we have given this war.

The tragedy is that there is, it seems, no reasonable compromise to be expected, but also no reasonable prospect of victory. The United States has defined victory in a way that has made its achievement impossible. Obviously a compromise must eventually emerge—but it can prove an embittering humiliation of the claims the United States has made, a compromise no better and probably worse than the compromises that could have been achieved before all the blood was spilled and the horrors committed.* Certainly the ideological victory cannot be won: the Vietnamese rebels will not be morally conquered or converted to freedom, and Vietnam remade as a free and progressive state. Certainly communism, as a vehicle of Asian revolution, must, whatever plausibly happens, emerge enhanced, its power to mobilize a society osten-

---

* As of the winter of 1966, the reasonable prospects in Vietnam seem four. A fifth prospect, military victory followed by a political consolidation of the country while social and economic reform proceeds, seems to us a near-impossibility.

The four prospects are, first, a negotiated settlement with the Viet Cong, possibly under international auspices, calling for a coalition government and eventual reunification of North and South—in short, a "neutralization." This would mean, most likely, the eventual capture of the South by communists. Second, a United States attempt to enter into negotiations, as above, thwarted by "our" South Vietnamese, who, on the analogy of the Dominican armed forces in 1965–1966, or Phoumi Nosovan in Laos in 1962, refuse to co-operate in such a settlement. Third, the emergence, by whatever means, of a "neutralist" government in Saigon. If the United States were to reject the "peace" party in Saigon, the war against the Viet Cong would then become, to our intense embarrassment, a naked United States-Vietnamese struggle —an "interference in the internal affairs of others." Finally, there is the possibility that the United States would withdraw to coastal enclaves, such as Saigon and Da Nang, and allow the Viet Cong to absorb the backlands. Such a plan has already been proposed by some observers. The trouble with the plan is that it surrenders the strategic initiative to the Viet Cong, is destructive of morale within the enclave, and in any case is unlikely to offer military security.

It is, however, a version of the best (or least bad) course, which would appear to be to halt the bombings of the North but hold on in the South, following a line of strategic defensive and tactical offensive, while relaxing our dominating pressure on Saigon politics so that dissident native forces favoring compromise might have at least the opportunity of emerging. An additional hope would be that the Sino-Soviet controversy might undercut Hanoi's and the NLF's positions, motivating a compromise that secures America's core interests—which are decent withdrawal from a Vietnam in which nationalist forces (non-Communist *and* Communist) have not been wholly obliterated.

sibly proved, its ability to defy the United States with all its military power demonstrated. And indeed, to foresee even this outcome of the Vietnam war in the winter and spring of 1966 is to be guardedly optimistic. This war can also prove the near-ultimate folly of American interventionism—that act of *hubris* and naïve ideology which will crack the edifice America has created for itself in the world in these decades of our international power and acknowledged political leadership. And if that is to be the outcome, and it is not impossible, hard though it may be for Americans to acknowledge it, it will be a cold judgment made by history upon those leaders who have wasted American power and generosity in folly, in programs ill-conceived and ruthlessly pursued—men ignorant of real life, real tragedy, real human possibility.

Thus this war has come to constitute a new dimension in the American national experience. While we have always given an ideological justification to our wars, they have also before this always been wars with real political or strategic causes and content. The causes may have been naïvely oversimplified or even unjustified—as in our imperialism of 1898 and after—or, as in the two world wars and the early Cold War, they may have expressed an instinctual grasp of the true strategic threat to the United States posed by a Europe wholly dominated by an aggressive and hostile power, or as in 1950 of a hostile Korea flanking Japan. In the past we have always fought wars over issues of control of people or of an area by a foreign government. In Vietnam, while there was an element of aggression by the communist North (and we have energetically attempted to publicize the war as simply one of international aggression, yet knowing that if it were only that, our problems would be slight), the primary issue is one of combating an intangible—a system of political values. One may now suppose, all protests to the contrary, that if it could be proven that the majority of the Vietnamese people wished to be ruled by Ho Chi Minh, the United States would still resist (or would wish to resist) this verdict. As the ideologues of the Church once held, combating heresy, "Error has no rights." The globalist practices a modern political translation of that belief, justifying it, as the Church did, as serving the true interest even of those who, in their blindness, have chosen error.

THE DANGER OF IDEOLOGICAL POLICY

All this, of course, is comprehensible. Our age has been one of ideological politics, ever since the notion of a "science" of politics and history gained influence in the eighteenth and nineteenth centuries. It may also be that this age is near its ending—at least in Europe, that part of the world which has suffered worst from ideology. In the politics of contemporary Europe, there is certainly a sharp skepticism toward ideology, a concern for practical political constructs, for existentialist judgments of political problems (as well as that certain renewal of nationalism evident in Gaullist France, and evidently coming within the next few years in Germany and in Eastern Europe). Even Soviet Russia is experiencing a retreat from ideology, though the movement is heavily rationalized and disguised, and includes—as we have remarked—some latent dangers.

In international affairs the United States is a late convert to ideology. Our version of ideology is, as we have seen, peculiarly benign—ours is an ideology created out of sentimentality. The hard Nietzschean commitment which men gave to Nazism—some of them serious and intelligent men—or the devotion with which thousands have thrown away their lives for communism, has seemed alien and repugnant to Americans. But our condemnations have perhaps been too easy. We have not before been in a position to die for ideology. To die for the nation is something else, or even to die for the nation and also for a generalized betterment of mankind. But in Vietnam, Americans for the first time find themselves in a situation where the ideological cause is dominant; the national commitment essentially a result of the ideological commitment—and investment; and the strict national interest and national threat negligible.

Some of the acts of ideological war were, of course, done by us in World War II—assassinations, terrorist actions, kidnapings, and the intimidation of civilians—but on our side, certainly, World War II was not simply an ideological war. Our agents did not murder Gestapo officers or collaborators because they were the servants—or victims—of an erroneous idea. We killed because Germany had conquered Europe and we were liberating it. We did not conceive of ourselves as killing Nazis primarily for Germany's own good—even though this may have been the result.

There is, in fact, an imposing discrepancy between the seriousness of our actions in Vietnam (taking Vietnam as the fully realized expression of the globalist and interventionist spirit) and the essential unseriousness of our political ideas. Nazism and communism, whatever else we say about them, were imposing visions of the world: a ruthless reordering of human society in the one case, a "scientific" collaboration with human progress in the other. Great acts might be justified in the service of goals such as these; pity could be suppressed. Both Nazis and communists have been Faustian collaborators with the devil—daring to commit great crimes for great goals.

Our ideology has no such precision or daring—and to our credit America wills no crimes. Our ideology is a kind of benevolent imitation of the real thing—with goals equally visionary but benign—and empty; we do not soberly expect the victory which our rhetoric proclaims. Our goals are ruthlessly pursued, but only at the cost of much scruple and soul-searching. Yet the intoxicating power of ideological politics is great, and our sentimentality does not make us immune to crime. The fact that ours is a benign ideology, and based in a sentimental historicism rather than "science" or a Nietzschean defiance of bourgeois limits, does not necessarily make it less dangerous to us—although it may be somewhat less dangerous to others.

Still, it drives us to do what cannot be done, to interpret reality in terms of illusion, and most ominous, to justify actions in terms of their "higher" meaning. Do we fight a counter-revolutionary war against a major part of the population of Vietnam? It is for Vietnam's own good; Vietnam's national insurrection must be suppressed because although many Vietnamese do not understand this, the national choice many make is wrong and will lead to tyranny while we bring them true freedom. Do we intervene to suppress a revolt in the Dominican Republic—and promise to do the same thing elsewhere in Latin America? It is because we would secure true freedom for these people and save them from freedom's counterfeit.

These ideas of ours have grown out of the later years of the Cold War; but they were until the early 1960's more rhetoric than action. They flourished at the verbal level under the Eisenhower Administration, but there was an innate conservatism in Mr. Eisenhower and some of his associates that checked them from following their logic as far as they might; their interventions— in Guatemala, Iran, Lebanon—were generally clandestine or guarded. And in Korea and Europe, where our commitments touched directly on those of the Soviets and China and promised unpredictable consequences, the old impulse was to great caution, and even, in Korea, to withdrawal. The tragedy of the Kennedy and Johnson administrations is that a new and self-conscious intelligence, energy, and style have been mobilized to serve the same naïve fundamental conceptions which have traditionally dominated our political beliefs. These new men have done what others had only talked of doing. The results in Europe, and more recently in Latin America, have been damaging enough; but in Vietnam they have produced a sinister result: the deployment of our great military power to seek not only naïve but intrinsically illimitable objectives.

The United States thus emerges in some sense as the last of the ideological nations. A national myth of separateness, ex- clusivity, and superiority was indispensable to our national for- mation. Now we have turned upon the world our conviction that we have found a new path, a new standard, for mankind. We are determined to give our new way to all, to save them from the world-historical communist challenge.

MORALITY AND POLICY

If this is wrong, where, then, does moral purpose lie in the con- duct of a nation's foreign policy? One cannot condemn the at- tempt to establish high goals—although one may sharply ques- tion the attainability and seriousness of those goals which are proclaimed. Politics—and indeed human action as a whole—is hardly possible without objectives which make the actions of the moment intelligible. Hope—which is what this obsession with the future comes down to—is indispensable to action; few have the stoic courage to deal with the anxieties and frustrations of the present hour without a sustaining belief in change, in newness, in what may be made of tomorrow.

But merely to articulate goals is not a moral act, and Americans must understand this. The *choice* of goals is a matter of moral decision, and in our history the goals have, of course, reflected all of the optimism and idealism which have been a part of this country's past conception of itself as a nation. Yet merely to choose high goals is not difficult; in a sense it is a trivial act, since no nation chooses its objectives without sincerely assigning to them a moral value. Even what today in America is regarded as the selfish nationalism of our past—of our years of manifest destiny—was quite whole-heartedly framed as a matter of high moral principle. Even Germany's pre-eminence in Europe was regarded by the Germans of the pre-1914 years as the pre-eminence of Europe's best and most civilized state, its most unselfish state. As recently as 1935 Professor Arnold Toynbee assured us that the security of the British Empire "was also the supreme interest of the whole world."[17] Earlier, Lord Wolseley had spoken for a century of Victorian Britons when he declared that if his supreme purpose was to maintain the greatness of the British Empire, "I firmly believe that in doing so I work in the cause of Christianity, of peace, of civilization, and the happiness of the human race generally."[18] Woodrow Wilson said after the American bombardment of Vera Cruz that the United States had gone to Mexico "to serve mankind"—and who will accuse him of conscious hypocrisy? Even the pan-Slav movement of the nineteenth century held that with Slavic predominance in the world, Christian love would become a political reality: "The Slavs are called to this creation of a Christian brotherhood of nations, the true realization of liberty"—as Hans Kohn paraphrases the Polish Hegelian philosopher August Cieszkowski—"because they are fundamentally peace-loving and freedom-loving . . . by their rise therefore a new era of social justice will dawn."[19] Even Nazism expressed an attempt, as George Mosse writes, "to capture and direct bourgeois dissatisfaction with existing industrial and political reality . . . to find a new meaning in life, a new dynamism which would enable [youth, in particular] to recapture their own individuality. . . . Fascism was far from being purely nihilistic. . . ."[20] Even Macedonian irrendentism, Panamanian revolutionism, or Quebec separatism, identifies its cause as in the higher historical interest of all men. And all are subjectively irreproachable in their idealism.

Politics would be without moral difficulty if we were to judge nations and movements by the subjective morality of what they *seek* to accomplish.

The moral questions become hard when we turn from goals to action. And on the relationship of goals to action there is an eloquent judgment to be found in Pasternak's *Doctor Zhivago,* his chronicle of Russia's revolutionary and post-revolutionary years. A figure in the novel says of the Bolshevik leaders, that they "aren't happy with anything that's less than on a world scale. For them the transitional periods, worlds in the making, are an end in themselves. . . . And do you know why these never-ending preparations are so futile? . . . Man is born to live, not to prepare for life."[21]

The truth is that the present is all that we have: we exist now, we can act today, our lives are determined by the events of this moment—this moment is the only time we truly possess. At the most stark, tomorrow may never come. But plans may also never be fulfilled. Expectations may be wrecked or betrayed. To rest our lives on beliefs—or fantasies—about how things may improve in the future can, at the extreme, represent a withdrawal from the real life of the present. In personal life this reaction is described as psychotic. But there are nations which in greater or lesser degree have withdrawn into fantasy—into fantasies of expedient conquest to be justified in the totalitarian redemption of history, into delusions of unearned pre-eminence, into political overextensions based on unreal appraisals of the world, into futile policies of reaction or attempts to perpetuate a particular time or particular condition. The Austro-Hungarian Empire in the nineteenth century, the latter-day Ottoman Empire and nineteenth-century Russia, China before the Opium Wars and the war with Japan, seventeenth-century Spain—all were irrelevant to the world in which they existed, moving through dreams to destruction.

Because this matter of living by fantasy can have the extreme consequences of totalitarianism, we like to think of it as only a problem of political extremism—and to disregard the interplay of fantasy and reality in the affairs of states like our own. But we are not immune to failure and irrelevancy. The problem is not merely one of totalitarianism, nor an analytic point of little moment to the life of the United States today. The futility of American foreign policy today is in part a consequence of America's preoccupation with, in Pasternak's words, "worlds in the making . . . never-ending preparations," a reflection of our unhappiness with "anything that's less than on a world scale."

The policies of this nation, or of any nation, are primarily valid only in terms of today's reality. They must be set clearly in terms of the best assessment we can make of what the future may bring, and they should try to create conditions that may improve the political future. But we are fools to expect very much of the future. Indeed, in our century, when expectations of the future have been the most exalted—as in the two world wars—the real results have been unparalleled horrors. It is the movements explicitly conceived to bring about a transformed future that have committed the most gruesome crimes.

We Americans are worse than fools if we justify acts which violate our consciences today because they seem to serve a redemptive future transformation of history, a "victory" over history —a victory which we know in our hearts to be sentimental and illusory. It is *today* that men die in Vietnam. It is *today* that the minimal conventions of order and restraint that exist are broken in the affairs of the Americas. It is *today* that Europe's reconciliation, the stabilization of Germany, the evolution of East European society are interfered with in the cause of larger and better reforms in some unforeseeable future. It is *today* that acts are done which affect our relations with China and Russia—and France and Poland. We do not know what Vietnam—or Russia— will be a decade from now, or what China will want, or the British or Germans. We do not know what radical transformations may occur an hour after these words are read. We cannot rely on the future. The future always astonishes us—even when it apparently fulfills our ambitions.

The moral reproach to be voiced against American policy today is not really, as some critics would have it, that we are near some new crypto-fascism, or that we are making ourselves into a reactionary world power. The real criticism is that we are acting stupidly—and cruelly: employing our immense strength in increasingly expedient ways, in pursuit of causes that are remote and intrinsically unserious—indefensible in terms of historical and political reality. This kind of thing, unchecked, can amount to a benevolent ruthlessness in pursuit of the unattainable; and then the world will be sorry, but our own children will be sorry too. The United States is too good a nation for this.

A NEW POLICY

But if we are to check this trend, we need honesty. We are as a nation capable of honesty. We first need honesty about ourselves. We need to stop sentimentalizing ourselves. We do not really sentimentalize about politics within the United States. In our own affairs we understand the relationships of goals and reality, the existential weight and importance of action in the present.

We know something about our domestic illusions, and guard ourselves against them—the illusions, as Scott Fitzgerald identified the chief of them, of "eternal strength and health, and of the essential goodness of people—they were the illusions of a nation, the lies of generations of frontier mothers who had to croon falsely that there were no wolves outside the door." Our failure is that we do not apply this intuition about ourselves in criticism of our actions toward others. We are prepared to listen to D. H. Lawrence, a man of Wilson's generation but an early, and acute, critic of American literature, who said in 1923 that "the essential American soul is hard, isolate, stoic, and a killer." Is this true? We will not deny it entirely when we consider the violence of this country, the record of the frontier, the darker reality of national life today that is hardly contained within political institutions achieved only after revolution, civil war, an intense conforming pressure in every element of national life, a semi-hysterical fringe politics larger and more influential than in any of the other English-speaking democracies. We certainly will acknowledge the seriousness of what Frederick Jackson Turner, historian of our frontier, has said of our "coarseness and strength combined with acuteness and inquisitiveness; . . . that restless, nervous energy; that dominant individualism working for good or evil." But when we turn our face abroad we deny these complexities—or we rationalize them. Yet America, to turn our national myth around, is a special country—in its inner violence as much as in its self-conscious idealism.

Our idealism is, after all, a social cement—a mass affirmation that helps to hold our society together today. We are, and have been, more than most peoples, divided, isolate: ". . . [N]ot only does democracy make every man forget his ancestors, but it hides his descendants and separates his contemporaries from him; it throws him back forever upon himself alone and threatens in the end to confine him entirely within the solitude of his own heart." Thus Tocqueville in the 1840's. Our interventionist policy arises from such sources; it, too, is a kind of social cement—a national mission, nearly a messianism, which expresses an American need for world identity that will confirm our national identity. It is a disguise for our insecurity and violence, a mask. Perhaps that is why men of undeniable intelligence, in the State Department and Executive Office, civil servants and political leaders, can so uncritically voice sentimental falsehoods, or prate egregiously illusionist interpretations of what other peoples do and say and think. Our indulgence in the historicism of globalism may indeed express a national search for external justfications that might take the place of flawed national realities. In a time of unfulfilled civil rights for millions within America, of urban and rural degradation which since World War II has worsened rather than been bettered, of paranoid political movements, of socially alienated elements in the national population, of renewed social radicalism and self-immolations and assassination, the United States cannot be called a wholly well country. But such matters as these cannot be mended by an increasingly intense and uncompromising political mission to the world and to history.

We may need to cure ourselves; but it is also true that some things are not to be cured. More than examinations of conscience, this country needs to acknowledge that it is, simply, a troubled human society like all the others. With that, we would have a sound start on a new beginning.

VI

A New Foreign Policy

Faced with the intellectual and moral dilemmas we have examined, the question of what the United States should *do* cannot really be answered with any list of new programs or of innovations in technique or political design. The popular and professional literature of the Cold War suffer from no shortage of such "answers" to hard questions, but these answers are nearly always trivial or rhetorical, and thus irrelevant. The United States might improve the training and promotion of its foreign service staffs, demand diplomats and foreign service agents who are linguists, put its foreign aid on a long-term basis, enlarge its conventional-warfare capabilities or improve counterinsurgency doctrine, and in fact change nothing important in its situation. Recommendations that America seek an undefined "victory" in a "war" that is also undefined, or that it "seize the leadership" of the world's "revolution," can hardly be described as serious. Those who propose less grandiose programmatic solutions—that we tighten or extend NATO, or enlarge and strengthen the institutions of the Atlantic community, or launch sweeping arms-control initiatives, or internationalize our aid programs, or take new steps to bind together the free nations of Asia—demonstrate their grasp that our present policies are deeply defective, but show ignorance of why they are so. New alliances, agreements, programs of co-operative international action are possible only when there is an interest and disposition among nations to support them. They are useless proposals when the interests or consent of nations is lacking, for good or bad reasons.

The specific proposals we will discuss in this chapter must thus be understood as subordinate to a shift in the American national style, and it is the shift in style that is crucial. Style is the habit of action and decision that derives from those assumptions that are made about political reality. We have argued that at the heart of America's problems today lie false or faulty beliefs about this country, about the world, about political action. If these are not scrutinized, nothing can change. If these assumptions are challenged, altered, reformulated, our national style will change. Politics is an existential art in which specific conditions and distinctions make all the difference; style determines the existential choices.

THE AMERICAN NATIONAL INTEREST

If we are to frame the terms of a new American policy that abjures illusion, we should begin with an appraisal of national needs. If foreign policy is not a quasi-theological mission but merely a means to certain human ends, those ends have to be stated. The primary ends of foreign policy are obviously the nation's security and well-being. Other less material objectives—our prestige, the standard we set for the world, the good we can do for the international community—are the consequences of a policy which is rooted in reality.

This simple truth cannot be stated too bluntly: a foreign policy is primarily a *defense,* a means by which the social organism defends itself against encroachments and seeks to achieve the international environment within which it can prosper. National greatness does not lie in foreign policy. A skillful foreign policy will ensure the external peace within which the conditions of a private national excellence may be achieved. But that is all a foreign policy can do. A society's true greatness lies within itself —in the condition of its intellectual life, the quality of its arts, the justice with which it treats its citizens and enables them to deal with one another. At most, a foreign policy can achieve a certain largeness of style—be far-sighted and generous, achieve its solutions habitually according to external standards that are in keeping with its internal decency, rather than in too quick, frequent, or expedient resorts to force or deception. But politics, like the art of war, is not of itself really enough to commend a nation to history. If a cause is mean, any victory won in that cause is mean as well; if a nation has few intrinsic qualities, its skill in war or diplomacy will be an exercise in triviality, or in human misfortune. As Sir Edward Creasy remarked in the mid-nineteenth century: "The powers of the human intellect are rarely more strongly displayed than they are in the commander who regulates, arrays, and wields at his will . . . masses of armed disputants. . . . But these qualities, however high they may appear, are to be found in the basest as well as the noblest of mankind. Cataline was as brave a soldier as Leonidas, and a much better officer."[1]

Political policy and military power are designed primarily to this end of national survival and continuity: that a given people endure as a people, and next, that the political institutions they possess endure. (The two are not the same, as any European knows. A people can endure while governments fall or are destroyed; in France there have been five Republics, and in Germany there have been three *Reichs*, to say nothing of insecure Republics.) Physical survival, then, is a primordial interest; in a nation it is collectively expressed with the unique power of a community in that it can successfully demand of individuals that they sacrifice themselves for the group.

For Americans the issue of survival or extinction has in recent times seemed largely unreal. But with the lesson of genocide in World War II and the development of nuclear weapons (which for the first time threaten the American homeland with the kind of disaster Germans knew in the Thirty Years' War, or Poles, Jews, and Russians in World War II), it has become, in fact and emotion, a matter which national policy must address. Political rhetoric to the contrary, survival as a nation may in a test prove weightier than any other commitment. The prevention of major nuclear war, then, or any nuclear war, or any large war, must be the first objective of American foreign policy. The next objective must be to assure that if the first fails, the war will be so limited and its development so controlled as to secure national survival. Policy must be designed to maximize these goals. They must, of course, be gauged in relation to other interests, but to ignore that national survival is primary would be folly.*

---

* A clear case of such folly is the present American nuclear guarantee to Europe—a pledge to use nuclear weapons, if necessary, to defend against

The second fundamental national interest is the survival of the American nation as a political society, as a democracy. The interventionist formulations of democracy's survival—freedom's survival—will often define America's freedom as bound up in the survival of freedom everywhere. "Freedom is indivisible," Mr. Rusk says. It was the Soviet foreign minister of the Popular Front years, Maxim Litvinoff, who said that "peace is indivisible." But this is rhetoric. Peace is divisible; freedom is divisible. This may be uncongenial, but it is a fact of the world today and of all history. War and peace coexist in every age, and so do liberty and tyranny. If the United States were isolated and ringed by aggressive tyrannies it would obviously find its freedoms in jeopardy. But that is not the same thing as to assert that there is a close material bond betwen the freedom of Americans and the freedom of Albanians. An American concern for the political condition of Albanians, Ghanians, or Vietnamese may be warranted on a score of counts, but among them is not a causal connection between the existence of political liberties in marginal and intrinsically unimportant regions and the survival of the American nation, or its democracy. A nation must limit its commitments and our interest is first of all in the security of those who are truly important to our national security and survival. We have a clear interest in defending Western Europe from Soviet control or from the control of any single hostile power, such as a revived and militant Germany. Europe is a core of industrial

---

Soviet attack, even though the status of Soviet nuclear forces has altered radically since the pledge was given. In 1949–1960 the United States possessed a devastating superiority over the Soviets. Today to use such weapons would likely call down reciprocal (and crippling) nuclear strikes on the American homeland. The American response to this dilemma has been incontinently to seek to maintain and even extend the paramount role of the United States in West European defense, nuclear as well as conventional, stressing the conventional alternative in the so-called strategy of the "pause." We have not, however, favored European, chiefly French, efforts to enlarge their responsibility for their own defense, for reasons having more to do with American pride and a fear of nuclear proliferation than with strategy. There is a theoretical possibility of reversing present American policy (which seems to seek the abandonment of nuclear arms by our allies, Britain and France, blurring the issue all the while by propounding implausible schemes for unworkable and unwanted mixed-manned forces) and building an independent nuclear defense in Europe on the basis of a modernized Anglo-French force; but this would require a basic revision in America's conception of its European political role.

intelligence and resources whose command is a crucial factor in the world's power balance. There are only a few other geographical areas whose hostile control would, in material terms, jeopardize our security.*

We have another kind of interest in the security and well-being of others who are either our friends, or, even if they are not, are serious and creative societies. Our commitment to India is unilateral but necessary. Nations need equals, societies of originality and intellectual power as well as of material resources. Even if Europe's or India's security were not strategically necessary, it would be an important interest in terms of the intellectual, social, and economic well-being of our own country—though clearly more important in the case of Europe than of India.

But granting these legitimate concerns for others, and the equally legitimate concerns that arise out of our human respect for others—out of human fraternity, charity, or even out of selfish fear of how suffering, callously tolerated, might eventually react to our harm—we need to understand what we can and cannot do. There is an inevitable limit on action. As individuals, the distress of others may move us, but we cannot always do very much to help; and often we can do nothing. We may help materially; the American impulse to share our extraordinary wealth is a sound one. But it is also true that the worst forms of distress are not material. Universal concern and universalized ambitions do not in any event produce universal competence. We cannot make Mali a self-confident nation, or liberate Haiti from its self-degradation, or give German society the inner stability it has lacked through history, or cure China of its xenophobia. We can only deal with

---

* The failure to make the distinction between the feasible and unfeasible, or between what might be termed important "real estate" and unimportant, is why Mr. Rusk, speaking to the NATO allies in Paris in December, 1965, was so unconvincing when he said: "If one commitment is not met in one place, ask yourself what other commitments elsewhere would mean. We will not ask the American people to neglect a commitment in one place and maintain one in another."[2] Again, this is rhetoric. Nations must always calculate whether they can meet a commitment by gauging the costs. To take the extreme case, no nation is required to lead itself into certain defeat or destruction to honor a pledge. The United States might reasonably pay a heavy price in casualties to defend Western Europe or Japan from conquest; but such a price could be plain folly in an arena like Korea or Indochina. Mr. Rusk's remarks are, in any case, better taken as a salutary warning against giving pledges too lightly, without counting possible costs, both material and to one's international reputation, than as an inflexible rule of diplomatic action.

the exterior consequences of these conditions, and not all of those. To try to do more may actually constitute a destructive intrusion, to compound disorder or at the least prove irrelevant. George Kennan wrote: ". . . [O]ur own national interest is all that we are really capable of knowing and understanding. . . . [We need] to recognize that if our purposes and undertakings here at home are decent ones, unsullied by arrogance or hostility toward other people or delusions of superiority, then the pursuit of our national interest can never fail to be conducive to a better world. This concept is less ambitious and less inviting in its immediate prospects than those to which we have so often inclined, and less pleasing to our image of ourselves. To many it may seem to smack of cynicism and reaction. I cannot share these doubts. Whatever is realistic in concept, and founded in an endeavor to see both ourselves and others as we really are, cannot be illiberal."[3]

Is it passive or illiberal to say that the American nation should look for national attainment and fulfillment within itself? The answer would seem to be that unless it finds it there the nation can have no valid world significance. Today we have made foreign policy into a search for external fulfillments—for surrogates for the real attainments we might achieve. But foreign policy, we ought to realize, cannot give others what we cannot give ourselves. Is it far-fetched to suggest that Americans have become obsessed with the grand drama of the Cold War, with the mere technique of struggle, and have come to accept as a first principle (self-evident and therefore unassailable) that our cause is indeed, as Vice-President Humphrey has put it, "all mankind's"? In fact it may be that we have used a fifth of a century of Cold War as a means of avoiding self-confrontation. The domestic social reality of America—the degradation of Negroes and Indians, the alienation of the young, the deadening effects of an easily come-by material affluence, a contempt for individual and solitary excellence— demands new attention. It may be that the best foreign policy for America is to attend sensibly to itself. It is one thing to defend ourselves against the hostile encroachments of enemies, or to understand that America is part of a supranational intellectual or moral community, and that nations need friends. But it is inadmissible to busy ourselves in the alleged cause of mankind, to strive to bring Laos or the Congo into the middle-class parliamentarian affluence *we* define as the twentieth century, while at home syphilitic Navajos stare out dully or with hatred **at** our white man's world.

America should do less, not more. There is a pernicious lure to action for its own sake, or as the unacknowledged (or unconscious) expression of disguised interests that are never admitted to the level of debate. Action without direction, or action divorced from a realistic appreciation of the inherent costs, difficulties, consequences, and ambiguities, is more likely than not to be destructive in its effects. This is especially likely to be true of vast programmatic solutions such as policies of "rollback" or "Atlantic interdependence" which are rhetorical and can be pursued only at the cost of more mundane but actual political accomplishments—such as political settlement in Europe or Franco-German reconciliation. A cardinal rule for Americans must be to do less. This is, in essence, Talleyrand's advice to a young diplomat: *"Surtout, pas trop de zèle"*—"Above all, not too much zeal." There has been too much zeal—noble zeal but sometimes also ignorant zeal, blundering zeal—in American policy for more than a decade.

During the years of the Eisenhower Administration there was a kind of reckless proliferation of American commitments far beyond the true national interest and actual national will to sustain—unqualified promises to Eastern Europe, to the Middle East, to Southeast Asia. In these years these commitments largely remained at the level of symbolic treaty or verbalizing; they were revealed as hollow by the French debacle at Dien Bien Phu in 1954, the Hungarian revolution in 1956, and the Iraqi revolution of 1958, in none of which the United States intervened. With the coming to power of the Kennedy Administration in 1961, a new seriousness, a new energy were infused into American foreign policy. But the aims of that policy, for all the self-conscious intellectuality, went largely unexamined. And the fundamental principles of that policy continue today. The foreign policy of the three most recent Administrations has been very largely a matter of pouring new wine into old bottles, and as the Biblical parable has it, the old bottles have burst. Crude efforts to reassert American authority in Europe, in Southeast Asia, in the Caribbean, have only served further to undermine the American authority by revealing limitations hitherto not perceived by the world.

But despite this negative admonition to do less, it remains true that the United States today is allied on five continents to a host of states—to some who are potentially of great power and world influence, to others who are nations by a kind of elaborate diplomatic courtesy only, and many of whom have accepted the United States commitment in good faith. It is one thing to say that America is overextended; but such allied states cannot simply be cut adrift as Americans reassess their past errors. America has its obligations, in international law and in simple humanity. We cannot abandon those who have taken our protection, or who have acted on our behalf at some cost. Yet to acknowledge that obligations exist and bind is not merely to stress the need for a continuity of policy and to understand that foreign policy reform is a matter of years, not months. It is also to stress an important admonition: since obligations can be painful, commitments should not and must not be proliferated needlessly. Any new and solemn undertaking must reflect the true needs of the United States as they are coldly, rather than sentimentally, calculated. Obligations are expensive—conceivably tragic in their costs; a wise nation will hold its solemn commitments to a minimum, and not magnify them heedlessly for reasons of empty national pride, rhetorical intoxications, or habit.

Within the realm of action there should be a slow cutting of commitments abroad: America should seek slowly to end its primary foreign involvements, substituting for them, whenever possible, alternative security arrangements which reflect current, not past, political conditions, and which leave more responsibility to local resources. Particularly this must be so in Europe or Japan, where there is a formidable potential strength. The essential American goals should, therefore, be three: to cut our emotional commitment to far-flung responsibility and to substitute arrangements which are calculated by *actual* need, within a framework of understanding for *actual* constraints on feasibility; to restore, insofar as possible, a primary balance of power in the world, *encouraging* rather than *fighting* the growth of local strengths which might function in counterpoise to that of present or potential enemies; and, finally, to see the United States itself chiefly as a *strategic reserve.*

It can be argued that the United States has consistently sought to restore local power, as in South Vietnam or, to take a more successful example, in Western Europe, and has only reluctantly taken up responsibility when local power has proven ineffective—as again, in Vietnam. The American effort, on examination, turns out to be somewhat more ambiguous than that; there has been a persistent unwillingness to free the reins where such power has been restored in fact (as in Europe) and often, too, an unwillingness to allow alternative security arrangements (such as neutralizations or peace treaties) to come to pass even when such arrangements would serve the American national interest. The common denominator has been the desire to maintain, and even magnify, the American presence, though we have sometimes, as in the case of the defense of Western Europe, desired to cut the actual material and economic costs to ourselves. The Cold War sprang in part from the collapse of Europe and Japan in 1945, which upset the world balance by removing the geopolitical constraints on the Soviets (and communism). Now, however, Western Europe and Japan are restored and could do a great deal to defend themselves against any assailant. They are in some measure hindered from doing so by the suffocating presence of the American tutelary power, which robs these regions, first, of the *need* to defend themselves (a dependency which is degrading and in the long run harmful to them) and, second, even of the understanding that they *can* defend themselves. The test for Western Europe or Japan, to take the simple case of military security, is not whether a nation, either singly or in association, can initially match the United States' war machine in size, or complexity, but whether it (and its allies) can construct a defensive system good enough to do the job. This we would argue (contrary to much official utterance which is marred by special pleading and a considerable lack of candor) is a relatively simple task for nations as advanced technologically and as wealthy as the U. K., France, or Japan, particularly if the United States chooses in some degree to help the process rather than hinder it.

Ultimately, of course, the issue of self-defense in full freedom implies the maintenance or acquisition of independent nuclear forces, as well as conventional ones—a complex subject which deserves more extended treatment than can be given in this book. Suffice it to say that Britain's nuclear forces are exceedingly

formidable and that France's soon will be—enough to deter
post-Stalinist Russia, at least, on any issue short of national survival, and as "credible" as the present American guarantee.
Japan's acquisition of a nuclear force remains a problematical
issue, and one over which the United States may not, even if we
wish, have decisive influence. But a restoration of a sound independent foreign policy in Japan or West Germany does not now
demand nuclear forces.

Communist China's rudimentary nuclear arms pose only a
slight threat to Japan, and the Chinese have not yet given evidence
of a real intention to blackmail their neighbors by brandishing
that force. Japan could, therefore, be stimulated to begin to ac-
quire reasonable conventional forces and to play a diplomatic
role in East Asia commensurate with her economic power and
technological sophistication. (Such a role might, incidentally, imply diplomatic dealings with the Soviet Union or Communist
China as part of this process, which the United States may find
moderately unwelcome.) We would argue that the long-term risks
to the United States in such Japanese diplomacy would be slight;
the Japanese in the mid-1960's and 1970's can no longer expect
the clear field of action in East Asia that they enjoyed in the first
half of this century. On the other hand, the re-emergence of Japan
would serve to steal much of Communist China's glamour and put
China's actual power into a healthy perspective.

In Europe, even if Germany had access to nuclear weapons it
would no longer enjoy the favorable conditions for imperialism
and aggression it did from the middle of the nineteenth century
until 1945. Whereas Germany previously outclassed its potential
opponents in Europe, this is no longer so, especially in the East,
where Soviet Russia has grown to great military strength, and
states like Czechoslovakia and Poland have sufficiently industrialized to offer some effective counterbalance to German power.
In Western Europe the independent British or French nuclear
forces would effectively deter any future German military adven-
turism in the West. The present (to say nothing of a future)
French *force de frappe* could effectively ravage a militant Germany, whatever its problematical efficiency against the Soviets
may be. As for a Chinese nuclear threat against Japan, the United
States nuclear guarantee in this case is likely to hold good (and at
small risk) for many years to come. Both Germany and Japan,

therefore, have suffered an over-all deterioration of their geo-political situation since 1939; and this is to the good. But they are more passive in today's world than is strictly defensible or, in the long run, wise.

A restoration of independent policy and independent defense forces is one alternative to the existing American security guarantees in Asia and Europe. The second, which is consistent with restored autonomy, is diplomatic settlement—"normalizations" and "neutralizations." Until now it has seemed that those normalizations to which the United States has been a party since World War II have been concluded in fits of absent-mindedness—or desperation. The Austrian State Treaty in 1955, which called for the mutual evacuation of Austria by the Soviets and the Western powers and the subsequent diplomatic and military neutralization of the country, might profitably have been seen as a prototype for a larger European settlement. However, the suggestion was hotly resisted as too risky, even though in the mid-1950's the United States had categorical strategic superiority over the Soviet Union, and the Soviets themselves, after the death of Stalin, were in a process of political retreat and painful consolidation and in no condition to press westward. Laos was neutralized in 1962 when the earlier American policy of building a military strong-point based on the conservative rule of a would-be "strong man" failed, and the outcome, whatever its ambiguities and dangers, has proved clearly preferable to the near-debacle of United States policy in South Vietnam.

The conception of America as the "strategic reserve" for a non-communist world within which plural powers and independent national policies would function is an austere doctrine. It would mean that the United States should not intervene to repel an aggression simply because aggression had occurred (or, as the argument sometimes is made today, because it seems imminent) but only when actual and legitimate American interest is jeopardized. Interventions to help a victim of actual foreign aggression do not compromise the government, provided that government is treated with a modicum of respect and the American "advisors" and "allies" resist the temptation to shunt it aside. It will always be an open question, to be determined in the specific context, whether any local aggression justifies the American involvement. The United States is a world power, but it does not follow that a war between two Latin American or African governments, where Soviet or Chinese opportunities for mischief-making are slight, is a proper occasion for American intervention—military or verbal. Equities are by no means always clear to distant spectators, nor, simply, do all interventions help; they sometimes compound the conflict.

WARS OF "NATIONAL LIBERATION"

As for "internal aggressions"—insurgency, or civil uprisings promoted or supported from abroad—the issue is complex, but we would argue that the United States should provide aid *only when the local government is clearly capable of receiving and using this aid through its own instrumentalities.* If, even with such aid, the donee government is incapable of suppressing the dissident movement, the United States will realistically have to stand aside. Civil wars simply cannot be fought by outsiders. We cannot expect that a victory in such a war, which is won by the forces of a foreign power, will establish the credibility and authority of a native government. Franco's victory in the Spanish Civil War was, despite German and Italian aid, largely his own. In the final analysis, the Soviet intervention in Spain, quite aside from its cynicism and malice, did much to compromise the Loyalist government and ensure its defeat. Similarly, if Lincoln had had to call on Bismarck or the Tsar in 1861 to suppress the Army of Northern Virginia, we may be certain that the South would never have accepted the verdict of arms. If a government cannot keep order within its borders, after reasonable foreign economic and military aid, and employ such aid as it receives through its own personnel, it will not and does not deserve to survive. The United States, moreover, cannot afford to identify itself with incapable governments or failing elites. Such identifications merely spread abroad the notion that *we* are failing or incompetent. Nor, given our vast power, is there any reason why we should identify the United States with incompetent elites who are, to employ the communist pejorative, in every sense "peoples of the past." In any case, as we have seen in too many real situations, the United States effort to give greater economic or military assistance than the recipient can absorb often robs the native government of what little legitimacy it possesses without significantly increasing its strength.

The firm distinction we have made between external *aggression,* which the United States should resist where its actual interests are at stake, and *internal* violence or dissidence is most important. We make this distinction because we believe that twentieth-century rhetoric to the contrary (by fascists, communists, and our own ideologues as well), internal disorder cannot really be stimulated by foreign powers. They can, at most, subsidize or strengthen movements which have come into being as a result of native discontent. A sound society cannot be ruined by agents of subversion; indeed, excessive support lent by an external power, such as the Soviet Union or China, can only rob the native dissidents of *their* authenticity, as was the case with the Greek civil war in 1944–1948. In any age of hypernationalism, foreigners cannot cross frontiers with impunity. The Fidelist revolution in Cuba was made by native dissidents, acting without significant support from communist parties abroad, whatever its later ideological coloration came to be. The abortive efforts by the communist Chinese to engineer revolution in Indonesia, or by the Soviets in Guinea, too clearly indicate what the fate of any such revolution must be when it runs up against the forces of nativism and nationalism. Whatever the risks for America may seem to be in a policy of abstention, they are inevitable. We must ask if genuine alternatives exist and whether the risks of non-intervention are less than of intervention. American tutelage and aid brought no internal security to the Iraqi regime of Nuri-es-Said in 1958, to the Cuban government of Fulgencio Batista, or to the Vietnamese government of Ngo Dinh Diem in 1963.

POLICY TOWARD RUSSIA

The most dangerous temptation for American policy-makers dealing with the Soviet Union would be to attempt to end the Cold War by inverting its terms: to end hostility and the danger of nuclear war (and diffusion) by entering into a kind of crypto-alliance with the Soviets in which we and they would secure each other's primacy in each half of a post-Cold War world, buttressing one another at the same time as we maintain a formal competition. (Such formal competition would permit both to preserve our messianisms intact as we draw back from physical danger.) There are today official and semi-official analyses which imply such a policy. These would impose arms control agreements on the world which in fact would consolidate the American and Soviet primacies. Calling for reform of NATO and a non-aggression pact with the Warsaw Alliance, these plans would have the effect of perpetuating the division of Europe, a Soviet primacy in the East (conceived as warding off a revived "social fascism" in the satellite states), and an indefinite prolongation of the American and Russian military presence in Eastern and Western Europe. Some propose that the United States support Russia against China, in this respect, at least, becoming Russia's ally.

We would insist that such proposals display a disastrous misconception not only of America's real interests in the world but of who America's real friends are. It would hardly seem necessary to insist at this point in modern history that the Soviet Union remains by ideological commitment inimical to American power and to crucial values of American political society. Ideology may be waning in Moscow, the Soviets may not wish to risk war for supranational considerations; but they are not so mellowed that they are reliable friends. Nor is it simply a Cold War statement to mention that Russia is also an erratic state whose record is one of betrayal, political instability, and excess. Russia deserves to be treated with the greatest caution and prudence for many years to come. Only a calamitous insensitivity to the depth and meaning of the free political culture of the West could produce the notion that the "normalization" and moderation of Soviet society that has taken place since Stalin makes Russia today—or very soon—"like us." This is a troubled nation with which we may indeed wish more cordial relations, which deserves a certain admiration for its talents and courage, with which on limited issues we need co-operative dealings; but Soviet Russia is nonetheless a state whose perceptions of values, interests, and of the political world around her differ from ours in crucial ways. The Soviets are in transition away from Stalinism, but to what, or with what success, no one knows. In any case, we may be reasonably confident that the Soviet leaders, whatever their covert admiration for us and ambivalent attitude toward our national successes, would not hesitate, as in Cuba in 1962, to seize an opportunity to hurt or embarrass us.

This state and its leadership have made a profound commitment, confirmed in immense sufferings, to values and objectives which contradict and challenge our own—which challenge our *political* survival, if probably not any longer our physical survival, and also the political survival of our allies and friends.

Perhaps the most pernicious current expressions of this long-persisting habit of sentimental appraisal of contemporary Russia are the recommendations that we support Russia against China, and the related appraisals that commend Russia's attempts to restore its authority over the communist bloc. One of the great liberating events in recent history has been the disintegration of that very authority, partly, at least, under the blows of the Chinese ideologues who here unwillingly do the Lord's work. The failure of Soviet authority has freed the West of a measure of physical threat, and has decisively undermined the univer-salism of Russia's ideological claims. Russian power—both material and ideological—has been cut by Communist China's independent policies and by the growing polycentrism of the East European governments and the foreign communist parties. Such develop-ments have been a prime objective of American policy since 1945. It is not a sound American policy to move now to bolster the Soviets in the fantasy of restoring a world stability and security which the growing pluralism seems to threaten. The real reasons for such recommendations do us no credit. One such reason is that as a nation we have enjoyed world power and wish to prolong it even though this is to endorse the prolongation of Russia's power. A second reason is a fear of China which the real facts do not warrant. A third is simply that we fear change.

If China becomes a true threat to Russia, the power of both Russia and China to threaten us is accordingly reduced. Their quarrel, in any event, is their own, and while war between them might (though not certainly) be dangerous to us, and deplorable in any human terms, an attempt by us to meddle in this affair or tacitly to align ourselves with one of the parties could aug-ment the risks. As for the increasing independence of Eastern Europe, it is not only a serious constraint on Soviet Russia's power and political standing, but it is a development of intrinsic value, by any standard of *moral* politics. It reduces that arbi-trary tension in Europe which it should be—and professedly is —our objective to eliminate.

Thus, toward Russia the United States needs to display guarded co-operation to moderate tensions and arms while remaining aware of the latent threat that Russian power and commitments pose. Specifically we should recognize and persuade the Soviets of the need to withdraw from Eastern Europe on safe terms that will satisfy their legitimate security concerns for the land approaches to Russia as well as their anxiety about the threat that a disorderly or aggressive Europe (or Germany) could pose. We ought, too, to welcome Soviet world policies that contribute to stability and peace (as in Russia's mediation of the Indian-Pakistan war, which is a product of its new concern for the containment of China) while remembering the differences between Russia's world interests and ambitions and our own. We must resist coldly, with diplomatic and military measures if necessary, extensions of Russia's physical power (as distinguished from its putative—and transient—influence) into new regions—for instance, any Russian attempt to establish military bases in Latin America, or to obtain military, territorial, or significant political concessions from neighboring states. (Russia, after all, is a traditionally expansive state; it already occupies or dominates major Asian areas which have little cultural or historic affinity to itself, and as well commands a military and political salient into Central Europe.) We must support the autonomy of the East European states, whatever their forms of government, not by interventions or unilateral guarantees but by encouraging their reintegration into the international community as autonomous and acknowledgedly legitimate states in conditions of re-emerging "normality," and particularly by supporting their reintegration into the European intellectual and moral community. The closer these states identify themselves with Western Europe, increasing and normalizing their contacts, the further they may be expected to moderate their domestic policies.* On the other

---

* The "normalization" of Eastern Europe and the Balkans does not necessarily imply their democratization, although in contemporary conditions the greatest pressures for these nations' evolution are likely to be toward moderation and popular consent. There are strong traditions and habits of authoritarian government in this area. Some Western policy-makers thus are inclined—implicitly, at least—to prefer national communism in Rumania, say, to the "social fascism" they see as the probable successor to communism. Our belief is that whatever Rumania becomes, the world will be a safer place when Rumania ceases to identify itself with any Soviet Russian interest, even its ideological interest. Moreover, we believe that for the United States to support, even implicitly, a foreign-oriented despot-

hand, it is unlikely that the United States by direct diplomatic or economic action can do much to hasten the break-up of the Soviet empire in Eastern Europe. It should be remembered that Tito did not break with the Soviets in 1948 because he had received American support or overtures; United States-Yugoslav relations were at low ebb when the Cominform dispute broke out. Nor was United States influence a significant factor in Poland's defiance of the Soviets in October, 1956. Nor has the United States been instrumental in motivating Albania's and Rumania's more recent challenges to Soviet authority. Indeed, one might argue that American economic aid to Poland since 1956 has had the effect of stabilizing an unpopular regime's power and slowing the process of domestic reforms. Hungary, virtually ostracized by the United States since 1956, has evolved far more rapidly in humane ways.

It is all very well to speak of building bridges to Eastern Europe, and no doubt they are of themselves a good thing, but it is questionable whether the United States itself is the best agent to undertake the cultural and intellectual reintegration of the "satellites" into the Western world. A too great American presence in Eastern Europe is likely to be perceived by the Soviets as a threat, and in any case as a galling loss of face. France, Italy, and even Germany have old ties to this region (Hungary, Rumania, and Bulgaria are not anti-German) and should be encouraged to reassert their interests, even if they will inevitably raise minor diplomatic problems for the United States.

The best thing America can do to speed the process of liberation in Eastern Europe is simply to seek the normalization of the European arena. It was the abatement of Cold War hostility, symbolized by the First Geneva Conference in 1955, that helped undermine Soviet authority in Eastern Europe; it robbed the Soviets of the rationale of hostile encirclement they had used to justify their imperial authority. Nothing so much keeps Poland and Czechoslovakia tied to the Soviets, and active within the Warsaw Pact, as their residual fear of Germany and uncertainty about boundaries, and these cannot be lessened within existing conditions in Central Europe. A German settlement on reasonable

---

ism in a country because we think, unprovably, its successor might be less attractive is—again to make a moral judgment as well as a political one—wrong.

terms would surely be followed within a very few years by the dis-integration of whatever authority the Soviets retain in the region.

Finally, what is needed most of all is to allow the Soviets to digest the bitter lessons of the contemporary history of communism. Russia wanted a Communist China. Now it has got it. We should permit the Soviets to learn the lesson, and take the consequences. The American impulse to meddle in this affair in support of Russia can hardly be comprehended except in terms of an ineradicable impulse to shape the affairs of others, or perhaps to save the rival partner with whom, despite the Cold War rhetoric, we sense more in common than we would wish to allow.

POLICY TOWARD EUROPE

It seems fair to say that present American policy in Europe has lost sight of its aims. Once these were merely to shield Western Europe from the Soviet attack, help restore European political, social, and economic stability, and so right the imbalance created by the devastation of Europe in World War II. American post-war policy did not look to a unification of Europe, construction of an Atlantic community, or the dozen or so vaguer schemes now put forward as "permanent" rationales for a tightly integrated American-European alliance. Nor had the world responsibility then so corrupted our vision that the United States expected to exercise a permanent tutelage in Europe or discounted utterly the possibility of independent European action in world affairs.

Europe today is once again secure, prosperous, and apparently stable as well. Sound policy must be based on a realization of these facts. Even the East European states are dramatically changed from their prewar condition of underdevelopment, chronic instability, and incompetent government. They have be-latedly, and at heavy cost, begun the modernizing experience which the rest of Europe began in the nineteenth and early twentieth centuries. The feudal heritage has been extirpated. The middle classes have survived the first shock of proletarian revolution (which in Eastern Europe was far less complete than in the Soviet Union) and are in process of coming to terms and intermixing with the communists. Having experienced a nominal "people's democracy" for a generation now, the masses of Eastern Europe, even in any post-communist phase, are unlikely to withdraw from the political process. "Popular" politics—mass politics, democratic politics—has not been practiced but it has effectively been preached.

Moreover, Eastern Europe has been industrialized. It is no longer the agrarian appendage to industrial Europe it largely was in the years before Hitler. One of the ironies of Stalinism is that at ruthless cost Stalin created industrially advanced and powerful states on Russia's frontiers, where incompetently led peasant societies had existed before. (One of the ironies of Hitlerism, as well, is that by attempting to turn Slavic Europe into an area of German exploitation, Hitler created conditions which have today produced a ring of serious and advancing industrial societies to Germany's east, which are now in occupation of regions once belonging to Germany.) Eastern Europe has become part of modern Europe. Together we and the Russians— we consciously and the Russians unconsciously—have created the preconditions, in succession to Hitler's devastations, of a powerful and increasingly independent all-European society. Our shared dilemma today arises from the fact that we both are not quite reconciled to the result; we are half desirous of denying its reality, half willing somehow to perpetuate a domination of new Europe which our own policies and actions have brought into being.

The first principle of American diplomatic policy in Europe, then, should be to acknowledge and deal with Europe's restoration and strength and seek a withdrawal of America and Russia. The Soviets—like us—will eventually have to leave Europe; it is inconceivable that thirty or so years after the cessation of hostilities in World War II, there should be no peace treaty bringing that war to a formal close. But there is a serious question as to the Soviets' ability to get out easily, without provoking political crisis or leaving a dangerous legacy of hostility.

Standing in the way of this objective as much as anything else is the fact that the United States in fact, if not in intention, persists in fostering in Western Europe a helplessness to deal with its political problems in the absence of an American tutelary and guardian power. Our policies in Europe, moreover, are predicated on an almost indefinite prolongation of the division of Europe—on the prolongation of that Cold War which on the other hand our diplomacy with the Soviets seeks to abate. America works for friendship with the Soviets; this is true to a considerable degree. But we have no notion, it sometimes seems, of what such an understanding and friendship would mean for Europe: the old divisions would be healed and America would find itself superfluous so far as the day-to-day security of the Continent is concerned.

American schemes—the multilateral force, or the integration of West Germany into a political community (or further in the future, an "Atlantic" community)—imply a permanent division of Europe, and of Germany within that Europe. There is a curious tension within our policy at this point. Because both America and West Germany profess to believe in the still-continuing threat of Soviet attack in Europe, we are locked in close alliance. But in fact neither Washington nor Bonn any longer believes, in fundamental terms, in the imminence of this threat. The result is that to an increasing degree both Washington and Bonn are hindrances to each other—Bonn to Washington, because the United States wishes to strike an accommodation with the Soviets, which will almost certainly require some considerable sacrifice of German national interest; Washington to Bonn, because West Germany cannot bargain for its occupied eastern zone, to say nothing of its lost territories still farther east, so long as it is tightly integrated into an alliance that is, and a possible future political entity which might be, inimical to Soviet concerns.

The chief result of overestimating the Soviet threat and the utility of West Germany's military contribution to NATO is that we have come to believe that Germany's interest in national reunion is an interest of our own—which it is not. That Germany seeks unification, which is to say a rectification of the losses it suffered in World War II, is comprehensible and legitimate enough. But it is not necessarily in anyone else's interest. The truth is that Europeans as a whole, as well as Russians, and most Americans— official policy notwithstanding—are content with Germany's present division. This is not, as such, an anti-German remark, for the truth is, as Germans know, that Germany has been a deviant in European society in this century, and that its present hard condition is a result of its own national follies. In any case, Germany cannot be reunited without the consent of its neighbors, and this consent cannot conceivably be forthcoming so long as they are afraid of the consequences of a German reunification. Thus, since no one in Washington seriously considers the possibility of, or would want, a settlement in Europe that would be imposed by force on the Soviets, such a settlement of the German, and European, problem can only come about by "normalization" of the European scene.

Such a normalization brings us once again to the question of a peace treaty for Germany. A European settlement means in fact a settlement of World War II. The conflict with the Soviets has obscured this fact, but it will re-emerge as the Cold War continues to wane. Neither we nor the West Germans are quite prepared for this; we have, if anything, permitted West Germany to retain political fantasies of solutions that spring from "rollback" or "victory" in a war we no longer wish to win.

It may also be true that the conditions responsible for Germany's past deviance from Europe's better tradition have now been eliminated. West Germany, certainly, seems firmly lodged in the West European intellectual community—freed of the old German (and largely Prussian-Brandenburgian) lure to the Slavic and Baltic regions, the old ambivalence between Atlantic Europe and an unspecified but unique mission in the East. Conditions suggest that the German future will be different; but the German past has yet to be fully laid to rest.

There must eventually be a peace settlement, and it will come fairly soon. Berlin cannot conceivably be maintained by rights of belligerent occupation half a century after the 1945 armistice. East Germany cannot long be the last colony in a decolonized world.

The objective of a European settlement should be to get Soviet troops behind Soviet borders and to remove the artificial or arbitrary constraints that still influence the conduct of the East European nations—to bring about the long-delayed European "normalization." The price certainly will include an American troop withdrawal, and constraints on Germany. Such an American withdrawal need not be on the worst possible terms, as sometimes seems to be the fear in Washington, and leave Europe helpless to Soviet invasion. Indeed, such a withdrawal need not be total; it could stop short in Britain, say, at least for some years. Nor should the treaty constraints on Germany be excessively harsh; a long time has passed since World War II, a new generation is coming to the fore in Germany, and Germans cannot forever be expected to accept a subordinate role in world affairs. Germany's present division might thus be formalized for a time, on the theory that once Soviet troops were withdrawn, popular pressure within East Germany would bring a rapid amelioration of the regime there. The military and diplomatic freedom of a united Germany might be limited. But it would be best if these limits were for a specified term—a twenty-year prohibition on nuclear weapons, for example—rather than "permanent," for the obvious reason that a limited term is likely to be observed and is enforceable, whereas an unlimited one is impossible to maintain.

These are not novel notions. The elements are those of the "disengagement" proposals of the late 1950's. But there is a vast difference between the feasibility of a disengagement designed to limit or mitigate a virulent Cold War as was the case in the 1950's, and a normalization which ratifies an already existing *détente*, a semi-reconciliation of the United States and Western Europe with the Soviets.

In any case, events will move fast in Europe. The NATO treaty is to be reconsidered in 1969, and it is difficult to imagine that it will survive that reconsideration in recognizable form, or that there will not by then be measures of disengagement or settlement. Most Europeans are prepared for a settlement; they have the power to force it against American wishes, and increasingly (not only among Gaullists in France) there is a will to do so. America has it in its power to help shape a useful settlement, or by resistance to provoke a dangerous one. We surely need now to face the prospect of this settlement and consider the price we are willing to pay. The Germans and Soviets must be encouraged to do as much.

A dialogue on normalization will open new possibilities in Europe. They may not all be agreeable possibilities—we have already discussed the European potentialities for violence and political excess. Nor can these possibilities be formulated in too great detail by the United States. The shape of the European future, so long as it does not threaten America's narrowly defined interests, is, after all, Europe's affair, not ours. The American role ought instead be to encourage the sound European politics which has dominated the Continent since the war, and to avoid those conditions wherein Europe's legitimate interests (which include the interest in being freed of American and Russian presence) are frustrated and provoke intemperate responses. America's policy record in Europe in the first decade after the war was brilliant; but our policy today includes elements of complacency and arrogance—not to speak of a shadow of hegemonism —which could wreck our earlier success and provoke the reemergence of European nationalism and political ambition on terms hostile to us and inimical to world stability.

POLICY TOWARD CHINA

We have argued that China, which bulks so large in American concerns, is, in fact, seriously overrated as a threat to American interests. Despite China's vast manpower, the actual numbers enrolled in her regular armed forces are not large; and we must remember that the size of a modern military establishment depends on *surplus* manpower, material, and monies and not on gross population reserves. China, for all her territorial extent and population, is a poor nation. Moreover, there are severe logistic constraints on her ability to send men and material *beyond her borders* in numbers sufficient for sustained battle. (The Korean War was fought close to the Manchurian industrial complex; the Chinese armies there were sustained by a Japanese-built railway network—conditions which do not obtain along the Indian frontier or in Southeast Asia. Nor was the Chinese military intervention a success. The initial onslaught caught dispersed American forces overextended; but once the Eighth Army had rallied, in strictly military terms the Korean War approached the proportions of a Chinese disaster.)

Thus China's practical capacity to harm her neighbors, and by implication the United States, is not large. China is poor; China is not a sea power; her land frontiers are formidable; and, in any case, her longest land frontier is with the Soviet Union—a nation which holds several million square miles of former Chinese territory. If the gloomy prophets of Chinese power are correct, it is far more likely to be the Soviets who suffer than the United States or Japan.

The horror with which the Chinese are viewed is in any case exaggerated. We have argued that, unwillingly to be sure, the net effect of Chinese assertions within the communist movement has aided the United States, not harmed it. China has drastically damaged the international communist movement, broken it into pieces, and wrecked its claims to universal relevance and consistency. Surely we should applaud this, even if China's revolution has wrecked some of our own universalist assumptions as well.

As for our core interests, China is not in the material or military position to threaten them for a very long time. In any case, if China is to be contained in the long run, the containment will have to be accomplished by those who have to live alongside China. The United States could not have "contained" Hitler if Britain and the Soviets had been weak and complacent. We argue that Japan is actually and potentially the great power of modern Asia—a much more formidable state than China. India, though it has severe economic and social problems, and a tradition of political passivity that puts it at a disadvantage in competition with the centralized Chinese state, could become a serious block to Chinese ambitions (if Chinese ambitions in fact extend to the Indian subcontinent, which remains to be proved). Furthermore, India, even if it never becomes a major military and economic power, remains a huge and hardly assimilable bloc—and with foreign backing against any Chinese incursion (a foreign backing which would in the face of *invasion* be wholly appropriate and justified), would be no casual victim for China. As for a Chinese-sponsored "war of national liberation" in India, we are inclined to dismiss the feasibility and strength of such a movement, on the analogy of China's Indonesian fiasco.

Japan's future is actually the more interesting and uncertain issue in considering the political prospects for Asia. Japan today is one of the great sophisticated industrial societies of the world (the third largest), and in the recent past Japan has actually functioned as one of the great military powers. Japan's political silence today is a comprehensible consequence of the disaster of World War II, but it is also an abnormal condition. This is not merely a powerful state, but by tradition an intensely activist and volatile one. Within the next ten years, at most, Japan is likely to resume an active role in world affairs. Within the same period it is reasonable to expect some degree of reaction within Japan against the extensive accommodations made to American policy and social values since 1945. One may hope and even expect Japan to continue to be a moderate and progressive state, but there are intense strains within this society—tensions and even contradictions in Japan's overt conceptions of its national identity and worth in the world today. Many of the traditional structures and values of Japanese civilization have been abandoned for systems and values of foreign origin. Some of these accommodations have been reasonable—which hardly reduces their emotional costs—and some have been unreasonable. Such a situation—the wholesale Japanese accommodation to the values of the liberal West before 1917—has once before produced a xenophobic "correction" and explosion. There is not likely to be a simple repetition of the experience of the 1920's and 1930's in Japan, of "Shōwa restoration" or imitative imperialism; but it would be unwise to believe that Japan will escape another crisis of national identity and purpose. Certainly China, already twice a victim of Japan, would be rash to deal with Japan as if it were not a serious rival.

An American policy that anticipated these issues would concern itself with easing and encouraging independent politics in Japan. In effect, this means allowing Japan to detach itself from us—rather than, as is the case today, attempting to perpetuate Japan's American ties and that Japanese subordination to our Far Eastern ambitions which is implicit in the present situation. The Japanese-American security treaty (due for renewal shortly)—which institutionalizes the military subordination, the American occupation of Okinawa, and the existing tutelage which is our present political relationship, with all its legacies of the occupation—is dangerous. We ought to want a Japan which has begun to redefine its world role in reasonable terms, rather than one that will eventually repudiate and hate America.

Our greatest need vis-à-vis China would seem to be somehow to disintoxicate the issue. China is a state hostile to America, but of limited power, that exists under serious material, economic, and geopolitical constraints. China is not a specter of revolution stalking the world. An American war with China would be a gratuitous and senseless slaughter, primarily of Chinese, and would neither defend nor advance any serious interest of the United States. It would, perhaps, be unlikely to involve us in war with Russia (which has already begun to signal its neutrality

in such a conflict), but it would be an act of supreme folly nevertheless. To use nuclear weapons would, in present or plausible
circumstances, be a crime—unjustified by any substantial cause.
It would also be a mistake, calamitously disrupting Asia and
loosing forces of incalculable consequences for this country.

Our confrontation with communism in Southeast Asia is not a
confrontation with China, however anxiously we seek to identify
China as the sole source and agent of our Asian frustrations. Our
interest in that region today and for the foreseeable future is to
achieve reasonable containment of violence and the international
consequences of the post-colonial domestic upheavals. We cannot cure Asia of its essential malaise, its unrest, and violent attempts to break out of its frustrations. We can hope to be a
party, one among many, in confining the international effects of
these conditions. Our present programs, which define that endemic unrest as international in its sources and meaning, have
precisely the opposite effect of turning Asia's native distractions
and violence into international wars—ideological or real.

Our true interest, for example, would have been in an autonomous and isolated Vietnam—even if it were unfriendly to us. This
kind of Vietnam could never have been large enough or powerful enough to conquer all of Southeast Asia. As for China's role,
given the record of the communist movement since Tito first
broke with the Cominform in 1948, few things in this world
would seem to be surer than that a strong, united Vietnam would
resist Chinese encroachments. On the record of the Vietnamese
war, unless the Chinese military are significantly more capable
than the Americans, the Vietnamese would seem to have the
strength to fend them off.

In Thailand our interest, like the interest we have already
tacitly acknowledged in Burma, is in autonomy, not in Thailand's
alliance with us. Like Burma and Cambodia, Thailand is a reasonably homogeneous state with a national identity and tradition.
Vietnam, less homogeneous, is also a society with an ethnic and
historical identity, though that history includes much civil violence and unrest. *South* Vietnam is a diplomatic invention of the
1950's, even though North-South rivalry exists in Vietnamese history. So is North Vietnam an invention, for that matter; but for
better or for worse it is governed by the native Vietnamese faction

that has dominated Vietnamese society and its anti-colonial movement since the 1940's. South Vietnam has been governed by a succession of regimes sustained—and since Ngo Dinh Diem, openly dominated—by the United States.

POLICY TOWARD SOUTHEAST ASIA

Actually, then, our policy choices in Southeast Asia are few; this is the result of our own ruthless rejection since 1954 of every alternative save the worst. We are the victims of our own folly in Vietnam. Today we obviously need to get out of the morass, and we are not likely to do so on good terms. The end will probably be a coalition in Saigon, eventually if not immediately, dominated by the Viet Cong. Possibly the end of the present war will be unification on terms resembling those of the 1954 and 1961 Geneva agreements and under some kind of international auspices. To achieve this, and some measure of "neutralization" of a unified Vietnam, would be a lucky result for the United States—even though it might quite reasonably have been achieved, without war, in the 1950's or even the early 1960's.

A settlement, a normalization, was potentially possible in the past, and probably on better terms than now are reasonable to expect. Vietnam thus emerges as a prime example of the futility of interventionist policy, creating the conditions for unnecessary defeats. Whatever the merits of the settlement we obtain in Vietnam, it will only come now after a war in which the most powerful of contemporary states threw itself against what is—by conventional standards—one of the weakest. The American reputation can only emerge damaged by this adventure, our military reputation hurt. Our army and air force, our Strategic Air Command, have been held to a stand-off by Asian guerrillas. The American political reputation must suffer too, for all of this could have been prevented.

Neither the Viet Cong guerrillas nor the Hanoi government are invincible, but to be defeated they demand a heavy price. Yet in the event they may prove luckless too; the rivalry between Russia and China may undercut their position. But they will have hurt the United States, and the eventual settlement can hardly be other than a compromise. There will be no American "victory" in Vietnam, whatever the Communists' sufferings.

Our concern today might well be with salvaging what we can after a Vietnamese settlement. If it is true that there is no good solution in Vietnam any longer, demonstrating that no country, America included, is safe from the consequences of folly, we must in prudence attempt to assure that we do not do again in Thailand, or elsewhere in the region, what we have so disastrously done in Vietnam. Despite some minor ethnic troubles in its northern regions, Thailand is capable of surviving, by its own political resources, anything short of foreign invasion—anything, that is, except being turned meanwhile into an American client. The vigorous and shrewd Thai leadership, like Cambodia's leadership, will doubtless resist our influence. If our fate in Vietnam proves humiliating, Thailand's hostile reaction against us is a virtual certainty. The motive of Thailand's leaders will be to save Thailand, as by compromise and cunning they have always saved it from foreign control—by China, by Japan, by Britain, by France. This surely is the end we ought to want as well. The worst service we could do Thailand and ourselves—or the best service we could do China and Asian communism—would be to choose to fight the Vietnamese war over again in Thailand. There are already nearly fifteen thousand American servicemen in Thailand. That is too many. To move into Thailand with great numbers of political agents and troops, to select a government faction to underwrite and dominate, to interpret the essentially local but communist-supported dissidence in northern Thailand as another manifestation of a worldwide aggressive pattern (and thus bestow upon this movement the mantle of the struggle of Thai "autonomy" and Thai resistance to white "imperialism") would be to prepare for ourselves and our friends another defeat.

It seems safe to predict that Southeast Asia will not be politically stable in our generation. The upheavals there will be a reaction to a renascent China pressing against its borders as a strong China has always done. Upheavals will also continue to come in response to the seeds of social and political disorientation sown in Asia by the European colonial powers between 1600 and 1954. These societies can no longer exist on traditional

terms: Asia's native societies and cultures have failed in crucial
ways under the material and intellectual challenge of Western industrial and political society. The Asian "revolutions"—
China's included—are essentially of Western provocation and
there is no end to them in sight. The spectacle is one which
should cause us concern, and which demands of us such help
as we can give; but we can, in fact, give little help that is relevant to the real sources of Asia's contemporary distress. How
do we address the emotions, the intellectual ambivalences, even
the hysteria engendered in a society whose self-confidence has
been decisively undermined by three centuries of humiliations?
The best that foreigners might do is avoid enlarging and inflat-
ing the crisis.

The American material or strategic interest in the region is
not great; Southeast Asia's fate will not directly jeopardize us.
A human concern for Asia's distress is one thing; to assert that
Southeast Asia is a pivot of world politics is quite another. We
owe help to Asia—"aid," so far as we can give it—but our political
interventions only inflame a socio-political crisis whose elements
are issues of culture, confidence, and identity. To the extent that
Southeast Asia is drawn into world affairs and modern ideological conflicts, the region will be a source of tension and even
of war. Our interest, as well as Asia's, is best served by the area's
isolation. Burma, instinctively, has already chosen isolation, even
though Burma's internal problems—including regional and ethnic
dissidence, and domestic (and Chinese-supported) communism
—are more severe than Thailand's. Both we and Burma have
been better off for Burma's choice. Somewhat similar, but more
exposed and more troubled, is Cambodia. It may be that Cambodia and Laos, at least, cannot survive an American failure in
South Vietnam. They are steadily drawn deeper into the struggle
there.

Politics, however, is a matter of present choices. The choice in
Southeast Asia is not, it seems, any longer, if it ever was, between American-oriented "progressive" states, backed by American arms, and Chinese imperial control. The choice, if there
is one left, is between either inward-looking, authoritarian, "socialist" and statist "neutrals," or a mosaic pattern of communist
or quasi-communist governments who are *actively* hostile to American interests within their limited capacity to harm.

POLICY TOWARD LATIN AMERICA

We have argued that the United States has misconceived its relationship to Latin America, by assuming that because we and the Spanish and Portuguese-speaking states of Central and South America occupy a "common" hemisphere we are linked by special bonds. The reverse is true; we and they share a colonial past but of widely divergent character. In political and cultural terms, the United States and Latin America are sundered by vast differences of geography, wealth, interest, and style. While this is not to say that *no* common interests bind us, both economic and military, the degree of commonality is easily exaggerated. Given the realities of today's world—the nature of modern international trade and strategic systems in particular—American national interest does not require a close integration of Latin American foreign and domestic policy with our own. This means that "Anglo-Saxon," largely Protestant, middle-class, mostly white North America cannot presume to devise a "Great Society" for the Iberian-Indian, Catholic, elitist civilization of South America. Nor should we delude ourselves that we are much loved in Latin America; for reasons which are both unjust and just, we are not. Indeed, one might hazard the guess that nothing would be so conducive to the ultimate improvement of relations between the United States and the Latins as a few years of distant dealings during which the United States did not insistently proffer its unwelcome advice and even aid, but genuinely respected the political and cultural autonomy of the Latin states. No doubt the Alliance for Progress, once begun, cannot be brought suddenly to a halt. But it can be scaled down and administered according to the general principles of American foreign aid. So far it has been marred by a taint of political bribery—it is, in effect, a subsidy to client states. Where Latin America and, especially, the Caribbean are concerned, the United States talks the language of political altruism but too often practices the reverse.

The objection that Latin America is a region of special economic concern to the United States, and that this interest demands a special American tutelage, is a colonialist argument. Put in these terms, most Americans would reject the notion:

the United States is not a nation that would wish, nakedly, to practice the politics it condemns in others. Nor does it follow in today's world that trade follows the flag: French and British commercial interests in West Africa, Japanese commercial interests in East Asia have survived the loss of empire. As for our strategic interests, South and Central America are very nearly inaccessible to powers hostile to the United States. Isolated by geography and our naval power, it is scarcely conceivable that an enemy, even a communist enemy, could secure and maintain a hostile lodgment in the Western Hemisphere or maintain truly significant military links with a Latin state. This was the lesson of the Soviet fiasco in Cuba in 1962.

American interests in Latin America are commercial, and require no special political position. The competitive advantages which the United States enjoys are immense. So far as political affairs go, our interest is chiefly that Latin America be secure from foreign aggression—that is, extra-hemisphere aggression. While the political calm of Latin America is desirable, and the absence of intra-hemisphere war clearly so, such desiderata do not give the United States special responsibilities beyond those of other American states. To play an honorable and influential role in inter-American conclaves is one thing; but to demand to speak with the lion's voice is quite another. We have been for a long time curiously insensitive to the harmful effects of our abrasive diplomacy among the Latins. We need to be abstemious in our dealings with this region and less indulgent (and sentimental) with ourselves.

Latin America is a primary example of a region in which the United States can promulgate a unilateral guarantee against external aggression, enforce it, and leave it, by and large, at that. The Monroe Doctrine can still be made to stand in today's world but it cannot be used to secure a narrow United States political advantage. What happens *within* Latin America is something else; it is of concern to us, but only to the degree that definable and legitimate interests of the United States can be harmed. The Johnson Administration has implied, and some Congressional jingoists have asserted, that it is our responsibility and right to promote a specific form of government in Latin America (a practical impossibility) and, if need be, to intervene by force to overthrow a communist or even radical government. This courts disaster. The Dominican intervention—to say nothing of earlier interventions in this century—has shown us how little such military expeditions can accomplish to establish traditions of orderly government. And the American intervention in Vietnam, repeated in a Brazilian, Venezuelan, or Colombian context, could open a wound from which the United States might bleed for years to come.

POLICY TOWARD AFRICA

America's general aim in Africa should also be to isolate that continent from foreign interventions—that is, to secure it against hostile and concrete interventions. It is impossible to exclude Soviet or Chinese political or cultural missions, or legitimate trade; nor should we try. Though Africa is not quite so inaccessible to hostile power as Latin America, the logistic difficulties in the way of intervention are immense. This is the record: the Soviets failed ignominiously in the attempt to capitalize on the Congolese disorders of 1961, and the Chinese have not even done as well. In Africa, communism is now perceived to be in conflict with nationalism; its appeal is fading. As for physical invasion, that could come about only if Moscow or Peking could secure a base in some such country as Egypt, Algeria, or Ethiopia—in effect, winning a "voluntarist satellite." Such a satellite would court immense physical risks and subordinate its own political interests to those of a distant imperial patron. This is a most unlikely event.

It ought to be feasible to quarantine Africa from the Cold War. Africa's strategic importance and accessibility are much less than Asia's, even though its indigenous problems are greater. In some sense Africa's very turmoil and poverty—and the absence of a sizable political elite—are a defense against alien manipulations.

Africa's problems are immense, and they can only be mitigated if for a period of time the continent is not exploited politically. It is to our interest that this continent be allowed that security and time in which to sort out its own problems, though with the disinterested help of the external world. The period needed may be very long, for Africa is, in material terms, an unlucky continent, and it has been badly used during the past hundred years.

What America can do to help, however, is limited by political and social constraints. Africa is already at fever heat because of the white man—his technology, political slogans, and venal civilization. Perhaps Africa needs less forced development and more of the calm that will come from detachment from world concerns which are beyond its present reach.

Eventually, of course, given sober and sustained aid, chiefly educational, native elites will come forward, and then we can do more to help. But even then we must not expect the process of development to be uniform. Ghana, Nigeria, Kenya, the French African States, are, in spite of their great difficulties, the happier successors to colonial empire; they have a tradition of schools and civil government on which to build. But countries like the former Belgian Congo are miserable victims of the worst colonial past, and are likely to suffer tribal rebellion and distracted millennial politics for decades to come. In such places, the best we can do is to avoid implicating the Cold War in these disorders.

As for the problem of the white states of sub-Saharan Africa, here, too, we would do well to stand aside. South Africa's racist follies are a scandal; and they are most likely, in time, to recoil on the white man's head. It is one thing to counsel moderation in South Africa or Rhodesia, or to help with such economic difficulties in native regions that might arise in South Africa from an eventual partition. It is unworthy to use South African or Rhodesian politics as a pretext to demonstrate an easy liberalism before Afro-Asia, to compete against Soviet demogogues. Given America's own racial scandal, it is more than unworthy— it is false.

FOREIGN AID

Aid to the poor nations is an absolute duty for the rich and lucky, and the American people, who are perhaps the richest and luckiest of all, ought to be willing to sustain foreign aid programs at reasonable—that is, sizable—levels; let us say, two or three billion dollars a year. There should be no governmental resort to the language of political crisis or panic to justify the aid. But along with the duty to give this aid is the need for a new sobriety and realism.

By a process of conditioning and habit, foreign aid has become an almost invariable American diplomatic tactic in today's world. We have extended foreign aid on the model of the European Recovery Program, taking it for granted that a program which successfully restored the shattered economy of a sophisticated and already highly developed continent could be, without radical change, a prototype for the development of Afro-Asia and Latin America. (The Soviet foreign aid program has not even that much claim to originality; it is not difficult to suspect that the aid given by the Soviet Union since Stalin's death— and it is considerable—has been less a tactic of influence and ideological conquest than a sterile competition. The Soviets imitate their great rival, the United States.)

In any event, the American foreign aid program to the underdeveloped world has been in operation for more than a decade and a half, and its successes are few. There are only a handful of cases, like Taiwan, of self-sustained growth in consequence of such assistance. In Indonesia, aid may well have been totally wasted; in Turkey and Iran, to take two Middle Eastern examples, the aid has been corruptly or ineptly used. In still other places, like Iraq in 1959, or Thailand in 1966, such aid given in excess may actually have tended to rob the government that received it of legitimacy. In such cases aid actually functions as an initiator of political instability.

These remarks are not a conclusive argument against foreign aid, only a warning: whatever the technical and political difficulties, in the present climate of the world there cannot be such a final argument. But we should be aware of the complexity and double-edged character of aid—its socially disruptive effects, its corrosion of the native value system, its effect of producing a rootless urban proletariat which is tinder for revolution.

Foreign aid, like the technique of alliance, is not of itself a good thing, or a bad thing. Any specific aid program (like any alliance) should be evaluated in terms of: the human interests at stake, the narrower United States interests, the capacity of the recipient to use the aid to good advantage, and the general efficacy of aid as a cure for his specific social problems. It may well be, in the worst instance, that the kind of programs that saved Western Europe after 1945 could prove only to accelerate Afro-Asian distresses.

What is needed is less mythology and more evidence. However rich a nation may be, the simple discharge of foreign aid funds on a vast scale, without serious plan, is not a moral spectacle. It is not that funds spent on foreign aid might better be spent within the United States—in Mississippi, say, or Appalachia. Let us admit that this is not, as the mathematicians say, a zero-sum game: this money, if it is not spent abroad, will simply not be spent. Nor is the sum involved, approximately $4.5 billion annually in recent years, ruinously large. But economy, as Edmund Burke observed, is a distributive virtue: it consists not in the saving, but in the spending . . . wisely.

Nor for that matter does it always follow that the United States is the best channel for aid, or the best agency for technological education; we have seen that the United States can be a poor choice as vehicle for the social transformation of a hypernationalist region like Latin America. It may be that aid that contributes to the overwhelming presence of the United States will actually lead to social and ultimately political instability, and bring about the very conditions we seek to prevent.

What is needed, perhaps, is a division of the United States aid program into two parts: the first part, the larger, would address itself to the immediate and relatively accessible problems of the underdeveloped nations—health services, drought and famine relief, and longer-range education and technological training. Such aid is, in essence, charitable. (Let us not shrink from the word. It derives from the Latin *caritas*, or love.) Whether such aid eventually contributes to the growth of a society, or whether it contributes subtly to its problems (its soaring birth rate or short-term political instability), it will have to be given in any case. The United States is rich and the others are poor. This is a moral obligation that life lays upon us.

But such aid would be better given through international agencies—and genuine international agencies, rather than regional "fronts" for the United States power. This is the American "tithe." Administered intelligently and over many years, such assistance will have its effects: in undeveloped regions a native technological class, capable of teaching its own nation what that class initially has had to learn from others, may slowly emerge. At that time, when the necessary preconditions of economic growth have been achieved, the nation may become eligible for another kind of aid—large capital doses to help finance an industrial transformation without the necessity of adopting totalitarian austerity programs, as was the case in the Soviet Union in 1928–1955 or is the case in China today. In all of this, one thing should be clear: the day when such preconditions are met will not come soon. It is callous and cynical of the Soviets, who inherited a partially developed country of vast natural wealth that rivaled the United States, to assert to Afro-Asians that the Soviet "model" is a blueprint for success. Americans should not contribute to this tragic illusion. Success in Afro-Asia will not be easy or certain. To pander to illusion out of a desire to compete with the Soviets for popularity would be ignoble.

As for the second class of America's economic aid program— aid with political purpose—the United States might here concentrate its efforts on a few, a very few, recipients, giving aid in massive doses to at most a half-dozen nations able to contribute to a regional power balance against the Soviet Union or Communist China and to function as primary stabilizing influences in the world. Recipients of such aid ought to be nations with at least rudimentary social substructures—nations capable of absorbing and using aid, for whom an eventual "take-off" into self-sustaining economic growth is not pure fantasy. The primary candidates for such aid are India and Pakistan. The importance of the Indian subcontinent is such that a strong political bastion in this region, operating in conjunction with a politically revived Japan, would function to contain Communist China in the South and Southeast. No doubt Pakistan would do less in this regard than India, but if there is not to be a regional power contest between India and Pakistan (to which the United States would merely contribute political instability), aid must be given even-handedly to both. There are other conceivable candidates in South America: Mexico, Brazil, and Argentina might become primary donees, but Mexico may not really desire aid, and it is a country of considerable accomplishment already; while Argentina—to use a word which has dropped out of the contemporary

diplomatic vocabulary—may not on its record *deserve* aid. Egypt
might be another candidate, should its political ambitions be
moderated. (Though we must not expect that the offer of such
aid would play an important role in bringing about such a moderation; the modern revolutions are highly "idealist" and in all
probability would spurn politically contingent offers, much as
the North Vietnamese regime has spurned President Johnson's
offer of development funds for the Southeast Asian region.)

Such major aid programs might be undertaken by way of
empirical experiment—to see whether, in fact, "it" can be done,
where "it" refers to the transition from the externally initiated
take-off to a self-sustained economic growth. We should remember that such a process of modernization, with all its ambiguity
and anguish, cannot be undertaken without a kind of iron national resolve. The great success story of modern times, the transformation of feudal Japan into a modern state in the nineteenth
and twentieth centuries, was undertaken without foreign aid.
It was undertaken against the prevailing intellectual belief of
the time, which viewed Asians as congenitally inferior to European whites. Japan helped itself, at great moral and intellectual
cost—and at some cost to the world. (We do not know that aid
given from abroad would have prevented the Japanese tragedy.
It is permissible at least to doubt it.)

It may be that the national *will* that is indispensable to moti-
vate serious change in a country's economy is most likely to
come when the country is united in opposition or rivalry to the
foreign world, as China is today, or as Japan was in the last
hundred years. But these are hypotheses that cannot really be
tested, though they can be studied. What is clear is that the
American impulse to share our fortune is sound—and good primarily in terms of America's own quality as a nation. Nevertheless,
present programs and formulations of American foreign aid are
intellectually disorganized, practically ineffective in too many
cases, and insensitive to the political implications and social
consequences of foreign interventions.

AMERICA AND WORLD REVOLUTION

The belief in universal crisis—a world revolution—is the identifying mark of interventionist policy. In this apocalyptic belief

the globalist actually joins hands with the Soviets and the Chinese communists, who purport today to call all mankind to a new history in which social relations and values will be utterly transformed. It would seem that behind the American opposition to the Soviets and Chinese in the last years has lurked an uneasy suspicion that they are, in some sense, correct in their world view. We, too, have conceived of our own national role as a rebellion against history, and believed the fate of the old is to be swept utterly aside.

We are inclined to agree, too, that the world is in need of a revolution. Communism has issued a universal definition of what that revolution should consist in. We, in turn, since we oppose the communist revolution, have increasingly attempted to define a universal alternative. The interventionists on the American Left, certainly, have adopted this interpretation of the world crisis, and the internal controversies of the Left chiefly focus on whether the style of the needed revolution should be pragmatic and progressive (as the established liberal movement would have it), or whether it must repudiate pragmatic change. The younger Left, elements of the so-called "New Left," regard the liberals' pragmatism as sterile. They are romantic revolutionists. Some are violent revolutionists, in theory at least, who oppose the communists chiefly because they see the communists (and especially the Soviet communists) as bureaucratic doctrinaires whose ultimate commitment—like the American—is not to revolution as such but to controlled and tamed revolution. Some of the New Left identify the Negro struggle in this country with the struggle of such groups as the Vietnamese: both of them, they hold, are capable of success only by a violent assault on established systems that preach reform but, in fact, practice exploitation. What is important in all of this is that there is a widespread American commitment to the idea of revolution, expressed in the rhetoric of nearly everyone from President Johnson to James Baldwin to Staughton Lynd. The United States, the world's richest, most powerful, economically and socially most homogeneous, politically most secure, most complacently satisfied of states, is rhetorically obsessed with the idea—and need—for revolution.

One must make use of the qualification "rhetorically," because revolution, after all, is a term with specific meaning. While some

Americans genuinely believe in revolution, most, while they talk about world revolution, actually mean something else. The "orderly fulfillment" of the "revolutionary aspirations" of the Third World means for them a kind of counter-revolution. It is a call for a forestalling of revolution—for measures which will prevent real revolutions which are, by definition, violent repudiations of the established system that destroy what exists in order to make way for the new.

One source of this rhetorical commitment of ours is the claim that the United States is itself a revolutionary society, an exemplar of successful and "orderly" revolution. This is not true in any sense that is relevant to the situation of nations today. America's revolution, middle-class in its values and parliamentarian in style, was less a social upheaval than the rebellion of a prosperous people against a distant but kindred rule that had grown irksome—that held back the burgeoning growth and national confidence of the colonies. Whatever it was, the American revolution was certainly not a rebellion of the poor and degraded against a malign fate. Yet the "revolution" of the Third World today is something close to that: a search for a radical alteration of society, a redistribution of wealth and power within international society, but also a radical revision of African or Asian society itself—its industrialization, which means a drastic cultural disruption and social change. This is surely change on the scale of the French and Russian revolutions.

The American revolution, as we have emphasized, was not a profound social upheaval, implying destruction of whole classes, cultural values, and property relationships; or an outburst of violence triggered by political and cultural humiliations. It was an ejection of an established colonial government and its replacement by another government whose members, in their formal intellectual beliefs, and values, hardly differed from those they replaced. Americans achieved liberty (in Edmund Burke's words) "according to English ideas and on English principles."

Our constant talk about revolution in the world—and a revolution to which we are akin—is a self-deception. We may genuinely want "revolution" insofar as we want the world happy, prosperous, and content—like us. We do not, however, want real social revolutions. (We do not even want real counter-revolutions in Russia or China; that could be dangerous.) What we want is reasonable change, even though history has seldom been reasonable. But it is dangerous to talk the language of world revolution. By so doing, we do not, of course, trigger the revolutionary process in the world; there are titanic forces loose in the twentieth century, and even a state like America is largely helpless to accelerate or slow them. The trouble—and danger —is that we deceive ourselves about our values. The very term revolution, moreover, implies a single process of change, relevant everywhere, with a conclusion—presumably a conclusion in a better, peaceful, satisfied, "post-revolutionary" world—that tempts us to seek to engineer it. There will be no such world. For there is no single revolution. There are a multitude of "revolutionary" impulses abroad in our world. There is the liberal idea of political and social individualism and private rights that seeks gratification in a new, more "progressive" political system. This idea was behind our revolution—and Britain's and in part France's. It is clear enough, though, that not even this impulse is very often gratified without excess. The French revolution, a great and liberating event, was also achieved at terrible costs to France, and to Europe.

There is the "revolutionary" impulse to material wealth in once torpid societies, and to the power which modern industry gives a state. The Asian and African desire to industrialize their regions is a quest for the conditions of decent material life, and it is also a quest for power—for an end to the humiliation of "backwardness," and perhaps (unadmitted) a quest for revenge. Japan certainly took a revenge on the West, which had humiliated it, and from which it had learned the methods of achieving modern power.

There is the nationalist impulse—or the impulse to communal or class independence, primacy, and power. This, too, was part of our own revolution; it is part of what is convulsing Asia today. And this is not modern. It is very old, and it can be ugly. The violent riposte against alien power sometimes takes grotesque form, and while it can be dressed in reason, it more often than not is manifested by unrestrained violence. Is the Viet Cong today fighting for the platitudinous principles defined in the propaganda manifestoes of the National Liberation Front

—or is it fighting to obliterate the last traces of a foreign race and nation's domination in Vietnam, and doing so with a savagery which gives some emotional relief for the past?

Modern ideas are loose in today's world—the liberal idea, the scientific idea, the idea of the individual's political and social autonomy, the Marxist idea. But the "revolution of our day" includes old ideas too, and ideas—or impulses—which exist in every era and are not to be rationally explained. Nazism included "reasonable" revolutionary impulses to rectify Germany's 1918 humiliation, to end the legal disabilities imposed on Germany in the Versailles Treaty. But it included much else too. In its response to the *anomie*, the deracination, which modern urban-industrial society imposes on many of its members, it may have been the most modern of all revolutions—a prototype for the future rather than the "revival of barbarism" it so often has been called.

Thus there is no single world revolution. There are old, new, and newer forces for change at work in the world; and the world is in transition—as it is always in transition. It is crucial to insist upon this, because any conception of a single revolution implies a dangerous monism—a crude scheme of history conceived with it temporal conclusion. It is a half-conscious articulation of that urge to a simple scheme of life with definite and attainable solutions which we all feel but must, if there is to be a reasonable politics in our day, resist. Resistance is necessary simply because, given modern nations' capacity to work harm, it is all too easy to commit vast crimes in an effort to short-cut the attainment of history's solutions—to reach the illusory day of rest. But the truth is that crimes are merely crimes. The crimes are real and the fancied solutions never come. The nation that makes war may do so for immediate and pragmatic reasons, and be justified. But when it makes war to "make peace," makes war to "save" a "peaceful revolution" or advance it, makes war to advance or prevent some political prophecy from being fulfilled, makes war to forestall some hypothetical calamity, makes war as a "regrettable necessity" justified by the higher interests of mankind—it is wrong, and it is very close to crime.

History is flux; politics is human experience, dense and contradictory, and without ultimate fulfillments. History may be a "revolutionary" experience, but it is enduringly revolutionary, that is, always promising, never fulfilled—the experience of man's endless condition of failure within success.

AMERICA IN HISTORY

The argument of this book reduces itself to a plea that this continuity of history, this complexity of human action, be understood. The urgency of our argument derives from our belief that the United States has a tradition of political messianism, and of a conception of itself as different, and better, than other nations—as a "redeemed" political society with a mission of redemption to others. Yet the truth is that while we are a nation with great and noble institutions and achievements behind us, we are not liberated from contradiction and failure.

The lure of national mission is insidious and corrupting. It turns us from those real victories which nations and men (for both are mortal) can, in time, win. But the sense of national mission is something more; it is perilous. To conceive of America's mission as one of transforming the political quality of our times may be foolish, but it is after all merely a hunger for the unattainable. But to believe that America has been specifically called upon in history to tame, or check, an illusory "revolution of our time" is to invite endless war and eventual destruction. At the very best, it begs a kind of life-in-death.

Disorder will not be expunged; America cannot extirpate the bloody-mindedness of all the world. And messianism, rebuked abroad, can only turn inward on itself. The penalty for this is savage. For like Philip and his Spain in another age "the spiritual reverse was . . . devastating, for Philip had believed with utter conviction that he was doing God's work, waging a holy war— and God had forsaken him. There was no easy answer to this one. He and his country could turn back upon themselves, search their consciences, and, while heresy triumphed abroad, pledge themselves the more fervently to the defense at home, within the citadel, of the true faith. But the old certainty was gone, and with it the belief in a . . . mission. In their place came the creeping disillusion, the hypocrisy, the divorce between faith and action that were to characterize over the next century and more a Spain sadly fallen from her high estate."[4]

If such is to be America's fate, it will be a great pity. Believing that we are unique in history—as indeed we are in power, security, and wealth—we shall only have proved the tyranny of that malign reality we had set ourselves to transform. A foolish ambition, blindly pursued, can lead to the irrelevance that was Spain's fate after the seventeenth century. The evidence of an American irrelevance to the contemporary world already exists. But there is another dimension to the danger.

Spain, in the years of its irrelevancy and decline was a tragedy chiefly to itself. In our day great states cannot easily be ignored by others, least of all a state, such as America, whose tradition is one of activism and assertion. Our resources of military and political power are too great for us to be ignored if the United States insists on imposing its own beliefs—or fantasies—upon the world.

We have in this book insisted that this country possesses the national intelligence and talent to remake its policies and regain its relevance to the problems of modern international society. But that we can do this does not mean that we will; certainly America's bitter persistence in illusion today offers no reassurance to those who feel anxiety—and even grief—at what is happening to this nation. If we go on in the ways we have set forth for ourselves now, irrelevance and isolation may be the best we may expect. National messianism turned inward chiefly harms ourselves. Turned outward, it can drive us to hurt others. National messianism, our moral isolation and separateness, our historicist beliefs about political possibility, could drive us into deeper interventions and widened conflict. These interventions, this conflict, could have no good end.

Such an outcome, such a conclusion to the modern American involvement in world affairs, could then prove to be something beyond grief, a betrayal of that adventure in justice which was, in 1776, our compact with one another and our promise to mankind.

Source Notes

In the following, one short title is used, *"D.S. Bulletin"* for *The Department of State Bulletin,* the official weekly record of United States foreign policy (Washington, D.C., 20520).

Chapter I

1. The Preamble and first two Articles of the United Nations Charter, to which Secretary Rusk refers, are as follows:

WE THE PEOPLES
OF THE UNITED NATIONS
DETERMINED

to save succeeding generations from the scourge of war, which twice in our lifetime has brought untold sorrow to mankind, and

to reaffirm faith in fundamental human rights, in the dignity and worth of the human person, in the equal rights of men and women and of nations large and small, and

to establish conditions under which justice and respect for the obligations arising from treaties and other sources of international law can be maintained, and

to promote social progress and better standards of life in larger freedom,

AND FOR THESE ENDS

to practice tolerance and live together in peace with one another as good neighbours, and

to unite our strength to maintain international peace and security, and

to ensure by the acceptance of principles and the institution of methods, that armed force shall not be used, save in the common interest, and

to employ international machinery for the promotion of the economic and social advancement of all peoples,

HAVE RESOLVED TO
COMBINE OUR EFFORTS TO
ACCOMPLISH THESE AIMS.

Accordingly, our respective Governments, through representatives assembled in the city of San Francisco, who have exhibited their full powers found to be in good and due form, have agreed to the

present Charter of the United Nations and do hereby establish
an international organization to be known as the United Nations.

CHAPTER I

PURPOSE AND PRINCIPLES

Article 1

The Purposes of the United Nations are:

1. To maintain international peace and security, and to that end:
to take effective collective measures for the prevention and removal
of threats to the peace, and for the suppression of acts of aggression
or other breaches of the peace, and to bring about by peaceful
means, and in conformity with the principles of justice and international law, adjustment or settlement of international disputes or
situations which might lead to a breach of the peace;

2. To develop friendly relations among nations based on respect
for the principle of equal rights and self-determination of peoples,
and to take other appropriate measures to strengthen universal
peace;

3. To achieve international co-operation in solving international
problems of an economic, social, cultural, or humanitarian character,
and in promoting and encouraging respect for human rights and for
fundamental freedoms for all without distinction as to race, sex,
language, or religion; and

4. To be a centre for harmonizing the actions of nations in the
attainment of these common ends.

Article 2

The Organization and its Members, in pursuit of the Purposes
stated in Article 1, shall act in accordance with the following
Principles.

1. The Organization is based on the principle of the sovereign
equality of all its Members.

2. All Members, in order to ensure to all of them the rights and
benefits resulting from membership, shall fulfil in good faith the
obligations assumed by them in accordance with the present
Charter.

3. All Members shall settle their international disputes by peaceful means in such a manner that international peace and security,
and justice, are not endangered.

4. All Members shall refrain in their international relations from
the threat or use of force against the territorial integrity or political
independence of any state, or in any other manner inconsistent
with the Purposes of the United Nations.

5. All Members shall give the United Nations every assistance in
any action it takes in accordance with the present Charter, and
shall refrain from giving assistance to any state against which the
United Nations is taking preventive or enforcement action.

6. The Organization shall ensure that states which are not
Members of the United Nations act in accordance with these Principles so far as may be necessary for the maintenance of international peace and security.

7. Nothing contained in the present Charter shall authorize the

United Nations to intervene in matters which are essentially within the domestic jurisdiction of any state or shall require the Members to submit such matters to settlement under the present Charter; but this principle shall not prejudice the application of enforcement measures under Chapter VII.

2. Dean Rusk, "Guidelines of U.S. Foreign Policy." *D.S. Bulletin,* June 28, 1965, p. 1032.
3. Quoted in *The New York Times,* September 2, 1965.
4. Rusk, *op. cit.,* p. 1033.

Chapter II

1. George Washington, Farewell Address, as quoted in Alexis de Tocqueville, *Democracy in America,* Vintage ed., edited by Phillips Bradley. New York, 1958, Vol. I, p. 241.
2. Thomas Jefferson to Priestley, letter of March 21, 1801, as quoted in Daniel J. Boorstin, *America and the Image of Europe.* New York, 1960, p. 19.
3. Tocqueville, *op. cit.,* Vol. I, p. 244.
4. Reinhold Niebuhr, *The Irony of American History.* New York, 1952.
5. Woodrow Wilson, speech on the S/S *George Washington,* July 4, 1919.
6. Charles A. Beard, *A Foreign Policy for America.* New York, 1940, pp. 4–5.
7. Tocqueville, *op. cit.,* Vol. I, pp. 243–244.
8. George F. Kennan, *American Diplomacy 1900–1950,* Mentor ed. New York, 1952, p. 60.
9. Kenneth W. Thompson, *Political Realism and the Crisis of World Politics.* Princeton, 1960, p. 67.
10. W. W. Rostow, "Peace: The Central Task of Foreign Policy." *D.S. Bulletin,* July 5, 1965, p. 27.
11. Dean Rusk, "The Unseen Search for Peace." *D.S. Bulletin,* November 1, 1965, p. 690.
12. Hubert H. Humphrey, "National Power and the Creation of a Workable World Community." *D.S. Bulletin,* June 28, 1965, p. 1049.
13. Kennan, *op. cit.,* p. 11.
14. Woodrow Wilson, Address to the First Annual Assemblage of the League to Enforce Peace, May 27, 1916.
15. Woodrow Wilson, *Congressional Record,* 63rd Congress, First Session, p. 5846.
16. Arthur I. Waskow, "The Limits of Defense." *Atlantic Monthly,* February, 1962.
17. Henry L. Stimson and McGeorge Bundy, *On Active Service in Peace and War.* New York, 1947, p. 259.
18. Robert A. Taft, Speech in the U.S. Senate, July 11, 1949, as quoted in Ernest R. May (editor), *The American Foreign Policy.* New York, 1963, pp. 214–215.

19. Kennan, *op. cit.*, pp. 84, 83.
20. Interview with Samuel G. Blythe. *Saturday Evening Post,* May 23, 1914, p. 3.
21. Tocqueville, *op. cit.*, Vol. I, p. 176.
22. Boorstin, *op. cit.*, p. 22.
23. Dean Rusk, "Guidelines of U.S. Foreign Policy." *D.S. Bulletin,* June 28, 1965, p. 1033.
24. Lyndon B. Johnson, "The Atlantic Community: Common Hopes and Objectives." *D.S. Bulletin,* December 21, 1964, p. 867.
25. W. W. Rostow, "Regional Organization: A Planner's Perspective." *D.S. Bulletin,* June 21, 1965, pp. 995, 1000.
26. Karl Polanyi, *The Great Transformation.* Boston, 1957.
27. Reinhold Niebuhr, *The Children of Light and the Children of Darkness.* New York, 1960.
28. Gerhard Ritter, as quoted in Werner Richter, *Bismarck.* New York, 1965, p. 80.
29. Lewis Namier, *1848: The Revolution of the Intellectuals.* New York, 1964.
30. Lyndon B. Johnson, "World Peace Through Law." *D.S. Bulletin,* October 4, 1965, p. 544.
31. Ray Stannard Baker, *Woodrow Wilson and World Settlement.* New York, 1922, Vol. I, p. 112.
32. Frederick Meinecke, as quoted in Thompson, *op. cit.*, p. 65.
33. Johnson, *ibid.*, p. 543.
34. Lewis Morgan, as quoted in Crane Brinton, *Ideas and Men.* Englewood, N.J., 1950, p. 426.
35. Denis W. Brogan, *Harper's Magazine,* February 1957, p. 27.
36. Lyndon B. Johnson, "The Search for a Durable Peace in the Dominican Republic." *D.S. Bulletin,* June 21, 1965, pp. 990–991.
37. Edward Hallett Carr, *The Twenty Years' Crisis 1919–1939,* 2nd ed. London, 1946, pp. 87–88.
38. Thomas A. Bailey, *A Diplomatic History of the American People,* 6th ed. New York, 1958, p. 552.
39. Woodrow Wilson, Address to the Senate, presenting the Peace Treaty, July 10, 1919, as quoted in May (editor), *op. cit.*, p. 162.
40. Milovan Djilas, *Land Without Justice.* New York, 1958, p. 3.
41. Charles Baudelaire, *Intimate Journals.* Boston, 1957.
42. George Ball, "The New Diplomacy." *D.S. Bulletin,* June 28, 1965, p. 1043.
43. Johnson, *ibid.*, p. 991.
44. Rostow, *loc. cit.*
45. Rusk, "The Unseen Search for Peace," *loc. cit.*
46. Alexander Werth, *France 1940–1955.* London, 1956, p. 5.
47. Albert Camus, *Resistance, Rebellion, and Death.* New York, 1961, pp. 31–32, 28–29.
48. George Ball, "The Dangers of Nostalgia." *D.S. Bulletin,* April 12, 1965, p. 535.

Chapter III

1. J. Huizinga, *The Waning of the Middle Ages*, Anchor ed., New York, 1956, p. 223.
2. *Kommunist* (Moscow), No. 2, 1953, p. 22.
3. Max Lerner, *The Age of Overkill*. New York, 1962, p. 97.
4. *The Times* (London), September 23, 1965.
5. Geoffrey Bailey (pseud.), *The Conspirators*. New York, 1960.
   Z. K. Brzezinski, *The Permanent Purge*. Cambridge, 1956.
6. Nicholas Berdyaev, *The Origins of Russian Communism*. London, 1937.
7. Tyler Dennett, *Americans in Eastern Asia*. New York, 1922, p. 5.
   Walter Lippmann, *United States War Aims*. Boston, 1944, p. 38.
8. Quoted in Tang Tsou, *America's Failure in China*. Chicago, 1963, p. 5.
9. Quoted by Louis J. Halle, "Our War Aims Were Wrong." *The New York Times Magazine*, August 22, 1965, p. 13.
10. K. S. Latourette, *A History of Modern China*. London, 1955, pp. 68–69.
11. *The New York Times*, September 4, 1965.
12. Robert Frank Futrell, *The United States Air Force in Korea, 1950–1953*. New York, 1961, p. 343.
13. *Ibid.*, pp. 344–345.

Chapter IV

1. John J. McCloy, "Foreign Economic Policy and Objectives," in *Goals for Americans*. New York, 1960, p. 342.
2. *The New York Times*, September 2, 1965.
3. V. I. Lenin, as quoted in R. N. Carew Hunt, *The Theory and Practice of Communism*. London, 1963, pp. 216–217.
4. Quoted in Max Lerner, *The Age of Overkill*. New York, 1962, p. 175.
5. *The Daily Mail* (London), December 4, 1964.
6. Roger Anstey, "The Congo Rebellion." *The World Today*, Vol. 21, No. 4, April 1965, pp. 174–175.
7. Quoted by A. C. Bouquet, *Sacred Books of the World*, Penguin ed. London, 1954, p. 147.
8. Hans Kohn, *The Age of Nationalism*. New York, 1962, p. 3.
9. Quoted in K. S. Latourette, *A History of Modern China*. London, 1955, p. 143.
10. Jacques Rabemananjara, "Europe and Ourselves." *Présence Africaine* (Paris), No. 3, 1956.
11. Jawaharlal Nehru, *The Discovery of India*. New York, 1946.
12. Karl Marx and Friedrich Engels, *The Communist Manifesto*.
13. Eric Hoffer, *The Ordeal of Change*. New York, 1963, pp. 22–23.
14. Gamal Abdul Nasser, *The Philosophy of the Revolution*. Cairo, 1954.

15. Raymond Aron, *The Century of Total War*. New York, 1954, p. 49.
16. Christopher Dawson, "The Dwarfing of Europe," *The Dynamics of World History*, Mentor ed. New York, 1962.
17. George Ball, "The Reallocation of World Responsibilities." *D.S. Bulletin*, February 24, 1964, pp. 290 ff.

Chapter V

1. Douglas MacArthur II, "America and Belgium—A Community of Interests." *D.S. Bulletin*, July 19, 1965, p. 122.
2. Hubert H. Humphrey, "The Interdependence of Mankind." *D.S. Bulletin*, July 12, 1965, p. 59.
3. Humphrey, "National Power and the Creation of a Workable World Community." *D.S. Bulletin*, June 28, 1965, p. 1049.
4. W. W. Rostow, "Regional Organization: A Planner's Perspective." *D.S. Bulletin*, June 21, 1965, p. 1000.
5. R. S. Baker, *Woodrow Wilson and World Settlement*. New York, 1922, Vol. 1, p. 18.
6. Lyndon B. Johnson, "The Search for a Durable Peace in the Dominican Republic." *D.S. Bulletin*, June 21, 1965, p. 991.
7. George Ball, "The Dangers of Nostalgia." *D.S. Bulletin*, April 12, 1965, pp. 535, 536.
8. *The New York Times*, November 28, 1965.
9. Mao Tse-tung, *On People's Democratic Leadership* (Peking). Foreign Languages Press, 1952, p. 10.
10. Tang Tsou, *America's Failure in China 1941–50*. Chicago, 1963, pp. 301–302.
11. *Ibid.*, pp. 498, 497; the Gallup Poll findings are quoted on p. 496 and are drawn from Gabriel A. Almond, *The American People and Foreign Policy*, New York, 1950, p. 105.
12. C. P. Fitzgerald, *The Birth of Communist China*. London, 1964, p. 26.
13. Aldous Huxley, *The Devils of Loudon*. New York, 1959, p. 77.
14. *Ibid.*, p. 175.
15. Leonard C. Meeker, "The Dominican Situation in the Perspective of International Law." *D.S. Bulletin*, July 12, 1965, pp. 62, 64.
16. Quoted by William Tuohy, "A Big 'Dirty Little War,'" *The New York Times Magazine*, November 28, 1965, p. 148.
17. A. J. Toynbee, *Survey of International Affairs, 1935*. London, 1937, Vol. II, p. 46.
18. Quoted in Kenneth W. Thompson, *Political Realism and the Crisis of World Politics*. Princeton, 1960, p. 151.
19. Hans Kohn, *Pan-Slavism, Its History and Ideology*, 2nd ed., revised. New York, 1960, p. 34.
20. George L. Mosse, *The Crisis of German Ideology*. New York, 1964, p. 312.
21. Boris Pasternak, *Doctor Zhivago*, New York, 1960.

Chapter VI

1. Edward Creasy, *Fifteen Decisive Battles of the World*. London, 1963, p. xii.
2. *The New York Times*, December 16, 1965.
3. George F. Kennan, *American Diplomacy 1900–1950*, Mentor ed. New York, 1952, pp. 88–89.
4. William C. Atkinson, *A History of Spain and Portugal*. London, 1960, p. 165.

Index

ABOUT THE AUTHORS

WILLIAM PFAFF and EDMUND STILLMAN have collaborated on two other books, *The Politics of Hysteria: The Sources of Twentieth Century Conflict* (1964) and *The New Politics: America and the End of the Postwar World* (1961). Both are with the Hudson Institute, and both have held Rockefeller Foundation Grants in International Studies and Senior Fellowships in the Russian Institute of Columbia University.

Mr. Pfaff, a graduate of the University of Notre Dame, has been a journalist, a correspondent in Europe, Africa, the Arab Middle East, India, and Vietnam, and an executive of the Free Europe organization. He writes a regular foreign affairs commentary for *Commonweal* (of which he is a former editor) and has contributed to *Harper's*, *The New Republic*, *Problems of Communism*, the Fund for the Republic report on blacklisting in the entertainment industry, and many ABC public affairs programs. He served with infantry and Special Forces units during and after the Korean War. Mr. Pfaff lives in Ridgefield, Connecticut, with his wife, Carolyn, a former Sydney (Australia) newspaperwoman, and their infant son.

Mr. Stillman is a graduate of Yale and the Columbia Law School, and is a member of the New York Bar. He was an American diplomatic officer in Bulgaria, Yugoslavia, and the Netherlands in 1947–1951, subsequently directed research and analysis for the Free Europe Committee, and has been an officer of a New York publishing house. He is the editor and translator of *Bitter Harvest: The Intellectual Revolt Behind the Iron Curtain* (1959) and *The Balkans* (1965), a volume in the *Life* World Library. He has contributed to *Harper's*, *Horizon*, *Show*, and other magazines. Mr. Stillman served with the Marine Corps at the end of World War II. He lives in Redding, Connecticut, with his wife, Mary, and their three children.